New Africa in America

Martin Luther King, Jr. Memorial Studies in Religion, Culture and Social Development

Mozella G. Mitchell
General Editor

Vol. 5

PETER LANG
New York • Washington, D.C./Baltimore • San Francisco
Bern • Frankfurt am Main • Berlin • Vienna • Paris

Mozella G. Mitchell

New Africa in America

The Blending
of African and American
Religious and Social Traditions
among Black People
in Meridian, Mississippi
and Surrounding Counties

PETER LANG
New York • Washington, D.C./Baltimore • San Francisco
Bern • Frankfurt am Main • Berlin • Vienna • Paris

Library of Congress Cataloging-in-Publication Data

Mitchell, Mozella G.
   New Africa in America: the blending of African and American religious
and social traditions among Black people in Meridian, Mississippi and
surrounding counties / by Mozella Mitchell.
      p.   cm. — (Martin Luther King, Jr. memorial studies in religion,
culture, and social development; vol. 5)
   Includes bibliographical references.
   1. Afro-Americans—Mississippi—Meridian Region—Social
conditions.   2. Afro-Americans—Mississippi—Meridian Region—
Religion.   3. Afro-Americans—Mississippi—Meridian Region—Race
identity.   4. Meridian Region (Miss.)—Social conditions.   5. Meridian
Region (Miss.)—Church history.   I. Title.   II. Series.
F349.M5M57   1994   976.2′676—dc20   93-42526
ISBN 0-8204-2425-0   CIP
ISSN 1052-181X

Die Deutsche Bibliothek-CIP-Einheitsaufnahme

Mitchell, Mozella G.:
New Africa in America: the blending of African and American religious and
social traditions among black people in the Meridian, Mississippi and
surrounding counties / Mozella G. Mitchell - New York; Washington
D.C./Baltimore; San Francisco; Bern; Frankfurt am Main; Berlin; Vienna;
Paris: Lang, 1994
   (Martin Luther King, Jr. memorial studies in religion, culture, and social
development; Vol. 5)
   ISBN 0-8204-2425-0
NE: GT

Cover design by Geraldine Spellissy.

The paper in this book meets the guidelines for permanence and durability of
the Committee on Production Guidelines for Book Longevity of the
Council on Library Resources.

To my mother, Mrs. Odena M. Gordon
My brothers, Albert and James Gordon
To Black families everywhere
To my adopted church family members in Tampa, Florida—
Sarah Mitchell, Lucy Mitchell, Daran Mitchell,
Phette Willis and Norris Myers
To my daughters, Marcia Miller and Cynthia Woodson and
grandchildren, Dena Woodson and Jamila Woodson

ACKNOWLEDGEMENTS

Sincere gratitude is owed to many for the creation of this work. First of all, it was a research grant from the University of South Florida that enabled the author to have the time off from teaching to travel to the state of Mississippi to engage in the research. The Mississippi State Archives and the Archives of Lauderdale County were sources of tremendous help. I am grateful to Clara Butler and her husband, to Annie Kent, and Gertrude Darden, who assisted me mightily through taped interviews and gaining access to important resource persons and places in the Meridian area. Also Reverend Otis Brown, Reverend Timothy Graham, Cleveland Graham, Mittie Jordan, Dessie Ree Wilson, and many others of the Graham family rendered invaluable assistance in the work. I owe a debt of sincere gratitude to Gertrude Darden for her hospitality in allowing me to live in her home and work on this research for an extended period of time. Mrs. Effie Hearon rendered much assistance in gathering information and materials, especially on the family tree.

Pat Schuster and Marianne Bell of the College of Arts and Sciences and the Information Processing Center of the University of South Florida worked untiringly in the typing, printing and editing of this work. Much appreciation is due them, especially Marianne, who did the final printed copy, a monumental task.

I also wish to thank members of my family who gave me encouragement and inspiration: Cynthia, Marcia, Dena, Josephine, and David Alexander, who read portions of the manuscript and delighted in the project.

My colleagues, Dr. Darrell Fasching at the University of South Florida and Dr. William Shea at St. Louis University, who praised the project and encouraged me continually to complete it. Finally, a debt of gratitude is due the production staff at Peter Lang, Kathy Iwasaki, Christine Marra and others.

TABLE OF CONTENTS

Rev. John Henry Graham, Sr.
and Mrs. Sarah Ann Anderson Graham

CHAPTER 1

INTRODUCTION

The state of Mississippi as a whole is an area of unique interest and significance. Whether myth or pure historical fact, most people have a mental image of this unusual state which stems from some point, or points, in Mississippi's past.

It may be for some a sense of peace and serenity, of place, of stability, of at homeness.[1] For others, the place might evoke images of bilboism, bigotry, and backwardness.[2] For still others, the very name of the state might conjure up images of hatred, brutality, murder, and countless forms of violence; such as one remembers in cases like Emmett Till, Medgar Evers, James Chaney, Michael Schwerner, and Andrew Goodman. The latter three cases, the 1988 book of Seth Cagin and Philip Dray titled *We Are Not Afraid* (McMillan, New York) and the Alan Parker film, *Mississippi Burning* (1989) vividly and dramatically recall to mind. But Mississippi is not the same anymore. The old Mississippi, experienced in fact as a horror to many who stayed through it all and others who escaped further north to avoid it, and as depicted in the fiction of writers such as Richard Wright and William Faulkner, has changed phenomenally.[3] Astonishingly. Not that there has been a total transformation. Not that hatred and discrimination do not exist there anymore, but social, political, economic, and even attitudinal shifts in the overall society of this state in the past little more than 25 years are unbelievable, to say the least.

Who among those who experienced the state would have believed, for instance, that only twenty-three years after the Goodman-Schwerner-Chaney murders the Meridian, Mississippi, City Council would approve renaming a street after the slain civil rights leader Martin Luther King, Jr. And that on May 31, 1987, a large crowd would gather at the 31st Avenue exit of Interstate 20–59, led by state and local dignitaries including Mayor Jimmy Kemp, City Councilmen and others, and carry out a formal and ceremonious program rededicating 31st Avenue as Martin Luther King Memorial Drive and honoring Dr. King in numerous memorials and unveiling the highway marker for the redesignation?

Who from those years would have believed that in June, 1988, Meridian, Mississippi, would make the top ten list of the thirty-ninth All-American Cities Award sponsored by the National Civic League (chosen from among ninety-five entry cities including Roanoke, Virginia, and Rochester, Minnesota, who also made the top ten)?

Who would have dreamed that in less than twenty-five years Mississippi would rise to the status of having the most Black elected officials than any other state in the United States; and that out of some ninety-six legislators in the state, more than twenty would be Black?

This governor vowed that Mississippi would never be last again and that he would devote this efforts first to spending money on the improvement of education. And one year later the state instituted teacher pay raises that moved Mississippi from number forty-nine to number thirty-four in rank of teachers' salaries by state; and the governor named two Black men and a white woman to the State College Board. Among his other goals for change was a determination to enhance local entrepreneurial opportunities, put in fifteen percent minority set-aside for businesses and state contracts, bid for high-quality industry from outside the state and around the world, develop new jobs and programs for business expansion, and reach out to minorities and women and get them into entrepreneurship.[4] In the summer of 1988, one read of the drop in unemployment and of Mississippi's ranking at the top among the states in the percentage of women in traditionally male jobs. Who would have believed a little more than twenty-five years ago?

The fact that Mississippi was the way it was twenty-five or so years ago and has changed as rapidly as it has is due to many factors, one of which is the peculiar character, culture and make-up of its people, history and conditions. Mississippi is a fascinating place for those who study it seriously. This research, however, does not concentrate on the whole state but rather looks at people of one geographic area—East Central Mississippi, especially Meridian and surrounding counties. Mainly it focuses on one group of people, basically from a religious and social perspective. Some attention will have to be given, however, to the state as a whole.

Overview and Method

This area in Mississippi will be viewed largely from the standpoint of one extended family and its ancestral head, who in the midst of extremely difficult and chaotic, post-Civil War times was able to establish and promote that family and exert a powerful and enduring moral, spiritual, and social influence upon it to the extent of enhancing its survival and present status. The Graham family and its various branches was headed by Reverend John Henry Graham, Sr. (often and more commonly referred to as Jack Graham). He was born a slave during the war in Alabama in 1862 and was sold on an auction block in Selma, Alabama, to a slave-owner from the state of Mississippi. Before being sold, he was named John Henry Mooney. (More details of his life will come later.) Having been born in the midst of the Civil War and growing up during Reconstruction, Jack Graham as a young man was able to fashion order out of the turbulence around him. Although the details of his childhood and youth are at best unattainable, we can conjecture from what we do know about that period in Mississippi and from the facts we have gathered about his later life that he had to grow up in a hurry. He had only a vague knowledge of his father, who did not accompany him and his mother to Mississippi.[5] Being the oldest and practically the only male with his family of a mother, two sisters, an aunt, a nephew, among others in the Clarke County area of Mississippi, Jack Graham was able to pull his family together, purchase land, build a house, and establish an enduring family tradition.

Examining the life of this man and his family and comparing it with others in the area within a hundred-mile radius of Meridian reveals a creative blending of African and American traditions and practices. Basic to both is the religious component. Jack Graham drew strongly upon the spiritual aspects of both traditions and made them the foundation upon which he was able to build a small society. He was a Baptist minister who pastored numerous churches. But he was much more than that. My contention is that he functioned more like an African chieftain, who, from the ancient memory of African social and religious practices, along with acute observations of practices around him, was able to become instrumental in the construction of a clan and a small tribal situation that was highly beneficial to the surrounding community as well as to the larger society. This is not to suggest that he was perfect, for he had his faults and shortcomings. These will be made clear also.

We will move from an examination of the character, values, make-up, development and achievements of the Graham clan to a characterization and similar features of other families of the area in question, as well as to the nature and make-up of the whole society so far as is possible. In the process we will look closely at the historical development of the Meridian area, aspects of the racial and ethnic make-up, the religious and cultural characteristics. We will look more closely and particularly at the African American component, their character, roles, contributions, and religious natures and impact. We will be interested in determining the extent to which African elements have blended into the progress and development of African Americans in this area, as they have in the life and character of the Graham clan.

Other writers and scholars in Black religion and culture have indicated in general and stressed adamantly the African survivals and unique character of African American religion and culture.[6] But none has taken a particular region of America or of a state and examined closely a particular family or society both historically, socially, and culturally to determine to what extent there has been a blending of African cultural survivals and American cultural influences on their character and make-up. Charles H. Long states, for instance, that:

> Even if [Black Americans] had no conscious memory of Africa, the image of Africa played an enormous part in the religion of the blacks. The image of Africa, an image related to historical beginnings, has been one of the primordial religious images of great significance. It constitutes the religious revalorization of the land, a place where the natural and ordinary gestures of the blacks were and could be authenticated.[7]

Although Long has not undertaken a systematic study of African American religion to prove specifically the extent to which Africanisms are present in any particular variety of it, he encourages such a study. He also suggests what it might do in order to be authentic. He believes that it should not be dominated by the Christian perspective but should "attempt to see what kinds of images and meanings lie behind the religious experiences of the black communities in America."[8] I agree with Long, for such an unbiased study would likely unveil a whole new world of religious meaning and manifestation in African America. One of my goals will be to keep an open mind so far as possible in examining the religio-cultural aspects of the particular community involved here and to hear and see which characteristics are African in origin and which are American, as well as noticing which may stem from both cultures.

The final portion of this study will focus on the turbulent period of the Sixties and what particular characteristics enabled African Americans to withstand the violence and upheavals of this period, not to run away from a terribly dangerous situation, to weather the storms, and to stick it out, you might say, and to reap the benefits that now accrue to Black people in the progressive development of that area and all of Mississippi today. As we know, thousands of African Americans did leave Mississippi throughout its history and during the sixties in order to find a better life.

Some never left, and some of those who left came back and are there today to share in the benefits. We will be hearing by way of interviews from those who stayed and those who left and returned as a means of better understanding African Americans of this geographical area.

My interpretive framework is Afro-centric, unapologetically. My tendency is to see the residual African customs and traditions beneath the overlay of Western religious character among the people of the study. For instance, one of the informants interviewed, Gertrude Darden, in her description of the environment of the area kept referring to the "common life," the natural flow of things, as what she treasured the most, living in harmony with nature, following the lay of the land. Immediately upon hearing this, I see the image of Africa, the African personality and philosophical stance.

John Henry Graham, Sr., as we shall see, was a genius at restoring the African sense of dignity, self-worth, self-sufficiency, to the post-slavery character of the group of African Americans he headed, and he used ingeniously the Biblical context in which to ground his principles, strength, unity, ethics, and by which to stabilize the community—land, family, religion, education, culture, and independence all figured into his social perspective. But he was home in Clarke County, Enterprise, Mississippi. And he was African. With the ancient memory intact, however so subtle, of life, family, culture, coupled with what he drew from his surroundings, he set out as a young man to rebuild the soul of Africa bit by bit. Gathering together the remnants of his disparate family a few years after Emancipation and starting his own family of procreation in his early twenties, acquiring plot after plot of land, building a house (plantation style), becoming the religious head (shaman, chief, medicine man) of that family and, later, other families in the community, setting out to possess the land by acquiring more and more and giving inheritances to his sons and their families on either side of his homesite, and thus expanding that family into a clan, Rev. John Henry Graham became the new African chieftain in America. And he established a situation and tradition that continues, and all indications are that it will continue to survive and be passed on to future generations.

The question to be answered is from where did Jack Graham derive the knowledge and innate understanding to achieve all these things. As I see it, he drew upon three essential sources: his observations of his surroundings (the white plantation owners and their families and other people of lesser status), the inner sense of human, spiritual and natural cohesiveness that was a part of his African character, and the Biblical understanding of family ties, and possession, and spiritual significance that undergirded the other two sources.

With these things in mind we look at a brief reconstruction of the history of Jack Graham.

A Brief Account of the Life and Character of John Henry Graham, Sr.

He was born a slave on January 6, 1862, in Alabama, where he and his mother belonged to the Mooneys. He was soon sold as an infant, along with his mother and other relatives, on an auction block in Selma, Alabama. His name was then John Henry Mooney. Purchased by the Grahams of Clarke County, Mississippi, along with other members of his family, he became a Graham, of course, as this was the custom of slave ownership. His legal enslavement lasted for only one year or less, as the Civil War was well underway, and the Emancipation Proclamation was only a few months away. He grew up, then, during a time of great upheaval and political and social disorganization, to say the least. Although no one is now living who could give the details of his childhood development and training, we can gather much from the facts we know of his later life and character and from the historical realities of the time.

For instance, we know that he received some formal educational training, no doubt in the schools established by Northern missionaries in the post-war period or during Reconstruction. All the many sources contacted described him as an extremely intelligent, learned man. Undoubtedly, much of his learning was self-attained. For from all indications, Jack Graham went far beyond the elementary teachings he learned in school. His achievements indicate that he was widely read. Early in life he was drawn to the ministry, and in his ninety-four year life span he became a renowned preacher, landowner, and community leader in several counties in the Meridian area, including Clarke, Newton, and Lauderdale Counties where he pastored numerous churches. When he died on March 15, 1956, he owned 363 acres of timber land in Clarke County, and it was evident that he had gained the respect and reverence of thousands of people. He was funeralized at Poplar Springs Baptist Church in Lauderdale County, where he had pastored 40 years; and the cars in the funeral procession going to the church lined the highways for miles. It seemed that everyone from all the churches he had ever pastored was attempting to attend the funeral.

Jack Graham's theology and preaching style were distinctive, and many others followed in the thinking and traditions he established. As mentioned earlier, most notable in his beliefs and practices are the blending of religion, family ties, education, and land ownership. These were the glue that held the Graham clan together, which was composed of his core family of a wife and thirteen children, sisters and brothers, mother and father, aunts, in-laws, and the like. The manner in which he set up the Graham clan is reflective of the background of the African social structure and the American situation, which includes Judaic characteristics stemming from the Bible. The basic foundation was the link between religion and land possession. In the churches where Graham pastored, he attempted to encourage improvement of the people socially and politically, as well as religiously, starting with his own family. He was very concerned about maintaining family unity. He kept a meticulous record of his family history in a family Bible published in 1854 and was passed down from former slaves and became a family heirloom. The tradition was continued by his son, John H. Graham, Jr., who also carefully preserved the strong sense of family connectedness.

From the records Jack Graham, Sr., entered in the Old Family Bible one can piece together the facts of his and his family's history. And from looking at the kinds of information listed, one may almost suppose that this is exactly what he expected to be done at some time in the future. First, on one single page in this Bible, he carefully listed in chronological order the full names and dates of birth (and deaths of those who passed away) of all his thirteen children, as well as those of himself and his wife, Sarah Ann Anderson Graham, born August 7, 1862, also in Alabama and sold on an auction block in Selma, Alabama. She died July 14, 1941. The Bible lists the marriage of John H. Graham, Sr., and Sarah Ann Anderson as having taken place on December 12, 1882; and the Clarke County marriage records for 1881–1888, p. 64, show the date of December 11, 1882 as the day the license was secured.

In addition to members of his immediate family, Jack Graham and his family kept records of extended family members, as well as records of what appeared to be slave-masters to whom they had been connected. A James Graham is listed as having been born in October, 1811 and died January 29, 1885. This, one may presume, was the slave master who purchased Jack Graham (who was then a Mooney) and others of his family in Alabama and brought them back to Clarke County.[9] The census of Clarke County for 1840 shows a James Graham and his wife, free white persons under 30 years old with five children under 15 years of age, and no slaves. However, Clarke County courthouse records show a deed of 40 acres of land sold to James Graham by a Sam Lee and wife on January 4, 1842 (p. 190, vol. c, *Deed Record*, Chancery Court). The amount paid for the 40 acres was $150.00. It can be assumed that this was the same James Graham who began to purchase land in the 1840's and accumulated a plantation and purchased slaves, among whom were John Henry Mooney (who later became Graham) and other members of his family.[10]

Also listed in the Bible is a Homer Graham, whose connection one has to figure out. Some clues help in this effort, however. The old family Bible is listed as having belonged to a Homer Graham, and the name Homer Graham is listed on the same page with that of Thamer Graham, who was John H. Graham, Sr.'s mother. These are reasons enough to assume that Homer Graham was Jack Graham's father. Also, not much is known about Jack Graham's father among the children and grandchildren, except the fact that his father was used as a stud to breed slaves, and that he died when Jack Graham was very young, and he himself did not know much about him. This too would help to explain why only his name would be listed as Homer Graham in the family Bible. Jack Graham also passed on to his children and grandchildren the fact that when his father died, he himself had to take on the responsibility of the family.

Other family and related data recorded in the Bible are Louvenia Graham[11] who is listed as having been eleven years old in 1880, apparently a younger sister of Jack Graham, as she was obviously born in 1869; Archie Anderson, born May 23, 1877, who grandchildren of Jack Graham's say was their grandfather's nephew, the son of his half-brother, Elijah Anderson; William Calvin Knoby, born October 24, 1895, identity unreconciled; Amos Esiah the Prophet, born July 28, 1897, probably a related preacher; Willie Dickerson and Alice Dickerson listed as having owned the Bible (9/25/1869). Ms. Lizzy Anderson, listed as having died December, 1925, who was the sister of Jack Graham's wife, Sarah Ann Anderson Graham; Mrs. Lizzie Bronson, another sister of Jack Graham's, and a Rev. Sandy Anderson, another half-brother of Jack Graham's who lived in Selma, Alabama, as reported by one of Jack Graham's grandsons by the name of Cleveland Graham. A man by the name of James Poor was listed as having been born October, 1819, who is presumed to be the former slavemaster of Thamer Graham, who Cleveland Graham said was a Poor before she was sold on the auction block in Selma, Alabama, to the Andersons of Clarke County.

All of these listings of family members and related persons show Jack Graham as having been very conscious of the importance of preserving family and a sense of history as a part of establishing meaningful roots and spiritual values and ethics, along with his passion for religion and land possession. It cannot be established when Jack Graham came into possession of his first plot of land, but we do know that it was early, for by the 1880's when he was in his late teens or early 20's, he was already in possession of land. He married in 1882, and with the assistance of his first young sons Charlie (born October 3, 1883) and Willy (born January 24, 1885), and the help of other neighbors and friends, he built on a growing plantation of his own and largely with his own hands a huge house in the 1880's, which lasted for at least 80 years. In this home he raised his 13 children, all except one, Arnol Graham, who died at an early age (having been born in 1892). Jack Graham steadily accumulated land and as his sons Charlie Graham and John Henry Graham, Jr. (born May 25, 1886) grew to manhood, got married and started families, he assisted them in purchasing their own plots of land and building homes on them in the same vicinity. These two sons absorbed within themselves the great value their father had instilled in his family of land-ownership.

Therefore, they too accumulated more and more land aside from that their father divided with them as a part of their inheritance. John Graham, Jr. had three daughters, Annie, Clara, and Gertrude, to whom he willed his land before his death at the age of 100 in 1986. Charlie Graham has numerous children with whom he divided up his land before his death on November 2, 1941. These children still possess that land of some 20 or 25 acres each (Mittie Jordan, Timothy Graham, and Cleveland Graham among them). This land was farmland and timberland on which they could raise crops and make a living for their families. Jack Graham had three other sons who grew into manhood, whose possession of the land is not as clearly demonstrated. It is not known what, if any, land Willy J. Graham (born January 24, 1885, and died July 9, 1936) had, but he was a preacher like his father.

Ira Wilson Graham (born January 29, 1891) was in the U.S. Army during World War I and died in France in 1918 in the influenza epidemic. He is listed on the WWI Monument in Quitman, Mississippi (county seat of Clarke County) among those who gave their lives for their country. Oscar Graham, born November 26, 1903, was the youngest son, who did not purchase a significant amount of land on his own but travelled around the country much and returned home to inherit his portion of his father's land, 40 acres, at Jack Graham's death in 1956. He has built a lovely new brick home on that land, which is next door to and includes the old family home of his father, which he was in the process of dismantling in 1988.

John Graham had 7 daughters (Daisy, born February 25, 1888; Sarah, Born July 5, 1889; Louella, born September 22, 1894; Bethena, born August 13, 1896; Odena, born March 23, 1898; Lula, born December 29, 1899; Mabell, born October 29, 1905). All of them except those who had died, inherited 40 acres of land in their father's will in 1956. But they had all married except one, and had their own families and land, and homesteads, and all lived away from the Graham homestead either in other parts of the state or further north in places such as Memphis, Chicago, Detroit, and New York City. Apparently Jack Graham had not instilled in his daughters the value of maintaining the lands of the old family homestead. So, they allowed their lands to be sold for a pittance to the lawyer who handled the will, and under the leadership of the youngest and oldest living sons who still remained on the Graham plantation.

Interpretation and Classification of Jack Graham

Some sociological and cultural anthropological studies help in understanding and placing Jack Graham. Hortense Powdermaker's *After Freedom* is an in-depth study of African Americans in the town of Indianola, Mississippi, a town located about one hundred or so miles northwest of Meridian, in the early 1930's. She classifies the African American society of that period in Indianola as divided into three general categories: upper, middle, and lower. Her discussion of the middle and upper classes among African Americans of that period proves instructive, even though she is dealing with a Mississippi town more than a hundred miles to the Northwest of the Meridian area. She found that only about five percent of Black people in Indianola fell into the upper-class category, while the majority were in the middle-class.

Some of her characterizations of these two classes were: the upper-class had adopted white social patterns in both form and meaning, while the middle-class had adopted the form only.[12] She goes on to describe the upper-class of that area as one in which the "structure of the family is patriarchal rather than matriarchal," and where "stability and cohesion of the family has made for stronger growth of family tradition: as a rule upper-class persons know more about their parents and grandparents than do" others of different class stratifications. She hastens to add, however, that not all of them have family traditions since some are newly risen into this class.[13] She states further, "This slow building up of family background and tradition...is comparatively new in [Black] life. To know about one's great-grandparents is extremely rare. To know and be proud of one's grandfather's calling is a mark of distinction."[14]

Powdermaker's findings concerning this African American community in Indianola and the middle- and upper-classes seem to be applicable to the Black community generally of that time. Most of what she discovered is certainly true of the upper- and middle-classes of the Meridian area, and especially to the characterization of Jack Graham. According to her descriptions, Graham would fall into the upper-class grouping as one strongly concerned with building family traditions.

However, something more figured into Jack Graham's thinking and purposes as he meticulously searched for and recorded names and facts in his family Bible. Powdermaker admitted her lack of a discussion of African survivals,[15] and because of this her study of Black life is not as meaningful as it could be. Jack Graham's and other African Americans' concentration on building family traditions, establishing a heritage, has deep roots in the African background, and it is supported by the Judaic traditions which they discovered in reading the Bible. The crucial importance of the family in African societies is well-known today. And it held a similar significance in ancient Jewish society. In African societies communalism was the practice. Not individualism but rather communalism gave the person her/his meaning in life. It was a three-way connection each person shared in the society. There was an unbroken bond between the living, the dead, and the yet-unborn. This may not have been true with the ancient Jewish social system, but strong family traditions are certainly stressed in terms of lineage—the patriarchal traditions of Abraham, Isaac, Jacob, Moses, David, and many others not so well-known, are found throughout the Hebrew Bible. Both the African and the Hebrew concern for family are steeped in religious context and meaning. And Jack Graham, being the religious man that he was, was certainly drawing upon the African religious and social cohesiveness stamped in his consciousness and the Judaic traditions he read of in his Bible. We see much evidence of this later on in the study.

Seeing his ready acquisition of land during the Reconstruction period and his access to an education (at least on a literate level), one could conclude, Jack Graham may fit into the category of freed house slaves who acquired property and got an education and thus advanced more rapidly than others of perhaps the field variety.[16]

> After emancipation, the house slaves were the ones most likely to be advised and at times more actively assisted by their masters. In any case they were far better equipped to cope with the new conditions than those who had been kept in the fields. They were more ready, also, to profit by the educational opportunities opened to them just after the Civil War, when a number of well-educated Northerners, fired by missionary zeal, came south to teach the [Black people].[17]

One of the cases Powdermaker cites is that of a grandfather who proved to be an excellent farmer. Acquiring property after the Civil War, he worked and planned his life and business so that when he died he left an estate of more than a thousand acres and about $10,000 in cash. He had sent all of his eight children through elementary school, some through high school, and two through college.[18] Such a propensity of landownership was one of the central criteria placing Blacks in the upper-class.[19]

Whether or not he stemmed from the house slave category,[20] Jack Graham certainly fitted the characteristics of quick acquisition of land, love of education and advancement. As we shall see later on, however, his tendency toward land accumulation and independent farming was something else that he drew from his African background and the Judaic traditions in the Bible he read. The way he divides up portions among his sons on either side of his homestead is equally attributable to influences from the African mind and the Biblical traditions.

E. Franklin Frazier, even though he denied the existence of African survivals among African Americans, makes excellent points regarding the African American family which assist us in seeing Jack Graham in a clearer light. Frazier points out that even though a large number of Black families of freedmen continued to be dependent upon the mother after Emancipation, as was the case during slavery, new economic conditions enabled the Black man to gain a position of authority in the family, along with the aid of the Black church. Frazier attributes the man's tendency to buy land only to the practice of assimilating a behavior pattern from the former masters. He states,

> The more stable elements among the freedmen who had been in a position to assimilate the sentiments and ideas of their former masters soon undertook to buy land. This gave the husband and father an interest in his wife and children that no preaching on the part of white missionaries or [Black] preachers could give.[21]

No doubt Frazier agrees with Powdermaker that these were probably former house slaves that were in such a close proximity as to observe and mimic their former masters. But while he makes a good point about the improvement in the family status of the Black male by the acquisition of land and other responsibility, Frazier falls short of actually accounting fully for this propensity for land accumulation by looking into the African background and the Biblical tradition. Frazier does, however, acknowledge the fact that the African American male found moral support in the Bible for the patriarchal family set-up. "There was, of course, moral support for a patriarchal family to be found in the Bible and this fact contributed undoubtedly to a holy sanction for the new authority of the [Black] man in the family."[22] Without a doubt this

Biblical sanction had a tremendous impact on Jack Graham's climb to the height of his family set-up. But so did his African heritage figure into his style of operation and function in the family and community. In the community Jack Graham became a religious and social leader, head chieftain. And Frazier has something to offer on this classification.

> The leaders in creating a new community life were men who with their families worked land or began to buy land or worked as skilled artisans. It is important to observe that these pioneers in the creation of a communal life generally built a church as well as homes. Many of these pioneer leaders were preachers who gathered their communicants about them and became the leaders of the [Black] communities. This fact tends to reveal the close relationship between the newly structured life of the [African American] and his church organizations.[23]

Certainly this passage is applicable to Jack Graham. He was both a landowner and a skilled artisan, as well as a pioneer in building and leading communities as a preacher and pastor of numerous churches. But he was more than this, as so many other Black preachers of his day proved to be. He became a tribal chieftain, a builder of his own clan, and a keeper, healer, and preserver of the people, even a shaman. The last sentence in the above quotation suggests this, even though it goes unnoticed in the mind of Frazier.

The Religious Character and Context of the Times

In 1871, when Jack Graham was nine years old, a race riot occurred in Meridian, Mississippi, that greatly concerned the United States Congress, among other things. It seems that the United States Congress was investigating and hoping to pass a law curbing or outlawing the early efforts at the formation of an organization in the state then referred to as the "Ku-Klux." Consequently, after the riot of 1871 in Meridian numerous persons of different races and classes and from different parts of the state were sworn in testimony before the Joint Select Committee of the 42nd Congress, Second Session, 1871–72. These testimonies were published in volume one of *Reports of Committees of the House of Representatives for the Second Session of the 42nd Congress,* Washington, D.C. Government Printing Office, 1872.

The Meridian riot occurred on March 6, 1871, as a result of bold and militant efforts of Black citizens to protect themselves and assert their constitutional rights and liberties amid the developing reign of terror which was carved out by early efforts of the organizing of the Klan organization in the state. The purpose of these efforts, of course, was to prevent and destroy the political, social, educational and economic progress of Black people, to advance the interest of the Democratic Party in Mississippi against the advancement of the more liberal Republican Party which at that time was the Party for Black voters and political office-holders (naturally, because of the Emancipation under the Republican Administration of Abraham Lincoln). The most notorious areas where the scare tactics were carried on were those of east central Mississippi in and around Meridian, the county seat of Lauderdale County.

Meridian is located five or six miles from the Alabama state line, and the procedure used by the terrorists was to frighten, threaten, and attack Black political office-holders until they would leave their positions, and to agitate against and bring false claims against white Republican office-holders and politicians who were in sympathy with the Blacks. One of the tactics against the Black office-holders and leaders was to have certain men from across the Alabama state line claim to be Alabama law enforcement officers and come over into Meridian and bring charges against the Black citizens and take them back to Alabama for supposed legal proceeding, and they would never be heard from again (p. 6). As Meridian law enforcement officials refused to protect the Black citizens against this encroachment, it was reported in the testimonies that a delegation of Black citizens of Meridian had gone to the Governor in Jackson about the matter and had returned and called a meeting of the Black citizens on Saturday, March 4, 1871, on the grounds of the courthouse to report what had transpired and to organize the Black citizens to arm and protect themselves against these violations of their rights.

There was clearly demonstrated a strong, assertive, and fearless attitude of Black citizens of the area for their equality and independence. They were not terrified by the developing Klan, but rather organized themselves to resist them. According to the testimonies, the assertiveness of these Blacks at this meeting were described by the whites of the Democratic Party as "incendiary" and the one leading Black spokespersons at the meeting, Clopton, was arrested, and it was at his "trial" on Monday, March 6, that the riot broke out (pp. 7 and 9).

Aside from all the interesting and revealing facets of these testimonies (regarding the character and nature of peoples of this period), which will be dealt with in another section of the research, the most pertinent for now is the religious involvement, the participation of the churches, and interweaving of the religious, political, and the social. Of particular interest is the participation in these affairs of a Rev. Mr. Moore who was both the Pastor of New Hope Baptist Church in Meridian, and a representative to the state legislature of the time, (also the participation of what was referred as an "African" and a "Negro" Method Church). The religious spirit of the actions then, of the actions of the congregation of Moore's Church during his time and afterward in keeping hope alive,[24] all stand out as worthy of note.

In the riot on Monday, March 9, 1871, Judge Bramblet, who was holding a 3:00 p.m. hearing or trial of the two Black men, Tyler and Clopton, who had been arrested for "incendiary" remarks made at the meeting on the Saturday before, was killed, as well as Tyler and Clopton. That Tuesday night, three other prominent Black men who had been placed in custody during the outbreak of violence, were taken from custody and murdered in the woods. According to the testimony of O.C. French, a member of the Mississippi State Legislature and Chairman of the State Joint Committee investigating the riot:

Three other men were arrested and placed in the care of the sheriff, it was not proven or claimed by anybody that those three men had committed any offense. They were known there as prominent colored men; that is the way they were designated before the committee. In fact, one of them went to the sheriff and asked for his protection. As represented by parties who testified before us, they were placed under guard for their protection. They remained under guard Monday and Tuesday. On Tuesday night, they were taken out of the room where they were under guard and carried off into the woods, and murdered. We could not get any statement under oath as to who murdered these men. (p. 7).

It was in this general sense of lawlessness that the circumstances and actions surrounding New Hope Baptist Church's Rev. Moore are made clear. Moore was also the representative to the State Legislature from Lauderdale County. He was there at the courthouse during the trial and consequent riot and would also have been killed had it not been for the fact that the body of the slain Judge Bramblet had fallen partially on him and he too was presumed dead. His house was burned down. Three or four search parties went out after him, a special train was chartered on the Meridian road to find and arrest him, but Moore succeeded in escaping back to Jackson, where he found protection (p. 10). Even after the Legislature adjourned, Moore would not dare go back to his home of Meridian, having been duly warned by the postmaster, among others, of the dangers of doing so (p. 17).

Furthermore, the church which he pastored, New Hope Baptist Church, founded in 1865 by Blacks who withdrew from the White Baptist Church of the city after the Civil War and established an independent religious institution, had also been burned at the time of the riot because it was a major center for Black organizational strength and activities of the day. Many, if not most, of the city's leading Black political and business men and citizens were members of this church. All of this attests to the central place religion held in the character and actions of the Blacks whose assertive efforts were a root cause of the eruptions that occurred. It was reported that many Blacks, possibly as many as 200, left

Meridian after the riot. But most remained there and retained the spirit
of assertiveness, strength, and resiliency as seen in the subsequent history
of the New Hope Baptist Church, which was rebuilt the following year,
1872.

The celebration of that church's 122nd anniversary in September,
1987, under the pastorage of Rev. Elijah Jackson, presents sketches and
descriptive phrasings which reflect the spirit of the people who stayed
and braved the negative forces which challenged them and continued to
build and expand the dreams of a people under a kind of siege. The
Program Bulletin describes the history in brief under four historical and
theological headings. "Little Hope," referring to the period after the
Civil War in 1865 when former slaves were dissatisfied with the White
First Baptist Church in Meridian and decided to withdraw from it and
form their own church, first located in a brush arbor in a field, where
branches were cut and placed around the area to enclose the section of
worship. The second period, "More Hope," indicates the work of former
slaves a few months later in cutting down trees and constructing a frame
building for their house of worship which they officially called New Hope
Baptist Church. The third period, "Fading Hope," reflects the tragedy
of 1871, when the Klan burned the church down amidst the activities of
the riot of Meridian of that period. The writer of the brief historical
descriptions for the bulletin states this:

> The meeting place of most Blacks of the community was New Hope Baptist
> Church where strategy was planned to counteract Klan activities. The
> meetings angered the Klan members and as a result they burned the church
> down, and ran the Minister out of town (Church Bulletin, September, 27,
> 1987).

The fourth period is described by the phrase "Renewed Hope,"
indicating the continued faith and vision of the people who, under new
ministerial leadership (Rev. J. L. Jordan, E. H. Tripplett) built a stronger
more permanent structure only one year later (1872) and rebuilt it in
1889, a structure which lasted almost a century.

In 1962 the present church was built under the pastorage of Rev. C. O. Inge, a fine brick edifice with spacious sanctuary, three choir lofts, and an open baptistery, pastor's study office, work room, fellowship hall with choir room, Sunday School rooms, library and kitchen, air conditioned, with numerous restrooms.

The Bulletin for the 122nd anniversary celebration closes its description with the words:

> From the beginning of Little Hope, More Hope, Fading Hope, and Renewed Hope, New Hope stands, not only as a dream deferred, but through faith, a dream realized with future dreams yet to be fulfilled.[25]

The spirit of these people in this particular church in Meridian, who underwent these experiences from generation to generation and continued under the worst of times to press forward against all odds, exemplifies the kind of strength, determination, endurance, and resiliency of the religious character and meaning instilled in the people of the area.

Endnotes

1. Peggy W. Crenshaw and Jesse O. McKee, eds., *Sense of Place: Mississippi* (Jackson: University Press of Mississippi, 1979).

2. T. D. Young, "Mississippi: Two Views from the Outside," in Peggy W. Crenshaw and Jesse O. McKee, *Sense of Place: Mississippi* (Jackson: University Press of Mississippi, 1979), p. 65.

3. Also as reflected in Hortense Powdermaker's study, *After Freedom: A Cultural Study in the Deep South* (New York: Russell and Russell, 1939,, and James W. Silver's *Mississippi: The Closed Society* (New York: Harcourt, Brace, and World, Inc., 1963); and many other works.

4. See William Raspberry, "Mississippi Reflects Dixie's Change," *Tampa Tribune*, Wed., Jan. 6, 1988, p. 7A.

5. Jack Graham's father was used as a stud to bear slaves in Alabama. He died when Jack was very young (interviews with Cleveland Graham and others in May, 1988).

6. See, for instance, Albert Rabateau, *Slave Religion: The 'Invisible Institution' in the Antebellum South* (New York: Oxford University Press, 1978); C. Eric Lincoln, *Race, Religion, and the Continuing American Dilemma* (New York: Hill and Wang, 1984); Gayraud Wilmore, *Black Religion and Black Radicalism: An Interpretation of the Religious History of Afro-American People* (Maryland, N.Y.: Orbis Books, 1983); John Hope Franklin, *From Slavery to Freedom* (New York: Alfred A. Knofp, 1967); and Charles H. Long, *Significations* (Phila: Fortress Press, 1986).

7. Long, p. 176.

8. Long, p. 174.

9. Powdermaker states that ex-slaves often included slavemasters as part of their lineage especially since their names stemmed from them, p. 56.

10. Interestingly, the *Deed Record* shows Jack Graham as having purchased 160 acres of land from the Farmer's Loan and Trust of Mobile Alabama for $360.00 on December 18, 1903.

11. She was also listed on an alternate page as having married on January 5, 1893.

12. Hortense Powdermaker, *After Freedom: A Cultural Study in the Deep South* (New York: Russell and Russell, 1939).

13. See also E. Franklin Frazier, *The Black Bourgeoisie* (New York: Collier Books, 1962), pp. 172–75, where the author speaks extensively of the emptiness and shallowness of the Black middle-class; also Harold Cruse, *The Crisis of the Negro Intellectual* (New York: William Morrow and Co., 1967) pp. 282–84, who agrees with him.

14. Powdermaker, pp. 62–63.

15. *Ibid.*

16. *Ibid.*, xiv–xv.

17. *Ibid.*, pp. 57–58.

18. *Ibid.*, p. 57.

19. *Ibid.*, p. 58.

20. *Ibid.*, p. xix.

21. Certainly the Homestead Act passed by Congress in 1866 is what most former slaves benefitted from in acquiring land. And Jack Graham probably took advantage of this opportunity since it was at least 18 years after Emancipation that he acquired land.

22. *The Negro Church in America* (New York: Schocken Books, 1963), pp. 32–34.

23. *Ibid.*, p. 33.

24. *Ibid.*

25. The history of New Hope Baptist Church, published as a part of the 122nd anniversary celebration in 1987, divides into four sections on "hope": "Little Hope," "More Hope," "Fading Hope," "Renewed Hope," each describing successive periods of struggles of the church to survive economic problems and racial onslaughts.

BACKGROUND, HISTORY, PROFILE, AND CULTURAL MAKE-UP OF THE MERIDIAN AREA

Visiting Meridian, one may wonder at its mixtures of urban and rural components, of industrial progressiveness and cultural simplicity. Or the question may arise, why can one not get a jet plane to Meridian? Why is there only the commuter shuttle that lands there? Why does one have to catch a jet to Jackson and rent a car or catch a shuttle plane or bus to Meridian? After all, Meridian is the third largest town in Mississippi and once served briefly as the capital. Questions such as these may arise and can only be answered satisfactorily by considering a brief account of the history and socio-cultural make-up of the area. Such was the question raised by one of the Freedom Workers who labored in the summer projects situated in numerous counties and towns in Mississippi in 1964, including Meridian, who wrote:

> I felt the sacrifice the [Black people] have been making for so long. How the [Black people] are able to accept all the abuses of the whites—all the insults and injustices which make me ashamed to be white—and then turn around and say they want to love us, is beyond me. There are [Black people] who want to kill whites and many [Blacks] have much bitterness but still the majority seem to have the quality of being able to look for a future in which whites will love the [Black people]. Our kids [in the Freedom project schools] talk very critically of all the whites around here and still they have a dream of freedom in which both races understand and accept each other.[1]

She adds, "There is such an overpowering task ahead of these kids that sometimes I can't do anything but cry for them. I hope they are up to the task, I'm not sure I would be if I were a Mississippi Negro."

It has been twenty-five years since this event took place, and the question remains to be answered, I believe, as to what in the culture, religion, and social make-up of the indigenous Meridians of the Black race enabled them to be "up to the task." For certainly, they have proven themselves "up to the task," having survived the tremendous ordeals of that period, and earlier, such as brutal slayings of Goodman, Chaney, and Schwerner, who were Freedom Workers stationed in Meridian during the same year mentioned in the letter. James Chaney was a native Black Meridianite, whose funeral was held there in the city on August 7, 1964. Although the killings did not take place at Meridian but rather in nearby Philadelphia, Meridian obviously felt the full impact.

This chapter will look into the background of the religious, social, and cultural make-up of the Black society of Meridian and some surrounding counties such as Lauderdale, Kemper, Clarke, that enabled these people to remain in their local home settings and withstand the ordeals they had to face historically without either undergoing mental breakdowns or abandoning the situation and escaping north, as so many of their race did, including the family of the present author. Although Meridian shares much in common with the rest of the history and culture of the state of Mississippi, this study will attempt to show that something of peculiar and distinctive interest and significance exists among the people in this locale.

During the turbulent years of the 1960's when most other cities in Mississippi such as Jackson, Greenwood, Philadelphia, were extremely violent in their attitudes and actions toward freedom-seeking Black citizens and civil rights workers, Meridian was viewed as "liberal" by comparison. They even had an unofficial bi-racial committee to help keep peace and harmony between the two races while in other towns there were daily beatings of civil rights workers, as well as frequent killings.

Great music, literature, and art have been contributed to American culture and the world by persons coming from this "backward" state. Black and white literary and musical figures, such as William Faulkner, Richard Wright, Leontyne Price, have come from this state (Price and Wright not far from Meridian). I would like to examine the cultural foundations that have been conducive to the stimulation of the artistic imagination, and to the human achievement in other areas such as politics and social life, where such figures as Medger Evers and Charles Evers and Fannie Lou Hamer are concerned.

There is much cultural and human interest in Meridian within itself, and Black people, who comprise about 45% of the population, have contributed much to it. One wonders, for instance, why, even though the town has progressed from the simple agrarian status to an industrial character, it has no major airport. There is something in the nature of the people which accounts for this. Meridian is the third largest city in this state of over 2 1/2 million people, comprising 46,577 people as of the 1980 census, next to Biloxi's 49,311. The largest city and capital, Jackson, by contrast, is more than four times the population of each of these two cities, having over 200,000 people. This too is an interesting phenomenon worth exploring. The 1978 manufacturing statistics reveal transportation equipment as Mississippi's leading industry. Meridian is shown as the center of that industry. It is also a center of lumber and forest products and textiles and clothing, which are high on the list, as well.

The Origin of the "Queen City" and Its Surroundings

A famous match between the L & N [trains] and the Queen and Crescent line in competition for a government mail contract occurred in 1883. Both had to go from Cincinnati to New Orleans. The Queen and Crescent made a four-minute stop in Meridian to pick up a fresh engine and engineer, and left behind the name 'Queen City' for the town that helped it win the race by four hours and ten minutes (Laura N. Fairley and James T. Dawson, *Paths to the Past: An Overview History of*

Lauderdale County, Mississippi[Meridian: Lauderdale County Department of Archives, 1988]), p. 103.

Meridian is located in Lauderdale County, which was founded in 1833. Counties surrounding the area include Clarke, Wayne, Jones, to the south and southwest; Newton, Scott, Jasper and Smith to the west and southwest; Kemper, Noxabee, Lowndes to the North; Neshoba, Leake, Winston, and Oktibbeha to the northwest. These lands and more were the home of the Choctaw before the intrusions of outsiders. There was an intermingling of several ethnic and racial groups with the Choctaws in the area prior to its takeover by Europeans. The earliest comers of French, English, and Scotch-Irish settlers and traders intermarried with the Choctaw bringing about some merging of cultures. And Black slaves who had been captured by the Choctaws from other groups when they sacked a French garrison remained with them, some even accompanied this Native American group when they were finally transferred to the reservations after their finally unsuccessful battles to resist encroachments.[2] The land began to be peopled by white families from Virginia, the Carolinas, and Georgia after 1800.[3] The state of Mississippi itself was formed in 1817, and as for the area that was to become Lauderdale County, it was in 1830 at the Treaty of Rabbit Creek that the fate of the Choctaws was sealed. "The treaty spelled the end to the Choctaw hold on the last of their Mississippi homelands and opened the door that permitted the birth of the county and its neighbors."[4]

By 1840 five thousand whites were settled in Lauderdale County, but few Blacks lived there, as few if any of the whites owned slaves. Although fifty-two percent of the state of Mississippi as a whole was slave and forty-eight percent white, the white settlers in the east central section of the state were at a survival level of subsistence and unable to afford slaves.[5] Fairley and Dawson found evidence that these early white settlers were poor but satisfied with their lives and resistant to change. "All evidence seems to indicate the first settlers arrived in the new county armed with little but faith, hope and a stubborn streak. Many came into the area with all their worldly possessions bundled onto an ox-drawn cart."[6] They state further that, "Contentment rather than wealth seems to have been the main goal of many of the early families."[7] Their study revealed that Black peoples' entrance into the area as slaves contributed greatly to the process of clearing fields and building the first homes. But indications are that these slaves were sympathetic toward the Native Americans "whose homelands their white owners had acquired." And seeing the abandoned gravesites of the Choctaws, the slaves interpreted the sad sounds of whispering pines as their ghosts mourning the loss of their homes. However, many of the Choctaws remained in the area helping white farmers harvest their crops in fall, and selling venison, baskets, and bows and arrows at other times of the year.[8] So, even at this early period of the area's history, it was an interesting cultural mixture.

Writing and publishing a paper in 1962 titled, "Progress Report, 1831–1962, Citizens of Color in Meridian, Mississippi," John Barksdale highlights the history and development of Black people in the city. According to his report they were there playing a vital role in the founding of the city. He states:

In 1831, Richard McLemore migrated from South Carolina, with some of his slaves to clear a plantation on the present site of Meridian. These dark-skinned toilers of the soil, worked diligently for the area's earliest "pioneers," and soon he was offering land free to white settlers he thought would make desirable neighbors. From then until the eighteen fifties, the first Meridian [Blacks] were to continue to clear this wilderness for plantations they were to build and farm on as slaves. In 1854, plans were made for two important railroad sites to be established in this area; since it was considered to form a junction, the name Meridian was chosen over the protest of the farmers who wanted the name "Sowashee," the name of a nearby creek. The [Blacks'] strong backs and tireless limbs became important now as he [sic] was to clear the path for what was to make Meridian an important transportation center—the RAILS.[9]

Fairley and Dawson detail the development of other areas of Lauderdale County prior to that of Meridian because the Choctaw legacy there of former villages could easily be turned into rural trading centers. Areas such as Alamucha, Chunkeyville, Hurricane Creek, Whynot, and others predated Meridian.[10] The authors noted one white settler, J. R. Romer's building of the first sawmill in the county with help of his four sons and three slaves. They also took note of a tradition of cooperation among the settlers in building their log cabin houses—neighbors helping neighbors:

> Log rollings and houseraisings were more than a way to welcome new arrivals. The community efforts were social events, with participants ready and willing to invest a day's work for the reward of a mealtime spread of fresh vegetables and game. A cabin could be erected in less than three days' time as communal labor speeded the chore.[11]

Religion and education captured the attention of the early settlers after they had taken care of their basic needs of building homes and farming. The first schools in the area had been Choctaw, however, set up in their homelands by Presbyterian Missionaries as early as the 1820's. Some individuals set up schools such as the Pickney Vaugh School and the River's School.[12] But a county law in 1846 provided for a board of school commissioners, among other things, which made possible the establishment of common schools as a more formal system of education. The first formal church congregations began to take shape in 1838 as Baptist and Methodist bodies. Fairley and Dawson noted the "civilizing" influence the religious bodies had on the populace:

> These early churches provided a civilizing influence in a still-untamed land, often passing sanctions against individual members who strayed into such sinful areas as dancing, drinking whiskey, allowing their hogs to run free over a neighbor's property and swapping houses on the Sabbath. The church sanctions, which could involve public disgrace and expulsion from the congregation, helped hold the line of "law and order," until the county's judicial system grew out of its infancy. Once accused of a violation of church rules, a member would be called in front of the congregation during a Saturday meeting. If the church members accepted the accused's

"defense," he would be forgiven and pardoned by the church. If not, the violator could face public disgrace and expulsion from the congregation.[13]

These moral sanctions and tough disciplinary practices at this early period in the county's history set the stage for what we shall see later as a tradition of restraint and conservative practices in the Meridian area.

In much agreement with John Barksdale, cited earlier, Fairley and Dawson elaborate upon Richard McLemore as the founding "Father of Meridian." They declare that he

> had put down, in 1834, his claim to 700 acres where the city now stands. The Virginia native and his wife, Nancy Perry Hill, built their first home at what is now the corner of Eighteenth Avenue and Eleventh Street out of hewn logs mortised with wooden pegs. Later, the pioneer would build another home at the present site of Fifth Street and Thirty-First Avenue. With his nearest neighbor eight miles away, McLemore began to recruit neighbors, sending back to the east word of the young county's potential and offering 'ample lands to many whom he thought would make desirable citizens.'[14]

McLemore's careful selectivity of neighbors is another trait that appears to have been passed on to later generations of residents in the city of Meridian and the surrounding area. It is manifested specially in Meridian's careful watchfulness of its citizens' character and behavior patterns and weeding out of the "undesirables," as we shall see later. It took decades before the village McLemore envisioned would materialize into the city of Meridian. In the meantime, he busied himself with significant tasks of organizing churches and schools in addition to attending his own family and business affairs.

The Development of Lauderdale County and Surrounding Areas— Character and Composition

Law and order was a strong emphasis among the populace, both slave and free. The churches played a major role in this before and after a system of civil justice came into being. Restrictions on the slave society in the areas of religion and education were meant to prevent possible rebellions. Although there were two types of Black worship, both biracial and independent (also, we may add the "invisible institution" worship groups or "bush arbors"), the fears of Black rebellion brought about two main restrictions—the Poindexter Code of 1838 and the Mississippi Code of 1857—throughout the state.[15] The former denied Blacks the freedom to preach and the latter prohibited any Blacks, free or slave, from meeting for any reason in groups numbering above five except under the overseership of whites in the case of religious worship. There was then no legal development of Black churches or schools before the Civil War. Law and order in the civil area for the general society was stressed in the development of the first formal court sessions in the county in the northwestern section in a spot called Courthouse Hill. Later came the institution of county and circuit judges and establishment of the first county seat at Old Marion, a step toward ending "rampant lawlessness." Fairley and Dawson cite the county's first capital punishment as taking place three miles from Old Marion. They record a report that a "criminal was hanged from an oak tree after a guilty verdict was pronounced in a hasty court session held around a wagon."[16]

Another characteristic of the Lauderdale County area in these early years which helps to explain its present character is reported by Fairley and Dawson. And that is the slow growth and settlement of the area in contrast to that of other regions of the state, such as those along the Mississippi River. The Choctaw is said to have delayed progress in Lauderdale and neighboring counties. Even the slave population remained small in Lauderdale County in the 1830's, as the farmers there were relatively poor by contrast with their richer neighbors in Western portions of the state. They are said to have been hard workers in their businesses, usually side by side with their slaves, if they happened to have them.

These farmers provided a sharp contrast with the comparative leisure of planters in western counties who could afford to sit back and watch their riches grow under the cultivation of hundreds of slaves. That fact, ironically, would benefit Lauderdale County, in that it escaped the devastating impact of the Financial Panic of 1837, when the good times for many speculators ended and banks failed abruptly.[17]

What provided a real boost to the development of Lauderdale County, Meridian, and neighboring areas was the coming of the railroad, the "Iron Horse," in the mid 1850's. In fact the 1850's were a time of increasing prosperity, with the increase in farming, such as cotton production, corn and other vegetables; and a flourishing industry with numerous grist mills, saw mills, a number of tanneries. Between 1848 and 1860 the slave population in the county grew from 2,218 to 4,711, which indicates the growth of a planter class. Fairley and Dawson note concerning the 1850's, "It would be an era of antebellum glory for some and a time of back-breaking labor for a small but growing slave force that helped make the prosperity possible."[18] Only about a third of the whites of the time owned slaves, most of those having fewer than five.[19]

Concerning the small town of Enterprise in neighboring Clarke County, where the Grahams were situated, Fairley and Dawson have an interesting account of its failed possibilities. In the 1850's Enterprise was a "thriving riverport town" which attracted much trade. By 1859 it was a boom town, and the Vicksburg, Jackson, and Brandon railroad (Alabama and Vicksburg) was originally headed for Enterprise, which would have made it the industrial and urban center that Meridian later became as a consequence of Enterprise's rejection of the railroad. Fairley and Dawson report:

> Enterprise citizens, fearing it would bring dirt and commercialism to their prosperous settlement, rejected overtures of railroad officials who hoped to connect with the M & O [Mobile and Ohio] there. A. W. Malone noted in his history of Meridian that Enterprise, then the largest town on the M & O, with 60 money-making merchants '...was fully able to come to the relief of the road, but her refusal to do so brought about her ruin.' As the steamboat era passed with the arrival of the tracks, Enterprise also faded while the infant village of Meridian reaped the rewards.[20]

Here then was the springboard for the rise of Meridian to urban and industrial prosperity. As soon as Ragdale [large landowner who purchased much of Richard McLemore's land in what is now Meridian, first name, Lewis] heard of Enterprise's refusal to deal with the A & V officials, he jumped in to lay out the red carpet from Meridian, "promising them all the land they wanted for railroad purposes and otherwise assisting them to the best of his ability."[21] Ragdale, along with another large landowners, John T. Ball, who had also purchased much of McLemore's land in the area now known as Meridian, "began an all-out, although still competitive, effort to promote their home, complete with large posters announcing the sale of lots and barbecue dinner."[22] After much debate, resistance, and conflict with other residents and farmers, Ball and Ragdale and others promoting the rails got their wishes. And on February 10, 1860, Meridian was chartered as a city by the state legislature. But only after the Civil War did Meridian reach its prosperity and become the most important railroad center in the eastern part of the state.[23]

The War Years

During the Civil War General William T. Sherman vowed to destroy Meridian as an important link between the South and the East because of its railroads. He arrived there in 1864, and James W. Garner quotes Sherman as declaring: "The destruction of the railroads intersecting Meridian is of great importance and should be done thoroughly. Every tie and rail for many miles in each direction should be absolutely destroyed or injured, and every bridge and culvert should be completely destroyed."[24] Houses and public buildings were plundered and destroyed, livestock seized, and businesses and Confederate establishments destroyed. Several days after the assault on Meridian, Sherman reported: "For five days, 10,000 men worked hard with a will in that work of destruction with axes, crowbars, sledges, clawbars, and fire, and I have no hesitation in pronouncing the work well done. Meridian...no longer exists."[25]

As John Barksdale declares, "Contrary to Sherman's infamous report, Meridian began to develop and has continued to grow steadily since that almost fatal date with destiny." It was rebuilt after the War as a railroad center and grew rapidly, and by the end of the 19th century Meridian was fast becoming a manufacturing center. Other towns and villages in the path of Sherman's Mississippi campaign in the surrounding area were devastated just as much as Meridian. Decatur, the county seat of Newton County suffered some thirty buildings burned. Lake Station had two livery stables destroyed, the machine shops, three locomotives, a railroad water tank, a turntable, thirty-five cars, two saw mills, and much lumber.

> At Enterprise, the chief place in Clarke County, the railroad depot, two flour mills, fifteen thousand bushels of corn, two thousand bales of cotton, two hospitals, and other buildings were burned. At Marion, the county seat of Lauderdale, the railroad station, and several other buildings were burned. Quitman, on the Mobile and Ohio road about fifty miles below Meridian, had two flour mills, a saw mill, depot, and other buildings burned while almost the entire length of the railroad between it and Meridian was destroyed.[26]

Lauderdale, Hillsboro, Bolton, and Canton were towns that suffered a similar fate.[27]

Before going further, it is revealing to look at the Civil War participation of some of the racial groups and other facets of Meridian and Lauderdale County life during the time.

Fairley and Dawson note that since so few of the families owned slaves, they "had no strong feelings about the ideological reasons behind the conflict."[28] Mostly, it appears, the people were concerned about protecting their way of life. With similar concern, apparently, the Choctaws and Black slaves also participated in the War. The Choctaws are reported to have been brave soldiers devoted to the Confederate cause. The authors tell of their battalion's formation:

During the war, Major J. W. Pearce of Haxelhurst organized a battalion of
Choctaw under the authority of the War Department, with Indians from
Kemper, DeKalb, Neshoba, Jasper, Scott and Newton counties forming the
'First Battalion of Choctaw Indians, Confederate Army.'[29]

One incident historically noted in which their loyalty and bravery was
displayed was the Chunky River train accident of 1863, in which sixty
Confederate soldiers lost their lives as a train carrying about 100
passengers, most headed for service in Vicksburg, plunged into the
flooded Chunky River. Choctaw soldiers stationed at their Newton
County camp were among the first to hear and respond to the cries for
help. They are reported to have been on the scene at once, plunging into
the raging waters and rescuing more than a dozen of the injured and
later helping to bury those who could not be saved. Major S. G. Spann,
who served with the Choctaw and headed the Battalion of Mounted
Scouts, described the Choctaws as exemplary soldiers, stating that they
were at their best "in the skirmish and sharpshooter service." As scouts,
he says, they served as "pilots through pathless swamps and jungles, and
over boundless prairies."[30]

As to the participation of Blacks of the area in the Civil War, on the
side of the Confederacy, Fairley and Dawson report that,

> Many slaves from area plantations accompanied whites to Civil War
> battlefields, according to pension applications and other records. Two
> former slaves who applied for Confederate pensions in Lauderdale County
> were Abraham Bell, who went to war as a servant of John W. Bell for two
> years, and Isaac Pringle, who was with F. M. Pringle in Civil War battles
> from 1862 until the close of the war.[31]

Decades later former slaves reported how some slaves "marched to the
front lines with their white masters, either out of loyalty or on orders of
plantation owners."[32]

Fairley and Dawson describe the activity of many slaves during the
time and quote their particular descriptions of the happenings during the
war.[33] Noting the freedom brought to the slave by the collapse of the

Confederacy in April, 1865, Fairley and Dawson indicate that it was hardly to be much enjoyed in the midst of the poverty and devastation suffered by both Blacks and Whites alike.

> Both whites and blacks faced new challenges as they struggled to cope. Many former slave owners, such as A.D. Hunter and George Chandler, strapped themselves in the general poverty left by the war, indicated they were relieved to be free of the responsibility of feeding and clothing their former hands. For most, finding enough food to feed their immediate families was a challenge in the post-war years. Former slaves, set free but still shackled by poverty, would join whites as the focus of all effort once again became survival.[34]

John Barksdale quotes the *Meridian Clarion* as declaring after the collapse of the Confederacy that Blacks could not possibly survive:

> They are a helpless people with no one to look after them, they have been turned loose like cattle with no food, clothing, medical care, minus knowledge and with no source of economic gain. It is an impossibility for them to survive...they will become extinct in less than a hundred years. My little daughter will see the last of the [Black people].[35]

Barksdale reports that this was the consensus feeling of many. But he declares that, "with little aid from the federal agencies appointed for their alleged well being (most notable—Freedman's Bureau) they did survive. Having been taught all manual chores and assimilating mechanical skills, and since Meridian was in a rebuilding process, the former slaves' services were recognized and ultimately utilized to the advantage of all. Thus, Meridian, with the [Black people] rose to become the largest city...in Mississippi and home of many of the state's most important industries."[36]

The Reconstruction and After

The twenty-year period after the war, 1865 to 1885, was probably and understandably the worst in Meridian history. They were dark days for both Black and White people alike. With both struggling to establish a way of life, politically, socially, educationally, religiously, and economically, there should have been little time for bitterness and hatred toward one another. Looking at the situation from the vantage point of today, one might say that all would have fared better if common bonds had been established between the races, who were now close to the same level economically, at least. But of course, there would have had to be some repentance, forgiveness, and acceptance of one another on an equal basis, among other things. And neither race was up to this kind of attitude or action, the whites least of all. The slavemaster sense of inferiority-superiority complex was far from dead.

Instead of the two races' seeing each other as mutual partners on the road to recovery, they obviously looked upon each other as the enemy in the way of their progress. An atmosphere of hostility and anger prevailed, and a racial and class war ensued that was at times hot and at other times cold. They drew the lines between them and dared not cross over generally. Of course, the whites were in control and dominated the process, but Black people for the most part wisely and expediently cooperated. Events were to happen that would do almost irreparable damage to the racial situation that even today has not been healed.

Yet the newly freed Black people seized upon the opportunities to become equal participants in the society both politically, socially, and economically. And this created severe problems. With Lauderdale County under federal control and military rule enforced by Northern troops and Black soldiers, and Black politicians elected to state and county offices, the former slaves were well on their way to playing their part in establishing a new way of life. But the other side—whites—for the most part were obviously not about to accept such a set-up.

By 1868, J. Aaron Moore, a black, was representing the county in the Reconstruction Legislature of 1868 which was composed of many former slaves elected under Republican control. Until 1871—when the first general election for county and local officers since the beginning of the

Reconstruction period was held—many discontented citizens fumed while under the control of strangers appointed by federal officers.[37]

As Meridian and surrounding areas began to grow and overcome some of the hardships, with the repair of the railroad and rebuilding of some mills and development of some businesses, the most devastating incident, outside of Sherman's march through it, occurred in Meridian, which in 1870 had replaced Marion as the county seat of Lauderdale. It was the Meridian riot of 1871, in which almost 30 people were killed. Fairley and Dawson record events leading up to the riot:

> Under Republican control Northern "strangers" and blacks did achieve a measure of power, with a Connecticut-born mayor, William Sturgis, in office in 1871. But, white Democrats refused to accept drastic changes. As tensions mounted, Joseph Williams, a black on the county's board of supervisors, was "called out of his house and killed" and another black supervisor was ambushed. Several Republican officers took their complaints about the actions of disgruntled whites to Governor Adelbert Ames, and on their return, black legislators, Warren Tyler and William Clopton, and preacher J. Aaron Moore, spoke at a rally. As events unfolded, the store owned by the mayor's brother, Theodore Sturgis, was set on fire, the blaze spreading until '...two thirds of the business houses of Meridian had been destroyed.' Tyler, Clopton and Moore were charged with inciting the uproar. On the following Monday, resolutions condemned the speeches made by the three men and a committee was appointed to request the removal of Mayor Sturgis from office.[38]

Fairley and Dawson in their accounts of the riot do not mention the activities of the developing "KuKlux," which was operating in the area attempting to undermine the political status of Blacks and Republicans, which all other accounts consulted do elaborate on extensively. James W. Garner, for instance, reports on the riot as an integral part of his chapter on "The KuKlux Disturbances in Mississippi."[39] He cites it as one of the subjects of investigation by the KuKlux committee of the U.S. government.[40] Garner comments that, "each race accused the other of responsibility for the affair," and declares that "political conditions were the remote cause, and when once the explosion came, the [Blacks] suffered the most."[41]

Another riot occurred ten years later in 1881 in the close-by town of Marion, in which the political conditions as the cause were even more evident. The contention was over voting rights, which was to be a problem of the area for years to come, finally erupting in the Freedom Workers' murders of 1964 (Goodman, Schwerner, and Chaney) and the firebombing of over twenty Black churches the same year.[42] It was reported to be the only riot in Mississippi in which Whites suffered the worst damage or loss of life. And it was motivated by the struggle between white Democrats and Republicans and Blacks. When Republican Ed Vance led a group of Blacks to vote at Marion Station, white Democrats were on the scene to try to prevent them. In the ensuing struggle a number of persons were wounded and four white men killed. After the riot the Democrats gained political control in the county.[43]

A number of other catastrophes happened in Meridian and neighboring areas in the 1870's, including devastating fires (one in downtown causing a drop in property values and a decline in the population from 7,000 to 3,000) and the yellow fever epidemic in 1878. On the other hand a number of good occurrences came about in this decade. At the beginning of the decade, on July 4, 1870, the state legislature passed a law establishing a free public school system. And the Lauderdale County supervisors appointed its first slate of school directors the same year and began developing its schools. Fairley and Dawson note the churches that were established in the area, which were of an interesting cultural mixture: Methodist, Baptist, Catholic, Episcopal, Presbyterian, Black, and a Jewish Temple.[44]

By the mid 1880's Meridian was well on the way to becoming a boom town in the midst of the industrial revolution that was sweeping the country. The rail lines were rebuilt to the point of making the city one of the most important centers of the South, competing with Atlanta and Birmingham. The increased manufacture of cotton, timber, and other products stimulated the economy of the Meridian area, stepped up employment and population growth. The lumber industry soared in the area, and Meridian became a lumber industry center.[45] By 1900 Meridian had grown to a population of over 14,000, and Lauderdale County to over 38,000, with a Black and white ratio of approximately 50–50. One source described Meridian's growth in the following terms: "By the end of the century...manufacturing was competing with railroading for first place."[46]

Fairley and Dawson mentioned one community in Lauderdale county populated largely by Blacks that was booming somewhat on the basis of cotton, timber, and rails: Wilsondale. Around 1900 its population was at approximately one hundred residents.

> According to records, Wilsondale was named for a black educator, Professor Wilson, who helped the Meridian and Memphis railroad secure a right of way through the area. A depot for the M & M track stood across from the 650-acre section owned by Wilson, who came into the area from Neshoba County and became one of the largest black landowners in the county.[47]

It is reported that in the early 1900's the community possessed the only Black owned and operated horse-racing track in the county. It was patronized by both Blacks and Whites. There was also a sawmill, general store, and school in this community. However, with the onslaught of the boll weevil and later the Depression this community disappeared.

Another small town of interest mentioned by these authors is Graham, Mississippi, located nine miles west of Meridian and a mile from Meehan. The village came into being in 1880 around the timber business of W. J. Graham. He was a successful pine products dealer who operated a sawmill and turpentine still. However, the town did not survive the Depression of the 1930's.[48]

By 1907 Meridian was claimed as the largest city in Mississippi, and apparently the most progressive, and remained so until Jackson overtook it as the state's largest city in 1930.[49] The literature provides a mixed view of the Black populace of the city of Meridian. Describing the laboring class in the early 1900's, one source presents not too encouraging a picture:

> To the [Black people] who make up 35 percent of Meridian's population, fall the jobs requiring unskilled labor. They are used especially in sawmills, cottonseed oil mills, and gins, where strength and hardiness are requisite. As in most Southern cities, the servant class is exclusively [Black], and, though Meridian is well dotted with [Black] districts composed of one- and two-room cabins with tiny dirt plot yards, a few white people maintain servants' quarters in the rear of their homes for cooks, nurses, or chauffeurs.[50]

The *Illustrated Handbook of Meridian, Mississippi*, issued and published by the Meridian Board of Trade and Cotton Exchange in 1907, was designed to appeal to and attract more businesses, trade, residents, and general development. It depicted Meridian in glowing colors. From the descriptions this document gives one can get a picture of the character and atmosphere of the place, or of that they wished to project, as both a place of progress and development and one of peace and tranquility, a happy family sort of town, with public schools and colleges. To protect this image the writers found it necessary to show a law enforcement and policies of law and order that were conducive to crime prevention. In the process of projecting a satisfactory image of Meridian, the document, unfortunately, gives a derogatory impression of Black people that is obviously discriminatory and prejudiced.

For instance, in describing the "Street Working Brigade," an upgraded form of a chain gang, as designed for those convicted in police court to work off their fines by devoting labors to cleaning up and beautifying the city, the document makes a degrading reference to Blacks. It is not clear what the writer means by the claim, "the treatment these convicts receive is eloquently testified to by the fact that after a [Black] once serves a sentence on the street force it is no unusual thing to see him in the police court a candidate for the second, and sometimes for the third and fourth times."[51] No mention is made of the false arrests and police brutality and other discriminatory factors that caused so many Black males of the time to find themselves before police court.

Describing Meridian as "one of the best policed cities in the South," the document continues as it depicts the police force as promoting a system of "prevention rather than detection of crime." What it labeled a "follow-up" was really a secret surveillance of newcomers and Black citizens as a means of "ridding the city of an undesirable class of people, before they have had time to settle and draw about them others of their stripe." Again, Black people are depicted in a highly unfavorable light:

In dealing with the petty crimes, for which a very large portion of the Black race is guilty, the department [of Police] has adopted in large measure the system pursued in many other cities with great success—a dependence more or less on certain informers who may be depended on to locate [Blacks] who are wanted by the chief. Again, in the selection of men for the position of police officers, the employing bodies have given close attention to not alone the moral fitness of applicants for positions on the police force, but have sought to gather to the force men who have peculiar faculties for learning the names and habits of [Blacks] and retaining in their memories pictures of these undesirable people. There are officers on the force who know the name and personal history of four-fifths of the [Black] men and women of Meridian, and who know instantly where to locate a man or woman when wanted. As the criminal [Black] is a predatory individual it is one of the systems of the department to keep a record of the movements of these fellows, and when a petty theft is committed and the evidence points to one of these men with police histories, the officers are enabled to judge with almost certainty to which neighboring city or town he has escaped.[52]

The amount of prejudice and stereotyping, police harassment and false arrests indicated by the practices described in the above passage is simply appalling. Realizing how widely distributed was this document, one is not surprised at the crippling effects it had in promoting such attitudes toward young Black males especially. One sees immediately images of Richard Wright's *Black Boy*, the movie *To Kill a Mockingbird*, and other artistic depictions of the Black male and white justice. It was simply an ordinary assumption: In the eyes of the white Meridian law officers every Black man was guilty more or less.

Fairley and Dawson, on the other hand, give a different view of Black people during the time from the standpoint of the Black entrepreneurial class in Meridian and educational development. They note the impact of Meridian's prosperity on the Black community.

> According to a directory of black-owned businesses covering the years 1896 to 1900, Meridian Blacks were taking full advantage of new-found opportunities in the professions and business enterprises as they left the hard times of slavery and Reconstruction behind. The heart of the black commercial retail district was between Fifth and Fourth Streets.[53]

According to other information in the directory the Black population was industrious, frugal, and prosperous. More than fifty business establishments were reportedly owned and operated by Blacks in 1900. These included drug stores, undertakers, real estate corporations, tailoring and millinery stores, hotels, cafes, groceries, and a variety of other enterprises. "That same year, the black-owned Queen City Savings Bank was to open. The directory pointed out, 'Doctors Howard, Sherrod and Young are a credit to the community. Fully as much can be said for John W. Harris, Strayhorn & Berry, S. A. Rivers, D. P. Early, E. H. Gaston, J. M. Nimrocks, J. W. Smith, B. F. Sims, L. Coleman, J. A. Winston, Emmet Evans, S. I. Curlen, T. J. Wilson, H. H. Hollie, and many other business men.'"[54]

Fairley and Dawson note the tremendous expansion of educational establishments across Lauderdale County by 1880, both Black and White. By 1900 there reportedly were seventy-three White and forty-three Black schools in the county.[55] As early as 1888 the first brick public school building for Black children was erected in Meridian, paid for by proceeds from a bond issue voted by the White citizens. It was named Wechsler, after the Jewish Rabbi Jacob Wechsler, who led the movement to provide school facilities for Black children. It was built on Fifteenth Street between Thirteenth and Thirty-first Avenues.[56] There were three Black public schools in Meridian in 1900 (Wechsler, East End, and Valley Street), and three private schools (Lincoln School, Meridian Academy, and Girls Industrial Home School). Schools of higher education at the time included the Meridian Female College, the Mississippi Medical College, the Moffitt-McLaurin Institute for Girls in the White community; and the Negro Normal College for Blacks. Another Black college, Haven Institute, which dates back to 1865 when it opened as a private school in St. Paul Methodist Episcopal Church, gained prominence during the existence. The property was transferred to Rust College after the Institute closed in 1928–29.[57] Finally, it must be noted that the Meridian Baptist Seminary, which was founded in 1896 in the New Hope Baptist Church, was the first establishment to offer high-school education to Black people. It wasn't until 1915–16 that Wechsler added the ninth and tenth grades, and in 1918–19 the eleventh, and 1919–20 the twelfth grades were added to Welscher as the first public high-school in Meridian for Blacks.[58]

The last fifteen to twenty years of the 19th century were designated by Fairley and Dawson as "The Golden Age" of the history of Lauderdale County, Meridian, and neighboring areas. Even the Black society is considered to have enjoyed a boom time in development. But while their work is a very good socio-cultural and developmental study, it does not deal satisfactorily with the political realities of the times. It was, in fact, a time of tension and struggle between Blacks and Whites throughout the state. Black people outnumber White people in Mississippi. In 1860, out of a total population of 791,305, 437,404 were Black and 353,899 were White. In 1867 Blacks were registered to vote, and in thirty-two of the sixty-one counties of the state Blacks were in the majority, though this was not true in Lauderdale County. Therefore, it is easy to see why so many Blacks were elected to local and state offices.[59]

However, since Blacks were so active in the political life of the state on all levels after the Civil War, Whites became paranoid over the possibility of being governed by them. The Whites were therefore constantly at work to undermine the Blacks' participation in politics. Buford Satcher summarizes the fears and the struggles:

> When opponents of Black politics became alarmed over the increasing strength of Black politicians in the state, they launched an intensive effort to remove them from the political scene. Fearing that Blacks would eventually control their lives, the opposition perfected tactics during 1874 and 1875 which greatly reduced the number of Blacks who participated in the state's government. Though thousands of Blacks were denied the vote in the election of 1875, they were still powerful enough as a group to elect enough Blacks to be effective in the years ahead.[60]

The opposition, of course, were White Democrats. Realizing that they had not eliminated Blacks completely from politics and that Black voters and office holders were still a strong factor and possible threat, the Democrats increased their efforts to remove them from the political scene. Black politicians, for their part, developed tactics to survive in politics. But by 1890, white fears led to the adoption of a new constitution which further eliminated Blacks from politics. And when that new constitution took effect it left 120,000 Blacks disfranchised. Yet Blacks continued their struggle for political survival and managed to retain political offices in the state throughout the 1890's.[61]

The fact is that in the years after the close of Reconstruction Mississippi became a closed society par excellence. Between the years 1875 and 1890, "inequality was effected by force and regularized by law, that is, by the constitution" under which the state still operated as late as the 1960's. Black people were "deprived of their constitutional rights by violence, intimidation, and fraud. All the social and economic sanctions available were applied with savagery." "When agrarian distress in the late 1880's seriously threatened the one-party white supremacy control, 'whippings, mutilations, robberies, rapes, and murders by bands of men became the order of the day.'"[62] Perhaps, as discovered by some of the Freedom workers of the 1960's,[63] the violence against Blacks was not as prevalent in Meridian as in some other areas, but Meridian was no political haven. Jim Crow was very much entrenched there as well as the constant threat of racial violence. And the area of east central Mississippi, which includes Meridian and Lauderdale County, was filled with the kinds of characteristics and acts described by Judge J. J. Chrisman on the floor of the constitutional convention in 1890:

> It is no secret that there has not been a full vote and a fair count in Mississippi since 1875—that we have been preserving the ascendancy of the white people by revolutionary methods. In plain words we have been stuffing the ballot boxes, committing perjury, and...carrying the elections by *fraud* and violence until the whole machinery was about to rot down. No man can be in favor of the election methods which have prevailed...who is not a moral idiot.[64]

The 1960's and After

The Civil Rights Movement of the 1960's brought about a political and social revolution in the state of Mississippi, as it did in so many other parts of the South. And the Summer of 1964 was the climax for Mississippi. Meridian and Lauderdale County found themselves at the center of the whole showdown. More than a thousand mostly white freedom workers from the colleges and universities of the North descended on the state, organized and trained mostly by the Student Non-violent Coordinating Committee (SNCC) and the Congress of Racial Equality (CORE), to assist voter registration of Black people denied the ballot and to set up freedom schools in which to train Black citizens in voter education and racial cooperation and equality. It was a testy time for Mississippi. James Silver sums up the reactions of the state to the prospect of this coming invasion:

> To meet the anticipated horde of barbaric invaders in that summer, a furious Mississippi legislature enlarged local police powers to the point of

legalizing home-grown vigilante committees, doubled the size of the state
Highway Patrol and gave it police powers, and lashed out against those
miscreants who might engage in the vague and wondrous activity of criminal
syndicalism.[65]

When three of the Freedom Workers headquartered in Meridian
(James Chaney, Andrew Goodman, and Michael Schwerner) turned up
missing and were later found murdered, this "liberal" city of Meridian
was visibly shaken, to say the least. The eyes of the whole nation and the
world turned on Meridian and the state of Mississippi, as the mass media
blasted the pictures of these three young men across the pages of
newspapers and magazines and on the screens of television, and the
search was on, involving the U.S. Marshals and other law enforcement.
Silver sums it up well:

> The cold glare of publicity had been on the state all summer in the massive
> search for the corpses of the three slain civil rights workers and in the quest
> for evidence against the murderers in a hostile community. Congress
> responded by breaking a Southern filibuster to pass overwhelmingly a civil
> rights law which established the nation's will on the side of the [Black
> people]. The stepped up federal presence in Mississippi, while notably
> inconspicuous to those whose bodies were fair game to a large lawless
> element, was also indicative of a rapidly changing public opinion.[66]

We can get a much clearer picture of Meridian and surrounding
areas and their socio-economic and cultural make-up by examining the
words and reactions of those Black people who left the area because of
the pressures and later returned as compared and contrasted with the
attitudes and reactions of those who stayed. Most of the people
consulted for these interviews were the grandchildren of Reverend John
Henry (Jack) Graham, Sr. Gertrude, Annie, and Clara are the only
children of Pearl and John Henry Graham, Jr., who died in 1986 at the
age of 100. He had spent all of his life in Enterprise, Mississippi, in
Clarke County, where he was born the third child of his father John
Henry Graham, Sr. His two older daughters Annie and Clara never left

the Meridian area except to attend college and graduate school. The youngest daughter, Gertrude did leave for a few years during her first marriage. They bring experiences and viewpoints from the middle-class.

The daughters came from a very religious background, their father having been a deacon in one of his father, Rev. Jack Graham's churches, and he himself a devoted worker, servant. The two older daughters are retired now from the Meridian-Lauderdale County and the Wayne County school systems. The youngest still works as a counselor in one of the junior high schools in Meridian. One of the daughters spoke of the strong influence the religious background had on her as a person and a professional, her husband having been principal of a high school in Waynesboro, fifty miles south of Meridian, and she a teacher there before their retirement. She is a former resident of Meridian, however, and Enterprise in Clarke County, where the Grahams and their extended families have their homesteads and heritages. She has several children and grandchildren, as does her youngest sister. The middle sister has one child, a daughter, and two grandchildren.

The oldest daughter spoke of having had a religious background that enabled her to be a better person and to deal with people in the community on a professional and religious level. "Having become a Christian and accepted the religious principles taught by my parents has given me a better insight on life and enabled me to deal with people, to do unto others as I would have them do unto me."[67] She spoke of how belief in religious principles makes a stronger person with strong convictions of right and wrong and asserted that she also tried to instill in her students the same values. Seeing that religion made her a better person socially, emotionally, physically, and spiritually, she said she tried to convey the same to the young students she taught in order to help them become better persons.

The youngest sister stated similar views, but added the fact that they were raised up in their grandfather's church, which he pastored even before they were born, and the grandfather's teachings influenced them as they did their father.

He instilled in us that there is nothing one can't do. He always taught us to
have a great belief in what you can do. He taught us to drive the cars, etc.
We grew up in the church and worked in the church as youngsters, and that
had a great impact on our lives. Having grown up in a Christian home as
poor people, yet we had a great desire for education. We didn't have much
money, but we had great courage from our parents and grandparents.
Therefore, I felt like there was no limit to what I could do. And I still feel
that way.[68]

With such a background she pointed out that she has been successful in
most things she has tried, and even with failures and other difficulties;
her religious experience has enabled her to work through these. She also
felt that being an honest person has a lot to do with success in one's life,
belief in working for what one earns and treating people fairly as one
goes along in life. Helping others, she says, caused some of the blessings
to come back to her in various ways.

This youngest sister was a teacher for many years, but teaching didn't
fully satisfy her. Neither did being a principal, which she was for three
years. Having done a lot of counseling as she taught students, she
discovered that her real calling was to be a school counselor. Her
position is now counselor to eighth and ninth graders in one of the
Meridian junior high schools. She is at one of the most prestigious
schools in the city, but those grade levels are also some of the most
problematic for children. And she is able to counsel these students more
successfully because of her strong religious roots and training. The school
is fifty percent Black, with a cross section of wealthy White and Black
and poorer classes of both races. Her academic training was at Jackson
State College (B.S. degree), Nevada Southern and Mississippi State
(M.S. in Guidance and Counseling). She also has an Education Specialist
Certificate.

The youngest sister's present husband was a very distinguished
gentleman, much older than she and was at the time of the interview
homebound because of illness. But he had made tremendous
contributions to the community of Meridian, the state and the nation,

according to the testimony of his family and the listing in *Who's Who Among Black Americans 1975–76.* Having been a prominent businessman who owned and operated a variety of businesses, he served for years as president of the NAACP of Meridian, on the state level, and on the Board of Directors of the National NAACP. He was also a devoted churchman, serving as Steward and Lay Leader at the St. Paul United Methodist Church. His wife described him as a very dedicated man who had a lot of respect in the Meridian area, as well as nationally, because he worked very hard in many capacities. He inherited his character from his father whom he often described as a Christian man who did not have very much education, but was a hard worker and a successful liver back in those post-Civil War times when people were very poor. His father had what he called a "cleaner shop" when bringing up his children. They would clean clothes for people. His father always advocated having several jobs and never depending on one job for a living. So the son himself lived this way.

His wife says he was a traveling salesman for some thirty odd years, going to several states. He was one of those persons who had to leave Mississippi for a good while because he could not do his kind of work there. She said being so heavily involved in the NAACP, both nationally and locally, he had to leave Mississippi. He worked so hard for civil rights until he worked himself out of some jobs.

One of his sales areas was contracting for the photography business and rings and jewelry business of various schools. In the state of Mississippi they would not contract with a Black, but would rather give the business to whites. But becoming a traveling salesman in this business he became well-known across many states. And when he would show up at many schools and universities they would show preference for him because of his civil rights reputation with the NAACP.

Describing her husband's community activities, the wife says he went to church on Sundays both day and night, and he couldn't understand why people would not go to church on Sunday. As president of the NAACP of Meridian for many years, he brought up many youth groups in the organization. He would lay aside everything to make the NAACP meetings. As a member of the National Board he flew to New York every three months to make the Board meetings. According to his wife it was he who helped to keep a balance in the racial situation in Meridian, because many of them "believed he was for the right and true civil rights part of the NAACP." He was honest and never accepted money for his chores, nor any payoffs or bribes, not even gas money for taking people to the polls to vote.

> So the better class of white people respected him and do so to this day. His life was spared. When his name would come up in KKK meetings, they'd say 'I'll take care of him,' so they just kept postponing things and nobody ever really did anything to him. And he has a lot of respect among the whites even to this day.[69]

Her husband was born in Lauderdale, a little town about seventeen miles north of Meridian.[70]

As to the very trying times of racial tragedies, dangers, and upheavals and the transitions to more peaceful and progressive times for Black people in the area, the Graham sisters had some interesting revelations. They acknowledged that Blacks in the state and their area have borne many burdens and trials, and numerous ones have left the state in order to find a better life and more tolerable conditions. The youngest sister's husband was one of those who had to leave because of his civil rights activities, but he returned to the area as things got better. And many others who left have also returned. These people lived through the times of the murders of Medgar Evers ninety miles away in Jackson, of Emmett Till, of Goodman, Chaney, and Schwerner only 30 miles away in Philadelphia, and many other tragic racial incidents. But their families remained in the area for the most part. They own their own homes in rather modest suburban areas of Meridian and Waynesboro, with large well-kept lawns, in some cases as much as an acre on corner lots. They own businesses and other real estate.

The oldest sister explained that the religious background and philosophy played a great part in helping her and the rest of the family to "weather the storms." "We were taught to respect people, first," she said, "that if we would respect ourselves and conduct ourselves in a certain way people would automatically respect us." She said this played a great part in enabling them to live through the struggles and crises involving Black and White peoples. She described the relationship of Black people and White people in the Meridian area as an "established" one, whereby they could "communicate with each other" and "compromise." She believes that the Whites were willing to do that because of their religious beliefs.

> White people who were church-going, who had a religious commitment, tried to establish this relationship, and they would often make the statement, 'We wanna get along together.' 'We got to live here together, and so we wanna to get along together. I wanna treat you right, and I want you to treat me right.' And of course, if they found out there were people in the community, especially ministers, that they confided in, they would talk to them and ask if they were satisfied. If they found out you were not satisfied, they went out of their way, to a certain extent, to try to do the things that would establish a pleasant relationship between the two races.[71]

She made reference to the situation during the civil rights movement when the Whites would try to get together with them and work out the problems so that they wouldn't have these demonstrations and riots and killings in the Meridian area which they were having in other parts of Mississippi and the South in general.[72]

It is well known that during the 60's when the Freedom Workers were in the state trying to register Black people to vote, in places like Ruleville, Jackson, and Philadelphia, a great deal of violence was carried out against the workers and others. But Meridian seemed to be the only one of the cities that had an unofficial biracial committee which had been operating for quite some time, trying to work through the problems between the races.

This is what the oldest sister was describing, how this "unofficial" committee really operated. She said that was one of the things that enabled them to build the relationship to the point of being as "pleasant" as it was. "And I think the people just didn't believe in violence," she said. She thought this was due to their religious background, churchgoing and Bible-reading that caused them to sense the wrongness of such actions.

The youngest sister elaborated on the involvement of her husband as president of the NAACP, and ministers of the community in the informal meetings and deliberations. She referred to a committee of ministers in the city, whom they would invite to certain meetings and dinners to find out what the grievances were among the Black people. The ministers could tell them what the dissatisfactions were because they were over congregations. In some cases, she said, the politicians would put another Black person in a co-chairman position of some sort to try to appease the Black community. She mentioned how the Democratic Party would have some of the Black lawyers as chairpersons or co-chairpersons of certain committees. The lawyers, she said, were already biracial in that they had clients from both races.

She mentioned the case of her husband, where some of the disturbances were caused by outsiders who were brought in to do dirty things in Mississippi. She recalled her husband talking about some people he knew were members of the Ku Klux Klan, who would get people from outside the state and "bring them in here with guns and line 'em up with their crosses in the street in front of his house." She said that there was a plumbing place across the street from his house. And the owner of the plumbing place would say to the Klans, "Well, don't worry about this NAACP man, I'll get him." But he just said that to protect her husband. She added,

> So, I say it was the better class of White folks that took care of Black folks in this town. They knew how we were thinking, what we were doing, even how they treated the family and children. They just knew all about us.

These are the kinds of people that were head of committees. They had a
lot to do with the progress of Mississippi and Meridian.

The sisters didn't think that Meridian escaped all the turbulence and
racial hostilities. There was much there and still is, the younger sister
felt. But her experiences were not so much because of the level on which
she dealt as an educator and well-prepared and respected person.
Speaking of the transition they had to undergo when integration came,
she explained that the kids in the schools got the worst of it. It was really
rough on the kids, she said, more so than with the teachers. Often the
White kids would come up with some kind of complaint because they
didn't like having a Black teacher. They wouldn't come out and say that,
but would give some other excuse to be transferred to another class. As
a counselor, however, in counseling Black kids she felt she really was
successful in helping them to prepare themselves and adjust to the
integrated school life. Yet, she was capable of handling all the kids well,
whatever their race or background.

The oldest sister related an interesting experience on the first day of
integration of her school in 1970.

I believe our school was one of the last schools to integrate. So I remember
that first day. They had alerted the police officers to come down. I guess
they anticipated trouble. So the officers were already there when we got
there that morning for the first day of school. Of course, we did not have
any incidents whatsoever. So, they stayed for maybe a couple of hours. I
guess they soon realized that everything was calm and we were not going
to have any violence. So they soon left.[73]

She noted that her husband was principal of the school. But they had
sent a White man down from the high school to be his assistant
principal, thinking perhaps her husband couldn't handle an integrated
situation. They expected the White man to soon replace him. But her
husband got the utmost cooperation from all sides and remained in his
position five more years, until his retirement. Even the assistant principal

cooperated very well. The traditional attitude of "We don't want to have any trouble" prevailed, although there were a few, as always is the case, who had a little trouble. But none of that got out of hand.

The sisters all seemed to sense that racial tensions still remain beneath the surface, but people try to be professional with it in the school system. They recognize that Whites are not satisfied and they can sense the dissatisfaction, but they are determined not to have any problems.

On the progress of Black people in business and professions, politics and otherwise prior to and following the Civil Rights Movement and in spite of the handicaps of prejudice and discrimination, the sisters believed that Blacks' ways of conducting themselves have played a large part. The oldest sister explained,

> I have found out that White people encourage Black people to do things for themselves, and they will help them if they feel they are intelligent and respectable people, and if they are thought well of in their community. It will surprise you, some of the encouragement that Blacks get. If they feel like you are ambitious, they will encourage and help you, if you're determined to do something for yourself.[74]

She described the limits of such encouragements in the case of the husband of her sister just under her age-wise. Her middle sister's husband experienced difficulties and a lot of friction in his business ventures because he was becoming too prosperous and moving up too fast in the lumber business, one of the chief industries of Meridian. For instance, where they are living in the suburban area in a large, plush home, on a generous land area, almost an acres, a corner lot, is an area where White people don't really want Blacks to live. They did all they could to prevent her sister's husband from buying that land but didn't succeed. She explained that her brother-in-law was able to buy his own equipment and hire his employees, track his timber, estimate it, and purchase large tracts of timber. One thing that accounted for his being prosperous was his connections in Kemper County, his place of birth and family home, joining Lauderdale County on the northeast side. The older people back there thought well of him, and they were big farmers from whom he could buy timber.

When her brother-in-law purchased the property on which his present home is located, there were two White doctors who also wanted to buy the property. But the land was owned by a Black woman who refused to sell it to White people. She sold it to the brother-in-law. So the Whites, in bitterness, tried to discourage him and undermine his business establishment. They would not let him have any timer at one time. But he survived the situations by having connections elsewhere and by some people's coming to his aid.

In an interview on the following day the middle sister gave added insights on her husband's difficulties and on Black-White relations.

> At the time, if You could buy your own equipment, a couple of trucks, tractor, pulpwood truck, you could do well. He got his equipment through hard work. And buying books of timber was a problem back in those days (books are big tracts of timber). So mostly his manager he was working for would buy the books of timber. In those times Black people were not very successful in dealing with banks, that was the hold-up. They wouldn't usually let Black people have loans. Eventually it got a little better when we had some more banks to come in here that would let Black people have loans to do business with. After this one particular man started letting Blacks have loans, then my husband could secure loans to buy these books of timber.[75]

She explained why she felt the Whites were reluctant to grant loans to Blacks. It was thought to be "one of the ways to keep Blacks under their feet, so to speak." One practice was to grant the loan if some White person would sign with the Black person. She felt that they didn't want Blacks to be independent. Even if one was capable, she said, they didn't want the person to be anything. She said:

> My husband started progressing pretty good. Then, they watch you, and if you're progressing a little bit more than they want you to, they have a way

of trying to stop you. I know there were any number of times that people
would call in to the plant and say that they wanted my husband to cut some
timber, and they wouldn't tell my husband. He said many times he heard
them mention his name.[76]

She explained that when they thought he was getting too much business,
they would try to freeze him out.

She also shed more light on the process of buying the lot on which
their present home is located. At the time the land belonged to Mrs.
Beatrice Matthison, a Black woman who owned about fifty acres out
there in the suburbs. She was their neighbor and friend when they lived
in the inner city. When she bought out there and built her home, she
was happy and wanted some Black neighbors near her. So when the
husband spoke about building out there, Mrs. Matthison readily agreed
to sell him about an acre. The younger sister and other friends were able
to buy lots from her also. The younger sister stated that it was the
general trend among middle class Black people in the city to try to help
one another "because they know what they have come through with the
other race, how they would try to take some of the better areas. And
there were certain areas, one while, they didn't want Black people to live
in. So we have quite a few Black people that are concerned about
helping their race."

The discussion moved then to the reality of the situation with Blacks
and Whites being that of a superior-inferior relationship. The sisters
agreed that the Whites would not block Black people so long as they are
progressing in their *place* and stay in their place, whatever that means
from either the Black side or the White side. Of course, it means, so
long as a Black does not get too close to what Whites consider a White
status. They have in their minds that there is only a certain level that
Blacks are supposed to reach, and beyond that level is for Whites only.
There is a subtlety with which this is expressed. The oldest sister pointed
out that there are only so many Black people allowed to rise to a certain
level, and the masses of Blacks are supposed to remain down on the low-
income level. She gave an example of this within the two previous years

when teachers' salaries have been rising rapidly. For a long time when their state's salaries were the lowest in the nation, the White people stopped entering the teaching profession in Mississippi. But now that salaries have risen considerably the competition for teaching positions has soared; and to block the Black teachers, authorities have come up with all kinds of tests and trials to pass in order to eliminate more Blacks from the competition.

The younger sister mentioned that Meridian is no longer attractive to young Black teachers. It is difficult to recruit Black teachers for the Meridian area because of a paucity of recreation. They say there's nowhere to go in Meridian. But she says they themselves are there because they are anchored there, but there's nothing to inspire new ones to come. This leads to the question of what happened to this city which was a boom town and the largest city in Mississippi up until 1930.

There seems to be something about the area, other than being anchored there, that keeps the Graham sisters there. They like the area, it's been good to them. They have prospered there. The youngest sister was away for nine years, living in the attractive city of Las Vegas, Nevada. Yet, she came back and has been there in Meridian for more than eighteen years since her return. She's doing well and is quite pleased with her life there.

As to why she left Nevada, she says she was only there with her first husband, who was in the military service and settled there when he was discharged. She in the meantime was working on a Master's degree at the university there. She got her Master's and went on for the Education Specialist Certificate, and after that she was ready to come home. Her marriage did not survive, and so she came home and found her present husband. She mentioned strongly that this was indeed home and she had sorely missed her parents. But she also had additional feelings about the place in contrast to Las Vegas. She simply did not like the strip life in Las Vegas, not the shows, not the slot machines.

You ask my oldest sister here. She came out there to see me, and she said, 'Oh, I'm not gonna play the slots.' I said, 'Oh, yes you are, you're in Las Vegas, you gonna play these slots!' So, she started playing 'em and hit the jackpot and there it goes. But I think it depends upon the lifestyle of a person. What is it that you want? the big life? the fast life? Or Whatever? But I just am satisfied with a moderate life.[77]

The oldest sister summed up the reasons for staying in the area with more solid evidence.

When you say, why did you stay, okay, why do some people stay and some people leave? I think our staying here was due to our foreparents. People leave for a reason, to do better. I think in our case, going back to my grandfather, he had established here in the early years, when land was cheap and this was unusual for Black people because most of them, I don't think, were interested in land and trying to better themselves and their situation. And he was, and of course, he had a lot of boys, and as a result he was able to acquire quite a bit of land. By so doing, he had something to offer his children, and the others did not. They saw where they could make a living here, especially the boys. And so they were able to purchase land. And of course, when they got married, my grandfather deeded them some land, and they were able to build them a house and carry on their farms. And at that time that was more or less what people did here. Most of them farmed, Black and White.[78]

Although her conclusion is wrong about most Blacks not desiring land and trying to better themselves, she looked back proudly on the fact that her foreparents and relatives were able to own their own homes and didn't have to live on somebody else's place and work for someone else. They themselves were the inheritors of this type of independence and self-sufficiency. The grandparents had instilled in them from way back that one should try to have something for the sake of independence. She elaborated on this concept in terms of land ownership, jobs, and education.

Land ownership, and of course, land is just like money in the bank. That's even true today, better than money in the bank. When we came along they told us the same thing, and this was instilled in us from one generation to another. We were fortunate to go to school and get a fairly good education. So we've always been able to have a job. That's one thing I've been grateful for. I felt like it probably came from my religious training and beliefs that I was always able to get a job. Of course, at first the salary was small, but if you have your own home, you can grow your vegetables and everything, and you were able to live at least a comfortable life.[79]

In the same light, she commented on why many people left the area,

because they didn't have anything to stay here for. I can remember the time, since I started teaching, the highest ambition of the Black child was to finish high school and go to Chicago, to Detroit, or one of the other Northern states, nothing here to keep them. The parent didn't have anything to give them, not even a plot of land to build a house. Going back to why we stayed, we stayed because we were able to accomplish something and to live a more or less independent life.[80]

She began to credit her grandfather for a lot of her fortune: "My grandfather was a minister, and he won the respect of the people far and near." At this point the youngest sister interrupted to express her pride in her grandfather. "Not even many White people had a house like my grandfather, this great big house with the great porch going all the way around it, all this, we thought he was really something." The oldest sister related an incident which displayed the respect and influence wielded by Rev. Jack Graham.

See, the reputation of the family goes a long way. I can remember once I was going to Quitman to take textbooks back after the close of school. I was driving in a 15 miles per hour speed zone. The white trooper stopped me, and he asked me who I was and everything. I told him. So she asked me, "Do you know Jack Graham?" I said, "Yes, that's my grandfather." So, then we just got started talking about families, and he told me about the good reputation my grandfather had.[81]

The trooper forgot all about her speeding. The youngest sister declared, "And if we wanted to borrow money at the bank at that time, it was, 'Oh yes, that's Jack Graham's grandchild, let them have it, they'll pay it back.'" The oldest sister added: "So, I think the accomplishments that the foreparents made and what we were able to do, and they were able to give us a little help, I think that's why we stayed, because we were able to live a more or less independent life."

John Barksdale summarized in 1962 the progress of Black people of Meridian and its surrounding area. Stating that they have distinguished themselves and their race and found reward in almost every field of endeavor, he declares,

> As they came from slavery to sharecropper; to landowners and became successful in education, religion, medicine, business, law, as well as in farming. Today there are just as many success stories such as funeral directing, insurance, printing, electrical, plumbing, plastering and housing contracting, food service, and clerical and administrative work, etc., skill[ed] and unskilled trades.[82]

This is an interesting picture of diversified professions and business involvement in Meridian as far back as almost thirty years ago when Blacks in most urban centers North and South were stereotyped as owning not much more than funeral homes, barber and beauty shops, restaurants.

Barksdale's statistical data regarding the Black people in the twenty-mile radius of Meridian help to see the words of the Graham sisters in a more meaningful perspective. According to him Black people numbered approximately 17,000 (37% of the population), constituting 6,000 families; forty-two percent were landowners; there were 3800 dwelling units occupied by Blacks. Sixty percent of the families were said to have telephones; less than two percent were without electricity and running water. But only 1500 were registered voters (not even ten percent). Within Meridian proper the author cited four elementary schools, two junior highs, one senior high school, and one junior college, that is, for Blacks. And there was only one public library for Blacks.[83]

One can therefore see that Black people were progressing even in the face of great odds. One may wonder what much greater strides they might have made had the society been a free and open one for them? No doubt others, especially the Euro-Americans, noticed the industry and ingenuity of this race of Africans in their thrust forward in spite of the great handicaps they threw in their paths. And that's obviously one reason they tried to hold them back.

The middle-class Blacks had worked hard to get where they were and are. They became successful either because of the roots established for them by their forebears, or because they struggled to establish themselves completely on their own or both. Some went away and got their start elsewhere and then returned to be successful. Those who stayed and took advantage of every opportunity or partial opening appear to have become more successful.

There are those of the nonprofessional working class who have a somewhat different picture to give of the Meridian area and life in this community. Some of these have stayed throughout their lives, and others have left and returned. Two of these are Mittie and her brother, whom I will simply refer to as C, who are from the rather large number of children (12) of Charlie Graham, the oldest child of Rev. Jack Graham. Economically, one might say they are in the middle income bracket, blue collar. They both were interviewed at Mittie's home in the city of Meridian. Both have spent time outside the area, C much more so than his sister, who didn't leave the state but, rather, spent some years in Biloxi, Mississippi. C left and returned more than once. He returned to Meridian in 1987 after being away the last time for twenty-three years. Both Mittie and C have their respective portions of the homestead land of their father and mother in Enterprise, Mississippi, in Clarke County, where they were born and grew up. There are one hundred sixty acres (eighty of which were purchased by their father and the other eighty deeded to him by the grandfather), divided among the children still living, each of whom has approximately seventeen acres a piece. Both C and Mittie have a strong religious background, having grown up in their grandfather's church in Enterprise, along with the numerous other children and grandchildren.

C described himself as not being educated like some of his relatives, but he learned a trade, welding, which is the very reason he left Mississippi—because there was not much of an opening in the area for Black people who were welders. And he wanted to better himself, find a good job. After finishing welding school at the age of 17, he and a fellow student were recruited by Mare Island Naval shipyard in Vallejo, California, during the war in the last part of 1944. He arrived there with only three cents in his pocket. The government furnished their room and board.[84]

Unfortunately, C found that the shipyard was not taking any welders who were not experienced in the trade. All of those were White. A few Black men were doing tack-welding, making $1.26 an hour. They offered him burning, a trade that goes with welding. But in anger he refused to accept it, and chose a job on the slab, building frameworks for ships, making $1.10 an hour. In six months he had saved $500. He stayed there until the war was over in 1945, when he and most everyone else at the shipyard were laid off. But he had gotten his foot broken working under a cruiser and was in the dispensary for treatment for quite a while. In 1947 he returned to Meridian and enrolled in Meridian Baptist Seminary,[85] but his professor (Moore) advised him and a fellow student named John Snowden that it would be better for them to go to Piney Woods School[86] where they could work their way through school. He enrolled there in 1949 and attended for one year only. He explained, "I was twenty-five years old when I went there. I didn't have any help. If I had had any help I could've stayed there and got a good education. I had it hard; I came up on the rough side of the mountain. My father had twelve children."[87]

It was a police harassment incident in Meridian that led C to leave Meridian for Chicago in 1950. He related the story in detail. He was

working for Dr. Rush out on Poplar Springs Drive for three days a week
when he had what he called "a little tragedy." The other two days he
worked for Rush's relatives or friends. One day a White lady asked him
to wash some windows for her. She had about fourteen or sixteen
windows. He asked her how much she was paying.

She said she was paying fifty cents an hour. I said, "Lady, I can't make no
money washing windows for fifty cents an hour. I'll wash 'em for forty cents
a window." That was just like I had spit in her face. She said, "No, I can't
pay you that. Well, you don't have to wash 'em, 'less you want to." I said,
"Okay," and I just walked on off and went home. I was wearing an army
garrison cap. And that weekend somebody raped a White girl out on Poplar
Springs Drive. And so I was at my girlfriend's house on 13th and 31st all
that Saturday evening. My neighbors told me that the law had been riding
around looking for me, going to the house. I said, "Looking for me?" They
said "Yeah." I said, "I wonder what they looking for me for?" So, I went
home from my girlfriend's house that night at about 11:30. At 12:00
somebody knocked on the door. My brother Roger got up and opened the
door. It was a White policeman. I had just laid down. The policeman was
trying to call my name. So Roger asked, "Who you talkin' 'bout, C?" They
said "Yes, is he here?" He told them I was home. So they called me. One
of them said, "Get up and put your clothes on." It was summer. I got up
and put on my clothes. So I told 'em, "I'm ready when y'all are." In going
down the steps, they asked, "Who been makin' whiskey around here?" I
said, "I don't know anything about anybody making whiskey." So one said,
"Yes you do!" I said, "Really, I don't know who been making whiskey
around here. I don't know nothing 'bout that." They said, "Who do you
work for?" I told 'em I worked for Dr. Lesley Rush three days a week and
went to school at night at the Meridian Baptist Seminary. One of 'em
looked at my hands and said, "I see, don't look like you been doin' no
work." I said, "What do y'all have me for?" They said, "I don't know. The
Sergeant down at City Hall wanna ask you some questions." I said, "Okay."
So they took me on downtown. I asked the desk sergeant, "What do you
have me for?" He said, "Dangerous and suspicious." They told the police
to lock me up in the cell. So they locked me up, and way in the night they
brought a drunk guy in. He didn't say nothing to me, and I didn't say

nothing to him. I sat up in the window; they had a bunk bed. I could see long cockroaches crawling around. I didn't lie down.

C was kept in jail all night and taken to county jail for breakfast, but he didn't eat. He was not hungry. They took him back to City Hall for questioning. He said he was not worried because he knew he hadn't done anything. In the questioning session, they said to him,

> "Get that cap over there and see if you recognize it." I picked up the cap and said, "I have a cap just like this." He said, "Where is it?" I said, "It's at home. But my cap has an eagle on it." He said, "We just want to know, did you know anything about this rape out on Poplar Springs Drive." I told 'em, "No I hadn't heard anything about it." So they said, "Somebody raped a White girl at Poplar Springs School." I told 'em I didn't hear anything about that. They said, "Where were you at such and such a time?" I told 'em where I was at. They said, "Have you ever been in jail before?" I told 'em, "No, my record is clean from here to the West Coast. I ain't never been in jail in my life." So, I answered so straight to 'em that one told the other, say, "Take this boy to the Desk Sergeant and tell 'em to turn 'im loose." say, "He's innocent." So they held me fifteen hours. I thanked 'em, you know, when they turned me loose.[88]

I quoted this story in full by C because it is almost a perfect illustration of the kind of surveillance of young Black males of the Meridian community the police kept, as described in the *Illustrated Handbook of Meridian*, 1907.[89] The Black male was placed in a precarious situation if he was poor and trying to make a living from menial jobs, or if he was just plain jobless at varying times. C's case was handled in the least harassing manner, probably because he had no jail record and could answer well for his actions. If he had had a record, he would not have gotten off so easily. Yet, there was no reason for his having to spend fifteen hours in custody simply because he had spoken as he did to the lady who wanted him to wash windows at fifty cents an hour and because he wore a cap similar to the one the authorities had discovered at the scene of the crime. Had someone asked him if he knew

Jack Graham, as in the case of the Graham sisters discussed earlier, and he could have told about being his grandson, perhaps life would have been more liveable in Meridian. But somehow this did not happen in this case.

C therefore did not feel safe in Meridian after this incident. Thus he sat down and wrote his sister in Chicago asking about the job possibilities there. His sister and her husband drove down in June and he rode back with them to Chicago. But conditions weren't that good in Chicago at all. He stayed, however, and tried his hand at one job after another—box factory, steel mill (where he finally got to use his training in welding, but it didn't last), working for the city, etc. Then, he went out to California, again and got a job welding for the Los Angeles Steel Mill for a while until that job ran out, and he was back in Chicago. After several other jobs there, he finally landed a permanent position with General Motors building gear casings for the traction motor. He worked there twenty-three years and retired and is able to draw both Social Security and his retirement. So he returned to Meridian in 1987 to farm his seventeen acres of land his mother deeded to him as his portion of the family's homestead.

C was married three times and has five sons and two daughters, all living in California. He explains why he came back to Meridian:

> This is my home. I wanted to come back. I got tired of living in large cities.
> I wanted to come to a smaller city where so much don't go on.

As to being satisfied with the size of Meridian, he replied that he was very pleased. "Compared to Chicago, it's just no comparison. They have a lot of gangs there. All in all, I lived there thirty-six years. You can hardly live comfortable there, gangs all over the place."

C's sister Mittie described her life in Biloxi, Mississippi, a seaport town, and explained why she left there and returned to Meridian.

> Since I've been back in Meridian, it's quieter. You take those towns, I was
> in Biloxi, that's a seaport town. Some of everything is there. There are so

many Vietnamese. They have just about taken over. They just do everything there. I feel much safer here. It's plenty churches there, plenty people go to church. They have good services and all, but I just feel safer here. With so many people coming in, you don't know what's going to happen. You see so many strange faces that you hadn't seen maybe this week that you didn't see last week. And the boats comin' in, the ships, the planes, people comin' in from Keysville, you see people comin' in all the time, so it's just plenty people down there. But I went to educational school down there. You know, I was in educational school down there heap more than I was here [in Meridian].[90]

Mittie found greater opportunity in Biloxi, which is larger than Meridian. It is the second largest city in Mississippi, next to Jackson, although Jackson is much larger. Mittie found less racial tension there than in Meridian also: "it's a mess, everybody mingles together, just everybody goes together, colored and white. I can eat with you, you can eat with me, yes. You can get a better job. Now, I can be at my house, people treat you so nice."

Mittie's little grandson was in the cub scouts, and she was the grandmother of the cub scouts. She would go to Keysville every Saturday. People would come and pick her up and take her out every Saturday.

It wouldn't be anything for these people to call me and ask me to come go out on the water and have breakfast with them. I'd go out and have breakfast with them at nine o'clock. And they were just nice. Some of them would say, White ladies would say, "would you come and take my husband out for dinner?" I'd say, "When I get dressed." I was driving. They'd say, "I don't feel like going would you take my husband out to dinner?" I would dress and take him out, and we'd go to the biggest hotel dining room and eat.

She agreed that in this seaport town the culture was different, much less conservative than Meridian, although she felt Meridian was a nice place, comfortable and peaceful.

You know what is good, if you're comfortable and don't have a lot, if you're comfortable, that's better than having a whole lot and not comfortable and at peace. If you're satisfied and your mind is satisfied and you're comfortable, that's better than having a good time and not comfortable.[91]

I detected a sense of resignation in Mittie. She had had an enjoyable experience in Biloxi, but she had had to make a choice between a town with greater opportunity and more open social life but with greater risks of safety and one which had fewer opportunities and more restricted social life but with an atmosphere of peace and comfort. She resigned herself to the latter.

Rev. Otis Brown and his sister Dessie Ree and brother Charlie are the children of Mrs. Lula Graham Brown, the eleventh child of Rev. Jack Graham, and her husband, Willy Brown. They live on their family's homestead in Lauderdale County about twenty miles from Meridian, in a place called Poplar Springs, Mississippi. The family home where the children were born sits back on the land, hidden by trees and bushes. It is preserved, not demolished, but no longer in livable condition. Dessie Ree has built a new brick home on the front lot for her family. And Rev. Brown has a frame house on a lot adjoining hers. Charlie lives in town. A narrow dirt road leads off the main road to the place where they live.

All three of these grandchildren of Jack Graham grew up in the Poplar Springs Missionary Baptist Church, which sits on a hill right off the main highway, now a beautiful modern structure, where Rev. Jack Graham was the pastor for 55 years and where he was funeralized in 1956. The grandfather is held in highest reverence by these grandchildren. They had rigorous religious training under his tutelage and have deep appreciation for their devout religious background. Rev. Brown, who was converted there in his grandfather's church, Poplar Springs, at the age of twelve, says, "He was a great leader in his preaching and teaching. He was very close to us, and we taken ahold of what he said. We followed his leadership, coming up through life as we grew up."[92] It was during the revival at the church that he was converted. He was baptized by his grandfather, and years later, still following his leadership, he was called into the ministry.

When he went to his grandfather and told him about it, Jack Graham was cautious. He told young Otis about his own "calling" experience. And Otis told his grandfather that his experience seemed much the same. They talked it over. And later Otis had another experience:

> Shortly, the Lord came to me again. When he came to me again, he was more understandable and gave me something to go on. So, when the Lord gave it to me the last time, weren't no way I could get out of it. I had to just come forth. And I went before my grandfather and talked with him again. And he gived me the appointment to a church.[93]

He meant, of course, as he explained later, that in time the grandfather ordained him there in the Poplar Springs Church and gave him an appointment to his first church. But he had gotten experience preaching in his home church first. Then he was called to Union Hill Missionary Baptist Church in Quitman, Mississippi, the County Seat of Clarke County, where Jack Graham lived. Rev. Brown pastored there fifteen years. He has never lived or pastored outside the state. He is pastoring two churches now: St. Mary's Missionary Baptist Church in Decatur in Newton County, where he has pastored for the last twenty-nine years; and Sand Hill Chapel M.B. Church in Hickory, Mississippi, where he has pastored for the last four years.

Dessie is the only one of this family who has lived outside the state. She lived in Mobile, Alabama, for two years and a half with her first husband, by whom she had one child, her daughter, Archie Nell. She was divorced from the first husband and returned home. She is married to her second husband, Otis Lee Wilson by whom she has a son, Terrence LeFrance, and she has never since left the homestead. As to her impressions of Mobile, she said, "Well, it was a little too fast for me." Since 1959 Dessie has worked at a hospital in Meridian. She sings in a gospel group that travels around both within and outside the state performing at churches. Rev. Brown used to be their manager.

The Brown children felt that they are still living there on the family property once owned by their parents, both of whom are deceased, the father, Willy, as early as 1948, because their grandfather instilled in them the sense of ownership of the land. And they have never let anybody take it away from them, as has happened in the case of so many African Americans who have owned land. Jack Graham himself held title to 363 acres which he willed to his children upon his death, because, they felt, he wanted his children to have the sense of being in possession of the land. Rev. Brown felt that practically all of Jack Graham's descendants had that spirit instilled in them. And they seemed to respect the property passed on to them, as well as to buy other land themselves, to keep it in their ownership. Speaking for himself and other family members, Rev. Brown stated,

> We like it out here in the country. It's better living than it is in the city. And now, our father, Willy Brown, who passed away in 1948, him and my mother bought this land here where we're living. My mother is Lula Brown. When they died and left us, they left us here, and so we just stayed here and kept the place going.[94]

Rev. Brown went on to suggest that there is really a good, positive feeling that this is his mother and father's property. A sense of dignity and independence was in his voice. "It's good to know that they thought enough of us to buy land, because they could've left us renting or on the White man's place, but they had the ability to get out and want something for themselves." Dessie Ree suggested that there is a spiritual closeness to the parents and grandparents, in being there on the land they purchased, a kind of tie, a spiritual connectedness.

Rev. Brown has seven children and eighteen grandchildren, all of whom live in Meridian and the Meridian area. They have never lived anywhere else. He explained why he thought they remained.

Well, the way I see it is that they probably done what we did. Our parents
stayed here. They didn't go anywhere. They lived here. So, the same thing,
it seem like, is for me. I'm living here, it's for us. I have two sons and four
daughters living. Two are still living in the city renting, but the rest of 'em
got a home for themselves. But I'll say, like my Pastor [his grandfather], he
stayed here, worked, and say, Mississippi loved him, he stayed here and
worked it. And then we done the same thing, and they have jobs, just didn't
go anywhere.[95]

The Browns gave their views of the area in discussing how their
religious training and background helped them to endure and remain
during the difficult times of the Civil Rights Movement of the 1960's and
after. They experienced the hostility and the tensions between the races.
But they stuck it out, held to their lands and their heritage. And they've
helped to bring about a change on their jobs and in the society. Another
young family member, Marguerite, explained that on her job as a janitor
in the junior high school she is now exposed to prejudiced teachers.

Teachers are prejudiced against Black, and they talk to you any kind of
way, and because they are White, they don't want you to talk back, don't
want you to look them directly in the face, you know, when they talking to
you; they want you to look down, I guess, but I just look at them, and I pray
for them. And if I feel like they're saying something to me I don't like, then
I respond back to 'em, and they don't care for that. But still, I pray for
them, you know, harder.[96]

Rev. Brown recalled some rather malicious experiences on his job
during the Civil Rights Movement. He stated:

I can say this, White people always, I guess always will have that sense of
being superior to the Black race. I worked on jobs during the rough times.
I worked with bad ones, mean people, during the Civil Rights. And we were
talkin' about what would happen to us, but we went right on, and we
worked. And when they talked to us, we wuz man enough to talk to them.
And it was a group of us men, Black men, and if the White acted like they
wanted to misuse you in a way, we let 'em *know* it, we humans just like you.

You got to respect us jest like you want us to respect you. And we done that on through, from the 60's on up. When we integrated we didn't forget the Lord. We always faced them with scriptures from the Bible. That was what whipped the White man, he can't stand the Bible. We used that on 'em, what the Lord say about it.[97]

Rev. Brown recalled one rather malicious act their White fellow workers used to try to frighten the group of Black men on the job.

And then the White man would run a joke on the Black man to try to condemn him, but we didn't let that stand. I'd look him in the eye and tell 'em just the truth of what we were gon' do. And so we went through that. We had a hard time on our jobs. We went on down through the time when, we'd have to go through federal aid on our jobs. And so this job here in Meridian at a brick and clay company. They tried to stop all that about the civil rights when it came. They tried to stop it in all kind of ways. They got an ole possum and hung 'im up and say, "That's the way we gon' do a nigger when he don't do what we tell 'im to do." We just ignored 'em and went on to work. Through the shop at night where we worked, they had it hung up. But we just went on and didn't pay no 'tention to it. So they wanted to integrate those water fountains (they had one for Black and one for White). So one of the black men was fraternizing with the White, that's where it started. He told 'em, "You can drink outta this one as well as we can drink outta that one. See that name." He told 'em, "That name don't mean nothing. This water run in my mouth like that water run in your mouth." So he got the water fountain integrated. So they went and told the superintendent. The superintendent came and say, "What's the trouble?" He said, "We drinking water." We had some people come in from Jackson, government people from New Orleans, one from Atlanta, and one from Washington. He came in, and when he came in that's the reason the superintendent didn't say nothing. So, the superintendent found out then, we weren't scared.[98]

He pointed out that their religion made them unafraid. He said, "You have to stand up and be a man; if you stand up and be a man or woman, whatever, a White man got to respect you. You look 'em in the eye, take time and talk wif 'em."

Dessie told of her experiences during the time among the White women at the hospital in Meridian where she works. She started working there when the Civil Rights Movement was strong. She also experienced the separate water fountains, bathrooms and other facilities. They as kitchen help had to eat in the kitchen on the meat block where they chopped meat, not out in the dining room where the Whites ate. She told of an incident involving a lady named Ellavie who was cleaning one of the doctor's offices. In cleaning his office bathroom, she used it before she flushed it. And his nurse, hearing it, somehow sensed what she had done. And she came in and told her, "Niggers don't use this bathroom. Y'all's bathroom is over there on F hall." F hall was on the other side of the building almost a block away. Dessie said when Ellavie talked to her about the incident, she advised her:

I told her, "Well, I'd use the bathroom anyhow. When you close the door to go in there and clean that bathroom, she don' know whether you cleaning or washing the commode or using the bathroom. She can't tell the difference." So she said, "That's true, ain't it?"[99]

Dessie also talked of experiencing the demeaning mannerisms expected of the Blacks during the time, such as not looking Whites in the face when talking to them.

Now a Black person, when they talkin' to 'em, they look down on the ground, fumble with their hands or either kick their feet around [what is often called shuffling]. Okay, that's their type of person. So when you look at them and talk to them like another human being and another White person talking to another White person, then they don't like that. but they say, "They crazy." They crack jokes like, you know, they say, "So and so crazy, they don' have any sense." The reason they say that, because they can't push you around. But when they talk to me, if they holler at me, I holler back at 'em and look right at 'em. I let 'em know, now, I'm just as grown as you.[100]

Dessie spoke of having a run-in with a White woman named Ron. When Ron would get angry with some of the rest of the Whites, she would take out her frustrations on Dessie by talking down to her in an abusive manner. She took this for a while, until it got too much for her.

> One day, I said, "Look, I wanna talk to you." She said, "Okay." She got a coffee cup and went in the break area, and I told her, I said, "Look, let me tell you something now, it's no children workin' here. I'm a grown woman. I'm older than you." I said, "Which you White, but still, I'm just as grown as you. And the way I feel, now you get mad with the rest of 'em and you take it out on me. Now I don't like that." I said, "Now, I'm gon' treat you like you're another human being, I'm gon' treat you like a grown person, I'm gon' treat you like I want to be treated." And she said, "Well, I didn't mean to be doin' that; I'm sorry you feel that way." I said, "That's the way I feel." I said, "That's the way you act." So she said, "I'm sorry you feel that way."[101]

After this incident Ron stopped for a while, and then she started abusing Dessie again. She called her attention to it again and even went to the supervisor about it. The supervisor made the excuse that Ron was having family problems. She told the supervisor:

> "Well, I have problems at home too. We all do." I said, "I leave my problems at home when I come up here to work. These people up here don' have anything to do with what's goin' on in my house." I said, "I come here for one thing, to work." I said, "And I'm treatin' you people right, and I want you to treat me right."[102]

Other incidents happened with Ron. She started complaining about their not changing the towels in the bathroom, and the like. Dessie came home and talked to her husband about it. He told her to talk to them woman to woman, and if they didn't like it, she could come home for good. She wasn't planning on coming home but rather staying there working. So she determined to confront the people and have it out.

So, I went there and I told 'em. I said, "Stewart, I wanna talk to you." She
said, "Okay." I went in her office. I was so mad the tears were comin' into
my eyes. I told her, I said, "I feel like, I didn't know you were that
prejudiced." And she said, "Well, what is it?" She handed me some tissue.
She said, "Sit down." So I said, "I don' wanna sit down." I said, "The way
you sound to me like I'm not supposed to use that bathroom. They said that
I used the bathroom like they do and I'm supposed to keep towels up." I
said, "I'm not supposed to run around, I'm up here working just like they
is, I'm not supposed to run around and keep things clean for them. They're
employees just like I am." I said, "We workin' here to tend the sick." And
she said, "That's true." I said, "Now, what's gon' keep them from taking
that towel down? If they wanna wipe their hands on that wet towel and
dirty towel, let 'em wipe on it. There're clean towels in there, all they have
to do is take 'em and put 'em up."[103]

Dessie says she didn't have anymore problems about the towels. But
there were other little petty things about the Whites leaving their eating
trays around and expecting Blacks who worked in the laboratory to clean
up after them. She had to get them straight on that. It seemed to be one
thing after another. She had to confront the supervisor again. They told
the supervisor that Dessie was mean and hateful and had a bad attitude.
Dessie replied, "I don't care what they say, I don' belong to nobody up
here." I said, "My mother and father had me, and they were Black." The
supervisor replied, "Stop feelin' that way. It's nobody up here
prejudiced." Dessie didn't say anymore about the situation to her. She
said, "Whenever they get on my nerves now, I tell 'em. I don't know
what these people think, the way we talk to 'em now, we just say what
we wanna say."

Even today there are still problems of prejudice and discrimination;
they do some petty things, make snide remarks, and the like. Dessie
concluded:

We just tell 'em, "All you White folks think y'all can do us any way, but
that's past history." And so they still call us crazy, you know. We just tell
'em now and go on. But they know they can't do the things now that they

wish to do. It's a lot of stuff that has gone on, with us working on these jobs. But a lot of people didn't know what was going on.[104]

Dessie and her brothers and other family members are decent working class people whose social status is middle income, middle-class but not upper-middle-class like that of some of their cousins. Their experiences on their jobs and in the society of the Meridian area are quite different from those of their cousins and others of a more professional class. They did not have so many encounters with the "better class of white people" who wanted to smooth things out between the races and keep them "satisfied," for instance. They had to defend themselves and bear a lot of indignities the others never encountered. It is interesting to note the strength and courage they drew from their religious background training, and Graham-family upbringing, which enabled them to stand up to the other race and correct them in their ethical shortcomings. It was as if they had to teach them how to be human and to treat Black people the way they themselves wanted to be treated.

Such people as these, and there were numerous ones, showed strength of character and purpose, determination in the restrictive and limiting circumstances of the White supremacist society of the southeast Mississippi apartheid system. But because of their strong religious orientation, they did not run from the circumstances but rather stood up to them and asserted their rights and dignity. In a later chapter we will look at the religious and moral training in more detail to see how it helped facilitate their survival, their efforts in gaining a sense of freedom within the confines of the system in this region; how it aided them in gaining and maintaining dignity and self-respect, in making a life, a good life in the setting; how it helped them in gaining and maintaining staying power. We shall also see that that religion was not compensatory, as Benjamin Mays and others chose to label Black religion.[105]

I found a sense of pride in the Black people of the area. It seems that there has always been this sense of dignity going back to the

nineteenth century at least, all the way back to 1871 in the race riot in
Meridian, which was caused partly by just such self-respect,
independence, and self-assertion on the part of the Black people in
finding ways to protect and defend themselves and their rights. This was
certainly characteristic of Rev. Jack Graham and his descendants. They
would not allow anyone to force them to knuckle under. They felt a
sense of being equal and expressed it. Rev. Otis Brown knew of the
White people's respect for his grandfather. He said they always called
him "Uncle Jack." He had the preacher's badge of honor along with the
strong character he exhibited in his surroundings. Brown said,

> I can remember the time they called him "Uncle Jack." They respected him
> as a preacher. And he didn't stand for no whole lotta things that did
> happen at that time. He didn't stand for it 'cause he always, when I was
> workin', I was around 'im a lotta times, he always talked with 'em, and he
> would be respected. He was a man that never looked down, he always
> looked up. When he talked he was gon' look you in the eye and talk. And
> when you look the White man in the eye instead of scratchin' your head
> and your back and get to itchin' all over, talkin' to the White man just
> 'cause of his color, cause my grandfather didn't do that, and when you
> mistreat 'im, he'd out and tell you, I seen 'im do that, "You done me
> wrong!" He would look at the Whites and tell 'em that, "You done me
> wrong!" They'd say, "Well, Uncle Jack, I'm sorry."[106]

Rev. Brown related an incident in which his grandfather had an
automobile accident. He had crashed into another man's car back in the
1930's. Brown was just a boy going around with him. He was arrested
and taken to court, he said:

> He was in town there to City Hall. The police had 'im, one by one arm, and
> another by the other. He had his arms up. He was tellin' 'em, "I didn't see
> the man, I didn't try to hit 'im. I *didn't try* to *hit* 'im." He told 'em, "Now,
> y'all know I didn't try to hit 'im." Whatever the fine was he paid it. And he
> never owned no driver's license or nothin' like that. He just drove without
> it.[107]

Brown said that everyone thought Jack Graham was a real man, a man among men.

Brown did not find a strong religious character among the Whites to whom he was exposed, no real religious sensibilities to whom one might appeal for sanity and justice. Some of them did have it, but not most, he said.

> Some of them were scared. I'm gon' tel you like it is, a lot of 'em, now they were scared of such as Christ, I'd say it like that. They were scared of the word of the Lord. Now, they didn't just have that much religion. They were scared of it. They had that much faith about that part, they believed in that part I won't say that they meant to do much right. But they feared...they feared.[108]

Rev. Timothy Graham, brother of Mittie and C, discussed earlier, and his wife Sarah, give another view of the Meridian area different in many respects from those views gotten from the others consulted. Rev. Timothy Graham was the fourth son of Charlie Graham, the oldest son of this grandfather. He was born on the Graham homestead in Clarke County and grew up in the Zion Spring Baptist Church pastored by his grandfather there in Enterprise, the same church in which all of the grandfather's children and most of the grandchildren grew up.

In discussing the turbulence of the Civil Rights Movement in the state, the Freedom Riders, and other acts of people, along with the dangers and violence of the White people of the state, Timothy made a point about the toughness of the times which caused so many people to leave the state out of fear. "But some of us stuck with it and just lived on and served."[109] He thinks Mississippi is a pretty good place to live. He is in the mid-middle class social range. He worked for the telephone company for thirty-three years and retired from it. He was converted at age 15 and one year later was called to preach. But he tried to "duck it" and didn't preach his first sermon until he was twenty-one years old. He is a trained minister, however. He attended Meridian Baptist Seminary, and has pastored three churches. He now pastors two, one in the rural area which he has pastored for thirty-two years, and the other in the city of Meridian, which he has pastored twenty-four years. He is a member of the National Baptist Convention, and Second Vice-President of the East Mississippi Baptist Convention, the state wing of the NBC, USA, Inc.

Rev. Timothy Graham's wife Sarah had the experience of leaving the state and living in St. Louis for eight or nine months before her marriage to Timothy, whom she met in 1945. Both Timothy and Sarah spoke about the Freedom Riders and Freedom Workers in the sixties. Timothy told of their having kept two of the White women Freedom Workers in their home for six months to a year. His father-in-law kept two of the males, and his house was shot into.

> We kept a young White girl in our house for six months. And we were living in the West end of the city at that time, and my mother-in-law and father-in-law lived on a corner, and I lived just up the street. And we kept some young ladies, and they kept the White men. And they shot into my daddy-in-law's house, just above the bed where some young men were sleeping. They shot out the top window; had it been the low window, they would have shot these boys and killed them.[110]

This was right in the city of Meridian that such violence was taking place. Timothy felt that Meridian had its share of violence, although he spoke well of the attempts by some of the White ministers and officials to get together with Black people and try to bring about better cooperation between the races (the "unofficial biracial committee" type of parleying). Yet, he said, there was the burning of crosses and damaging churches and property in order to frighten people in the area.

Sarah recalled her experiences in the city with Whites living around her and her family's opening their doors to the White Freedom workers when they came to town.

> I was reared right here in the city of Meridian, and the community I was reared in, it was always Whites around me. We were on this side, the White

were across the street. So I always kind of associated with them, to a certain extent, not that I could go to church or to their house and eat with them or anything like that. But I have played with them. When it comes to all this about integration, we opened our doors when integration first came in, and the Civil Rights people were coming into the community. We opened our doors, we were some of the first people to open our doors to 'em, and I kept 'em, we kept 'em in our house. In fact, I kept one girl about a year, maybe a little longer than a year, a White girl. And she slept in the bed with Edna, my daughter. And I cooked for 'em and everything. They came to my house to eat. But we never had the problem of anything. Mickey Schwerner and James Chaney and Goodman, we had gotten kind a close to Schwerner and his wife, Rita, when they first came here. And James Chaney was just raised up 'round here.[111]

Perspective

So far we have looked at some basic aspects of the history and culture of the Meridian area as a way of establishing the context within which to view the tendency toward blending African and American religious and social traditions among Black people in this area. We have seen glimpses of the changing social, political, and economic conditions, and particularly the racial attitudes and relationships during slavery, the Civil War, Reconstruction, and on up to the 1960's and afterwards. And we've looked at these from the standpoints of historical documents and personal testimonies, especially of members of the Jack Graham family grouping. In the following chapters we will do a more detail examination of religious and social practices that are indicative of a blending of traditions from Africa and those encountered in America.

The position taken is that the Black people of this east central area of Mississippi could not escape the fact that they were Africans in spite of the "Middle Passage" and the deliberate stripping of African Americans of all visible signs of African culture to make them amenable to slavery.[112] No one can stamp out the memory, the consciousness. Images and impressions in the mind may be suppressed in the unconscious for a time, a long time even, but at conducive and necessary moments they rise to the surface of consciousness again. The African personality, character, worldview, conceptions, thought patterns, feelings, customs,[113] and practices, and the like, were preserved in the consciousness of the slaves and were transmitted into the new environment and combined with new external encounters to produce a new person. And this occurred especially when the slaves were emancipation and began to experience the freedom to create a life of their own, apart from the one previously imposed upon them. This came out in some families more than others. I am using Jack Graham and his family as a prime example of how this took place in many ways among Black people of the area in question. My contention is that Jack Graham began to create a new Africa where he was situated in life.

Endnotes

1. "Dear Blake, Milestone, August 9," written by Martha, in Elizabeth Sutherland, *Letters from Mississippi* (New York: McGraw-Hill, 1965), pp. 192-93.

2. Laura N. Fairley and James T. Dawson, *Paths to the Past* (Meridian: Lauderdale County Department of Archives, 1988), p. 17.

3. *Ibid.*, p. 18.

4. *Ibid.*, p. 23. See also *Mississippi: A Guide to the Magnolia State*, Mississippi Agricultural and Industrial Board (New York: Hastings House, 1938) pp. 55-59; "This treaty removed all but a small portion of this nation to what is now Oklahoma" p. 59. Article 14 of the Treaty spelled out terms for allotting lands to each Choctaw head of a family who chose to remain and become a citizen of the U.S. "Other articles gave special land considerations to chiefs, compensation to other individuals and outlined plans for removal to the West." But many of the protections guaranteed the Choctaw in the treaty were later denied. It was made difficult for the Choctaw to sign up for the land promised under Article 14. "Fraud and force eventually drove most of the reluctant Choctaw to Western lands and consequently today, of what was specifically designated for Choctaw individuals and families in the treaty '...not a single piece of land had remained in Choctaw ownership" (Fairley and Dawson, p. 24). Internal quotations from Bob Ferguson, edited version of speech delivered at 150th Anniversary of Signing of Treaty of Dancing Rabbit Creek, in Goldman Collection held by Lauderdale County Department of Archives and History.

5. *Ibid.*, p. 25.

6. *Ibid.*, p. 25.

7. *Ibid.*

8. *Ibid.*, p. 26.

9. John Barksdale, "Citizens of Color," 1962, Lauderdale County Department of Archives and History.

10. Fairley and Dawson, pp. 28-29.

11. *Ibid.*, p. 31.

12. *Ibid.*, p. 34.

13. *Ibid.*, p. 35.

14. *Ibid.*, p. 37. Internal quotation taken from Henry Sale Halbert, "Creek War Incidents," in *Transactions of the Alabama Historical Society*, ed. by Thomas McAdory Owen (Ala. Hist. Soc.: 1898), Vol II, p. 118.

15. Randy J. Sparks, "Religion in Amite County, Mississippi, 1800–1861," in John B. Boles, ed., *Masters and Slaves in the House of the Lord* (Lexington: University of Kentucky Press, 1988), pp. 65, 66, 67. Also Larry M. James. "Biracial fellowship in Antebellum Baptist Churches," *Ibid.*, p. 52; and Fairley and Dawson, p.40.

16. Fairley and Dawson, p. 40.

17. *Ibid.*, p. 41.

18. *Ibid.*, p. 42.

19. *Ibid.*

20. *Ibid.*, pp. 47 and 52; internal quotation is from *The Meridian Star*, May 8, 1960.

21. *Ibid.*, p. 52. Internal quotation from A. W. Malone's history of Meridian in *The Meridian Star*, May 8, 1960.

22. Fairley and Dawson, p. 52.

23. *Ibid.*, p. 53.

24. *Reconstruction in Mississippi* (Gloucester, Mass.: Peter Smith, 1964), p. 13.

25. Federal Writers' 'Project of the WPA, Miss. Agricultural and Industrial Board, *Mississippi: A Guide to the Magnolia State* (New York: Hastings House, 1938), p. 230.

26. Barksdale, p. 1.

27. Garner, pp. 14–15.

28. Fairley and Dawson, p. 57.

29. *Ibid.*, p. 60.

30. *Ibid.*

31. *Ibid.*

32. *Ibid.*

33. *Ibid.*, pp. 60–65.

34. *Ibid.*, p. 65.

35. Barksdale, p. 1.

36. *Ibid.*

37. Fairley and Dawson, pp. 67–68. The "strangers" referred to here obviously means Northern appointees as well as former slaves.

38. Fairley and Dawson, p. 70.

39. James Garner, pp. 338–53.

40. *Ibid.*, p. 349.

41. *Ibid.*, p. 351. A more detailed account of this riot is found in the "Introduction" to the present volume.

42. Seth Cagin and Philip Dray, *We Are Not Afraid* (New York: McMacmillan Pub. Co., 1988), p. 2.

43. Fairley and Dawson, pp. 71–72.

44. *Ibid.*, pp. 72, 75.

45. *Ibid.*, pp. 78–82.

46. *Mississippi: A Guide*, p. 230.

47. Fairley and Dawson, p. 84.

48. *Ibid.*, pp. 87 and 163. Efforts are underway to find out if this man Graham was related to James Graham, the former slave master of Rev. Jack Graham, especially since Jack Graham also was into lumber business.

49. *Ibid.*, p. 91.

50. *Mississippi: A Guide*, p. 230.

51. F. M. Runnels, Ed. *Illustrated Handbook of Meridian, Mississippi* (Meridian Board of Trade, 1907), p. 15.

52. *Ibid.*, pp. 15–16.

53. Fairley and Dawson, pp. 97–98.

54. *Ibid.*, p. 98.

55. Ibid., p. 99.

56. Barksdale, p. 1; Fairley and Dawson, p. 99.

57. Fairley and Dawson, pp. 99–100.

58. Barksdale, p. 1.

59. Buford Satcher, *Blacks in Mississippi Politics 1865–1900* (New York: University Press of America, 1978), p. 1.

60. *Ibid.*, p. v.

61. *Ibid.*, pp. v-vi.

62. *Ibid.*, p. 15.

63. See "Introduction"; Also Lewis Lomax, John H. Griffen, Dick Gregory, "Mississippi Eyewitness," *Ramparts Magazine*, 1964, pp. 9 and 11.

64. Quoted in Silver's *Mississippi: The Closed Society*, p. 16.

65. Silver, p. 247.

66. *Ibid.*, pp. 250-51.

67. Interview, May 19, 1988.

68. Interview, May 19, 1988.

69. Interview, May 19, 1988.

70. The husband had over eight awards for outstanding leadership hanging on the walls of the study. The *Who's Who Among Black Americans 1975-76* listed him as a business executive. The businesses listed numbered three current ones (a florist and gift shop, an insurance agency, and a photo service), and three previous ones. He was noted as founder and president of the Meridian Negro Business and Professional League 1946; President of the Meridian NAACP; Member National Board of the NAACP 1957 (this lasted 23 years); member of J. F. Kennedy National Committee of Constitutional Rights and American Freedom, 1960. One of his many awards was a citation by the Oranges and Maplewood Branch NAACP for "Outstanding Courage and Distinguished Leadership in the Cause of Equality and Justice for the Negro People of Mississippi."

71. Interview, May 19, 1988.

72. *Ibid.*

73. *Ibid.*, Interview, May 19, 1988.

74. *Ibid.*

75. Interview, May 20, 1988.

76. *Ibid.*, The "plant" was the wood yard where he got his business contracted.

77. Interview, May 19, 1988.

78. *Ibid.*

79. *Ibid.*

80. *Ibid.*

81. *Ibid.*

82. Barksdale, p.1.

83. *Ibid.*

84. Interview, Meridian, May 23, 1988.

85. First highschool for Blacks in Meridian, founded in 1896. See Fairley and Dawson, p. 100.

86. Piney Woods was then a Black private highschool located in Piney Woods, Mississippi, about twenty miles south of Jackson. It is now a public institution.

87. Interview, Meridian, May 23, 1988. His father had died in 1941, three years before he went to California.

88. *Ibid.*

89. See Section four.

90. Interview, Meridian, May 23, 1988. Mittie was 77 years old and her brother C was 63.

91. *Ibid.*

92. Interview, Poplar Springs, May 25, 1988.

93. *Ibid.*

94. *Ibid.*

95. *Ibid.*

96. *Ibid.*

97. *Ibid.*

98. *Ibid.*

99. *Ibid.*

100. *Ibid.*

101. *Ibid.*

102. *Ibid.*

103. *Ibid.*

104. *Ibid.*

105. Benjamin E. Mays, *The Negro's God as Reflected in His Literature* (New York: Anteneum Press, 1969). Also Hans A. Baer, *The Black Spiritual Movement: A Religious Response to Racism* (Knoxville: University of Tennessee Press, 1984).

106. *Ibid.*

107. *Ibid.*

108. *Ibid.*

109. Interview, Meridian, May 23, 1988.

110. *Ibid.*

111. *Ibid.*

112. For a discussion of this, see E. Franklin Frazier, *The Negro Church in America* (New York: Schocken Books, 1963), pp. 1-15.

113. I deny categorically Frazier's contention that "slavery deprived them of their accustomed orientation towards the world," *Ibid.*, p. 9.

CHAPTER 3

LAND POSSESSION, RELIGION, AND FAMILY TIES

"Now the Lord said to Abram, 'Go from your country and your kindred and your father's house to the land that I will show you. I will make you a great nation, and I will bless you, and make your name great, so that you will be a blessing'" (Genesis 12:1–2).

Love of the Land

Land is the central image in the biblical vision of life both on earth and in heaven. It is central in the experience of those in possession of it and those dispossessed of it. The status of the Jews from beginning to end in the biblical history revolves around either their being in possession of it or being dispossessed of it.[1] The beginning of Abraham's essential life, his most vital existence is initiated with God's promised gift of the land to him and God's promise of descendants who will possess the land. The land is not promised to a man and wife alone, a couple, but to a family that eventually is to become too numerous to count. The same type of link, of family ties and land possession, governed the apportioning of the conquered lands by Joshua in chapters fifteen through nineteen of the book of Joshua. The land was divided up among families (See 15:1,20; 17:2; 19:1,17,24). And these are religious communities, the descendants of Abraham, people who are expected to be living in accordance with the divine covenant made with Abraham and renewed with other patriarchs after him.

The significance of this biblical picture hardly escapes the truly sensitive and perceptive biblical interpreter who sees the Bible as a guide for life. It certainly did not escape Jack Graham, who in the late 1870's and early 1880's gathered together the family members and began to build a social and religious community. One of his first acts was to purchase land and build a house. Mrs. Sarah Graham Gregory, who was interviewed in 1988 at the age of 99, the second oldest daughter and the only one living, said of her father's house-building and land-purchasing, "When I was born he was on his own land, and he was preachin' too, when I was born." She said,

> Him and a White man named John McLemore built that house. And it was awful rough lumber, and Papa took his jack and planed all that lumber himself, all the outside he built but not the ceiling inside.[2]

She said she and the two oldest sons were around trying to help but they were too young to really do any real good other than pick up things and hand them to him. She said her father covered the house with shingles which he made himself. "He had a, I don' know what they call it, but he had his drawing knife while he's making shingles."[3]

The desire for land was strong among many Black people, going back a few years before Jack Graham was old enough to exercise any initiative in that direction. Two years after the Civil War had ended and the slaves in Mississippi were freed, when Jack Graham was only 5 years old, Black people were anxious to possess land. Buford Satcher tells of an incident in December, 1867, at the end of the harvesting season when many Blacks did not have jobs. Crime had increased, livestock especially was being stolen.

> It was common belief among Blacks at this time that land would be allotted to them.[4] In the wake of that opinion, a marginal number refused to sign labor contracts for the next year and some refused to leave the plantations.

Governor Humphreys was the first to react to these activities. He informed Blacks that he had learned of their intentions of seizing land for the purpose of establishing farms and of their hopes that Congress would devise a plan for distributing it among them. Likewise, he added that Blacks had avowed that if Congress did not organize such a system by January of 1868, then they would proceed to take land themselves, even if it meant going to war, an act of which they felt sure of succeeding.[5]

It is evident from numerous examples and testimonies that land is very important to Black people in east central Mississippi, and other parts of Mississippi and all over the South really. But our concern is with this area as an example. In his publication in 1962, John Barksdale states with pride that of the 17,000 Black people within a twenty-five mile radius of Meridian forty-two percent were land owners.[6] It is amazing that in less than one hundred years after the close of the Civil War, when practically all of Mississippi, and especially the Meridian area, was in a state of almost abject poverty, Black people of this area should have advanced to the point of forty-two percent land ownership. It would have had to entail great strength of mind and character, dogged determination and stubborn persistence on the part of these people to overcome the seeming insurmountable odds of racial hatred, segregation, discrimination, and outright oppression and acquire land and hold on to it even through serious economic crises such as the Great Depression. With the little help they received in acquiring it, it is nothing less than astonishing that twenty-five percent of Blacks throughout the South owned land, even if it was not more than forty acres in many cases.[7]

The overwhelming majority of Black people in Mississippi became share croppers in a new system of slavery. Powdermaker describes how the masses of them were exploited by self-serving White landlords and plantation owners, whose lands were restored to them for the most part after the War. The Blacks for the most part were given nothing but a mandate to continue to labor for the former slave masters.[8] Yet some small numbers of black people were cash tenants and renters. In the confusing and chaotic conditions after the close of the Civil War some

Black people, former slaves, managed to acquire land. In a few cases those who had served in the category of house slaves were assisted by their former masters.[9]In other cases a group joined together and purchased a large plot and formed a small colony and worked and paid off their different portions of the land. Others were assisted by a few sympathizers and philanthropists.[10] Individual landowners among Black people date back to the close of the Civil War when land was cheap. A few were able to purchase some of this. Every indication is that wherever they had the resources they eagerly invested in land and periodically would continue to accumulate more and more land and pass it on to their descendants.[11] One man cited by Powdermaker owned as much as 1600 acres which he divided up among his eight children before his death.[12] Quite a number of landowners started from scratch and worked hard and saved their money and began to purchase land and eventually became rather well-off.[13]

The question I wish to pose is, why was the desire for land so strong among so many Black people? And another is, why did they struggle so hard to hold on to it? Why do those even who live outside of the state hold on to the land they inherit from their parents and some return to live on it and farm it? I know of no one who has dealt sufficiently with these questions. Certainly, the religious significance of land in the Jewish scriptures influences this attachment, the sacredness of the land. But there is also another significance here that is not immediately apparent, and that obviously escapes the awareness of those Black people themselves who maintain a strong love of the land. The feel for the land is an integral part of the African heritage, which is still very strong in descendents of Africans in America. And having been dispossessed of their homelands and brought to a foreign place where they worked the land, another land, for the benefit of a strange race of people must have been a traumatic experience for people who came out of a culture where views of land possession were almost entirely different from the views of those whom they were forced to serve as slaves.

John Hope Franklin points out that,

> The African concept of land ownership stemmed from the importance of agriculture in the [people's] way of life. The land was considered so important to the entire community that it belonged not to individuals but to the collective community comprised of the first occupants of the soil.[14]

The importance of the local dignitary in the community, the "master of the ground" attests to the land's significance. This man was also the grand priest of the religion and the administration of the soil, and not even the political ruler could make any decision about the land without his consent. Individuals were granted the right to use certain portions of land but it was not permanently owned. For when it was no longer in use by a person to whom it was granted, it reverted to the community ownership.[15]

This African tradition is exemplified in the novel by James Ngugi, *Weep Not Child*, in which the Kenyan father relates the creation story of his Gikuyu people. According to the story, in the beginning there was a type of chaos—wind, rain, thunder, lightning. The earth and forest shook terribly in and around Mt. Kenya. Animals of the forest whom the Creator (Murungu) had recently put there were afraid. There was no sunlight. The whole land was in darkness. In the darkness at the foot of the mountain, a tree rose, small at first, but grew, called Mikuyu (God's tree). There was only one man and one woman (Gikuyu and Mumbi). God first put them under the holy tree, and immediately the sun rose, the darkness melted away. The storm ceased. Animals were at ease, all gave homage to the Creator and to Gikuyu and Mumbi. *The Creator took Gikuyu and Mumbi from his holy mountain and showed to them all the land and told them: "This land I hand over to you, O Man and Woman; it is yours to rule and till in serenity, sacrificing only to me, your God, under my sacred tree."*[16]

Here we see the supreme importance of the land as sacred because it was given as a gift of grace to the first man and woman by the Creator God. This is the same way in which the land is regarded by other archaic peoples such as Native Americans and ancient Jews. This is also, then, the Biblical view of land. When asked by his son, "What happened to

the land?" Which had been taken over by the British in colonial rule, the
father answered:

> I am old now. But I too have asked that question in waking and sleeping.
> I've said, "What happened, O Murungu, to the land which you gave to us?
> Where, O Creator, went our promised land?" At times I've wanted to cry
> or harm my body to drive away the curse that removed us from the
> ancestral lands. I ask, "Have you left your children naked, O Murungu?"[17]

Although the exact transmission of African cultural traditions cannot
be traced satisfactorily in African descendants in America, yet the
memory, the dreams of the ancient homeland could not be stamped out.
Their love and desire for the land here in this country, I dare say, was
an awakening of an ancient memory, a desire for home. And I intend to
demonstrate this in the particular examples, as well as the communal
links involved in land possession and religion.

The Setting for Jack Graham's Assumption of the African Chieftaincy Role in the New Africa

Descendants of Africans brought to the New World in Jamaica who
embrace the religion of Rastafarianism still look upon themselves as a
captive people in a strange land. They lament that Black people in the
West have been laboring for centuries in a land they can never call their
own, building a strange country, a people who belong to Africa but are
here building a strange world. Their labor is unappreciated, unrewarded,
and they are being oppressed. These brothers appreciate the "natural
beauty and fertility of the Jamaican land and the strength and wisdom
of the Jamaican people," but they "cannot reconcile themselves to the
type of society which now exists, since in their view it demeans both land
and people." These Rastas long for return to the African homeland of
Ethiopia, the Promised Land.[18] Their position is perfectly rational and
understandable within the context of their total religion. Their refusal to
be a part of the alien society which controls Jamaica is also
understandable from a socio-political standpoint.

Yet other religious and social responses to the new world situation in which Africans found themselves after slavery may be just as supportable within a different socio-religious context. One is that in the United States Africans have given liberally of their labor to build this country, and it rightly belongs to them. And the people who embrace this belief, the majority of African Americans in the U.S., are just as determined to share equally in the benefits of this country and to receive justice therein.

There is no evidence that Jack Graham ever debated whether to become a part of this country or to seek to return to his African homeland. It is clear from the record of his actions that within the political, social, and economic confusion and chaos of the post-Civil War period between 1865 and 1880, he as a young man in his teens drew upon all the resources within him, as well as those without, to bring order to the environment in which he moved. With the knowledge and insights available to him he set out to build what I am calling the New Africa in America where he was. And I call it this because the society he fashioned among his own family and the churches that came under his direction possessed internal and external characteristics of both African and American traditions.

There has been much debate between scholars over the years as to whether Black people in the United States who are descendants of Africans enslaved in this country retained any traits of their African background or traditions. Realizing that the slaves in this country were deprived of their African languages, religions, and social customs, many concerned persons have tried to answer the question. The slaves could not speak their language nor practice their religions because they were placed in groups of Africans who were of different cultural groups who spoke different languages and practiced different religions. Their family structures were destroyed and cultural continuity was severed. The only common language they could use to communicate with each other was the master's. And they were also forced to adapt to other aspects of the new social surrounding. Melville Herskowitz and E. Franklin Frazier were the leaders of two opposing camps of sociologists, anthropologists and historians who made claims regarding the question. Herskowitz claims that there are Africanisms among African Americans, though not as evident in the U.S.A. as among Blacks in such areas as the Caribbeans where languages and religions and other cultural manifestations from Africa have been discovered in highly visible forms. He cited certain traits among African Americans such as the dance, the shout, distinct African music, spirit possession, etc.[19] E. Franklin Frazier, on the other hand denies the existence of any remnants of African culture among Black people in the United States.[20]

There has not been a resolution of the conflicting positions on the issues of African cultural survivals among U.S. Blacks. Charles Joyner adopts the more realistic viewpoint. "The nagging question is not whether there were continuities or discontinuities with African cultural patterns—clearly there were both—but rather, given the nature of the 'peculiar institution' [of slavery], how slave folk life developed from the interaction of various African cultural traditions and the new natural, social, and cultural environment."[21] Throughout his work, he demonstrates the continuities and the interactions between African cultural traditions and certain encounters in the new environment.

John Hope Franklin agrees with this viewpoint. He notes that there were sufficient common experiences for Blacks in the New World to cooperate in the fashioning of new customs and traditions which reflected their African background.

> There were at least two acculturative processes going on side by side in the New World. As Africans of different experiences lived together, there was the interaction of the various African cultures which produced a somewhat different set of customs and practices which manifestly had roots deep in the African experiences. At the same time, there was the interaction of African and Western cultures which doubtless changed the culture patterns of both groups.[22]

In making the last point Franklin adds a rather pertinent observation, namely, that "where European practices were relatively weak the opportunities for African survivals were correspondingly strengthened." He also observes astutely that the acculturative process varied in different places under different circumstances. "In some places it was all but stymied where there was sufficient consensus of experience among the Africans to take the Western culture and reinterpret it almost wholly in terms of their own experiences."[23]

It is with these points in mind of varying degrees of acculturation and African survivals' being strongest in areas or at times when European culture was weakest that I wish to assert that Jack Graham arose on the scene in the Meridian area when Euro-American life had collapsed and was in a state of turmoil. The system of slavery upon which the whole socio-economic fabric was founded was completely disbanded. Former slaves and former masters, the whole populace were in a state of quandary. No one was certain as to which route things would take. It was indeed a time for those who possessed creativity and imagination, intellect, skill, and ingenuity to act with all deliberate speed to steer this fallen world on the road to recovery. And Jack Graham, among the Freedmen, demonstrated the precise genius necessary to bring order to the chaotic conditions of these Africans set free with no kind of guide or support from the larger society as to how to build a life as free individuals.

Where did Jack Graham get the knowledge and expertise to perform the yeoman's tasks that he did? It was both from his African background and from whatever schooling he was exposed to and from observing certain other individuals as the occasions may have permitted. For when he was born in 1862, the world into which he entered was fast falling apart in a state of war. The Euro-Americans were battling it out against each other and his people, the African slaves, were caught up in the midst of social and political upheaval and destruction. When he was about two years old in 1864 Sherman marched through Meridian and surrounding areas, including Enterprise in Clarke County, where the

Grahams lived, and wiped them out. So as a toddler Jack Graham saw the White man's world fall apart.

Growing up as a boy he witnessed the society at its poorest and weakest. Everyone, Black and White, had to start again more or less from scratch. Everyone had to play the survival game. The red clay hills and virgin forests of this east central Mississippi area must have brought back memories of the African bush and the family and home life, farming and hunting and fishing, along with social and political possibilities that were there. But even if it didn't, the creative genius of the African mind was obviously set in motion by the challenge of the natural environment and the needs of families and friends and neighbors. And Jack Graham witnessed Black men and women struggling together to establish a life for themselves. When the constitutional conventions were meeting in 1865 and 1868 and Black and White men were trying to put the political life of the state back together, Jack Graham was probably getting some schooling—either in one of the schools set up by the Freedmen's Bureau or one run by some White missionary groups and benevolent societies.[24] Jack Graham must have seen Black men holding local political offices during his boyhood years, and observed their attempts to help the society reorganize life and regain a sense of control amidst the lingering turmoil. He may have been in one of the schools in Clarke County on Monday morning March 6, 1871, when news circulated that a bloody riot was in progress twenty miles away in the city of Meridian. Or if he didn't hear of it Monday, he had to hear of it sometime during the week.

On July 4, 1870, the state legislature passed a law establishing public education for all its citizens, Black and White, making the likelihood of Jack Graham's getting an education even more probable. And Jack Graham grew to manhood as the east central Mississippi area began to grow gradually back to economic, political and social strength. But Jack Graham had to grow up in a hurry because he was the only able man in his family, with a mother, aunts, and other relatives, mostly females, dependent on him to take over leadership of the family as soon as he could arrive at a viable age at which to do so. And with the society in the upheaval that it was, he had few if any models, like so many others of the Black race of the area. The only models he had were in his head, in his genes. From what we have said in the introduction to this volume, he rose to the occasion, using all that was within him of his African origins, as well as what he encountered without, to become the architect of a new African society that even today bears the marks of his genius.

At a very early age, Jack Graham became an ordained Baptist minister and began to pastor rural churches. He married at the age of twenty and somehow came into possession of some land. And he continued to acquire land, both timber land and farmland for growth of cotton. The earliest record of his purchase I was able to locate was in the *Deed Record* of Clarke County Chancery Court, where Jack Graham was shown as purchasing 160 acres of land from the Farmers Loan and Trust of Mobile, Alabama for $360.00 on December 18, 1903. But prior to that time we know that he was steadily accumulating land and prospering very well. He built his home in the 1890's on a portion of that land.

Of course, Graham started out as a landowner, farmer, and business man at a time when Meridian and the surrounding area, including his county, had begun to recover economically in the 1880's. And when it became a boom town in the 90's, owing to the rebirth of the rail lines and the lucrative timber and cotton production, Jack Graham and his family in Clarke County and many other Black people of the area progressed right along with it.[25] The land he owned, eventually amounting to a total of 363 acres by 1956, when he died, was located in what Fairley and Dawson referred to as the "extensive pine region extending to the South and West of Meridian." It is therefore evident that Jack Graham was able to make a profit on the sales of timber from his lands. Furthermore, as Meridian became a center for compressing and shipping cotton, producers of cotton in the thirteen cotton-growing counties surrounding Meridian were able to sell their harvests with ease.[26] And Graham, being among the smaller land-owners, was obviously able to make a profit on his cotton productions, as well.

Jack Graham as the Self-Styled Tribal Chieftain in the New Africa

Without being entirely conscious of it Jack Graham in the most easy and natural way set out to restore Africa in the New World. This is what we come up with or the conclusion we may draw as we analyze exactly what he did in assuming the roles of family head (of an extended family); religious leader (shaman, medicine man, chief, etc.) of the peoples and families of the various churches he pastored as well as of his own extended family, the Graham clan; possessor of the land, businessman, educator, and spokesperson and benefactor of the group he headed. Furthermore, the manner in which he combined the religious with all other aspects of life (social, political, and economic), and the stress he places on kinship ties and possession of land are reflective of the leadership role played by an African chief of the family or tribal chief.

It is fairly common knowledge that the family played a key role in the organization of African society, serving as the basis for both economic and political life. And religion permeated all the phases of life. John Hope Franklin summarizes the nature and role of the religious head common in African religions:

> Because of the family character of African religions, the priests of the religions were the patriarchs of the families. They were the oldest living members of the descendants of the initial ancestor, and had therefore inherited the earthly prerogatives of their predecessors. Thus, they had dominion over the family grounds, water, and atmosphere. It was the family patriarch who entered into communication with the souls of his ancestors and the natural forces in his immediate vicinity. He was therefore authorized to conduct the ceremonies of worship.[27]

While there was not an exact transmittal of the role of the African religious head in the character and functions of Graham in his community, there were characteristics in his actions and operations among the group far too strongly reminiscent of such African leaders to be passed over without acknowledgement of the direct correlation.

Graham could hardly trace his family roots farther back than his mother and father. And his father died when Jack Graham was very young, so that he didn't remember much about him. Thus, in a great sense, as he assumed the headship of his family, he became the patriarch and initiator of a new African people in a new land.[28] The combination of Chieftain and religious leader and practitioner, which Jack Graham's self-styled role reflects, was discerned by Frazer in his studies presented in *The Golden Bough.* He cited numerous examples in which the chieftaincy in different areas in Africa, (East, Central, West, and South) is linked with the roles of medicine men, rainmakers, healers. He cites, for example, peoples of the Upper Nile where the medicine men are generally chiefs. Also, he states, "In Western as well as Eastern and Central Africa we meet with the same union of the chiefly with magical functions. Thus in the Fan tribe the strict distinction between chief and medicine man does not exist. The chief is also a medicine man and a smith to boot; for the Fans esteem the Smith craft sacred, and none but chiefs may meddle with it." Finally, in South Africa it was found that the power of rainmaking was a part of the "fundamental glory of ancient chiefs and heroes."[29] Once again, Graham's functions in such regard are not direct transmission but rather a reflection and a creative transformation of such a role in a new environment.

Graham's socio-religious leadership function of re-establishing family ties which had been severed by slavery, building his own family, deeding out land to his oldest sons and their families,[30] training and educating his children and grandchildren, and serving as the moral and ethical guide and overseer of the entire religious community of several churches in different counties[31] all of this reflects both the chieftaincy role background, as well as the patriarchal and tribal headship functions in the ancient Jewish traditions, to which Graham was exposed in very thorough biblical orientation. This character and function of Jack Graham can best be illumined by looking at the descriptions of the man by those who knew him and could discern the respect and reverence he inspired in the community he served.

Reflections on Jack Graham Which Illuminate the Chieftaincy Characteristic

The reflections included here are on the various characteristics of Graham in assuming the roles of family head, religious trainer and leader, businessman, landowner, counselor, guide, skilled artisan; as well as on his personal traits as a human being. They are made by his only living daughter, his grandchildren and one person who was not a blood relative. Mrs. Izella Zan Beasley has some interesting revelations both about the family ties and land possession in her own and Jack Graham's family, and about the reputation of Jack Graham.

According to Izella Zan Beasley, born in Clarke County, now living in Meridian, Mississippi, whose father, Mr. Alex Mercer, was Sarah Ann Anderson Graham's first cousin, her grandfather, Wash Mercer, a former slave, also accumulated much land after his emancipation, and at his death had 370 acres, of which each of his children received 40 acres apiece. Mrs. Beasley reported some interesting facts also concerning the family ties and relations on Jack Graham's wife's side of the family (Ms. Sarah Ann Anderson Graham). Her family were sold in Selma, Alabama, to the Andersons of Clarke County, along with a part of the family of her later to be husband John Henry (Jack) Graham (who was then a Mooney). Most of John Henry Graham's family were sold to the Grahams of Clarke County. But his brother Sandy (Anderson) was sold to the Andersons along with Sarah Ann, who was later to become John Henry's wife. Sandy and the other members of John Henry Graham's family were Mooneys up to that time.

Elijah Anderson and Archie Anderson were Sandy Anderson's sons, nephews of John Henry Graham, Sr. Sarah Ann Anderson Graham had a sister named Lizzie Anderson Henderson, who also lived in Clarke County. Mrs. Beasly stated, Rev. Jack Graham was most intelligent, he was a business man. After his father, Alex Mercer died, and his first cousin, Jack Graham's wife Sarah Ann Anderson Graham died, Mrs. Beasley's mother, Mrs. Viola Goodwin Mercer married Rev. Jack

Graham, a marriage which lasted 13 years, until Jack Graham's death in 1956.[32]

Mrs. Sarah Graham Gregory describes her father, Jack Graham, as having been a versatile craftsman. When she was a child she said she would follow him around when he was working on things. And when he would put tools and other objects down, she would pick them up and try to do everything he did. So she learned a lot that way. He was a perfectionist in his work, she said, and required that of his children.

> People used to in them days, if they would slit they shoe or anything, they'd need the patch on, papa used to do all of that, patch the shoe and put a sole on 'em. *Papa could do anything.* I'm talkin' 'bout, now, he didn't do no patchwork. He did spark-down good work, cause he didn't believe in half-doing something. Don't bring him no patchwork! Yeah, he made us, wherever we had anything to do, he'd see that we done it complete.[33]

She said of her father's handling of his land that her father gave each of the boys a portion of his land when they got grown except the youngest, and left the rest of it to him and the girls when he died.

All of Jack Graham's thirteen children were members of Zion Spring Baptist Church which their father pastored in Clarke County. Most of the grandchildren and great grandchildren were members of that church. The grandchildren interviewed give interesting and revealing testimony as to the kind of person and religious head and family leader the grandfather was. Rev. Timothy Graham, son of Charlie Graham, says Jack Graham

> was a great leader. He was a great Baptist preacher; he served these churches in Clarke County, and he served some churches in Jasper County, and Lauderdale County (Poplar Springs Baptist Church).[34]

As to the kind of training he tried to instill in his members, Timothy says, "Oh, he was very strict. He believed in his faith. He was a Baptist and he believed in the Baptist faith, very strongly." He says his

grandfather was an "outstanding preacher during his day." He described
him as an "expository preacher" who did much dramatizing of the stories
of the Bible and did "hooping" also.[35] Asked if Jack Graham would
first develop the sermon clearly, he said:

> Oh, certainly, he would explain his text well. He would stick with his text
> during his preaching. People thronged to hear him preach; he baptized a
> whole lotta people. I meet people now that I don't even know. They tell me
> that J. H. Graham baptized them. They were converted under his
> preaching.[36]

Timothy's brother Cleveland and his sister Mittie had great reverence
for their grandfather. To them he was a sacred figure. Mittie said, for
instance, "We just thought, if anybody goes to heaven, we thought
grandfather, he would." She went on to describe him and other members
of the family and their connections.

> My grandfather was really a Christian man. And I had a uncle, Uncle
> Willie, my father was the oldest son in the family, and he had a brother
> next to him, Uncle Willie, he was a minister. He married my mother's
> sister. My father and my uncle married sisters. And Uncle John married,
> Uncle Willie, they had one child, but this child died. I don't think it was
> quite a year old.[37]

Cleveland related some of the everyday life regarding his
grandfather, revealing very clearly the tribal chieftaincy-Biblical
patriarchal figure, the ritual leader, guide, benefactor:

> My grandfather used to buy cars ever so often. He had some T-Model cars,
> Chevrolets. So I used to open the gate for 'im. He lived down below where
> we lived. He had a old gate, you don't see these kinds of gates nowadays.
> This was a slide gate, wooden slide gate. We would lift it up and slide it
> backwards for the traffic to come through. And when the traffic would
> come through, I would pull it forward and leave it like that between two
> posts and a piece of wood like that. So that was my duty. I volunteered for
> this. Every time I'd hear my grandfather crank his car up, I'd meet him at

the gate and open it for him. When I'd see 'im coming, I'd be at my house, I run down there and open the gate for 'im and close it. I loved him that much. I thought he was the greatest man in the world. I thought he could say anything and God would do it for us.[38]

Cleveland also explained the land situation in regard to the grandfather's relations with his son, Cleveland's father, and the family.

We lived on my grandfather's land until we grew up to a certain age. Then my father taken us and bought eighty acres of land. He taken a milk cow that my grandfather gave my two older sisters, Mittie and Vivian, and made a downpayment on eighty acres of land. I never will forget her name. She was a black and white cow named Mamie. And then we picked cotton and helped pay for the land from then on. And my older brothers sawed wood like stove wood and fire wood for White people. We all helped pay for the land like that. So we finally paid for it and all. After we bought that land, my grandfather deeded my father two forties, and so that made us have 160 acres of land. He deeded a forty on the southeast corner. So we have that land today.[39]

The barter system of paying down on the land is interesting in this account. Also of striking interest is the communal nature of paying off the land, as well as the grandfather's paternal act of deeding a portion of his land to the son and his family. One sees that family ties are very strong here, and they are linked to the land. Because of the love of the land and the family heritage, the ancestral and sacred character of the land, none of the grandchildren have sold their land. The other living sisters and brothers of Cleveland, Mittie, and Timothy dwell out of state, but they maintain their land also (between 17 and 20 acres each). Cleveland only recently returned to the area after many years up north. He explains how he makes use of his land.

I started a fruit orchard some years ago. I set out approximately four hundred trees, and so I was living in Chicago. And I'd come down every year and have 'em worked out. So one year, it didn't bear, and the next year, I had 'em worked out, and the cold came and destroyed the blooms, and they didn't bear that year. So this year, a couple of years later, I didn't work 'em. So just about half of the trees are dead, but the trees are loaded with fruit, peaches, ten different types of peaches.

Reflections on the Religious Leadership of Jack Graham as Combining African Ritual Traditions with American Religious Practices

As so many interpreters, sociologists, anthropologists, theologians, and other scholars have pointed out, although African Americans were exposed to and accepted the Christian faith from their White slave masters and other Whites, they did not swallow whole what they received. Rather, they took that religion and adapted it to their own experience and needs such that they created that faith anew.[40] Slaves in Mississippi, as elsewhere in the South, were largely a part of the biracial churches, relegated to special sections. The churches that they became most receptive to were the Baptist and Methodist varieties. The reason for the attractions to these groups is commonly accepted as their close similarity to religious beliefs and practices of the African cultural background. In the revivalist movements, camp meetings, etc., the Blacks participated along with the Whites. But slaves were preached a different gospel from that delivered to the Whites. They were admonished to accept their menial status as slaves to which God had assigned them, and to be obedient and subservient to their masters. But the master's form of Christianity is not what they accepted. They transformed the religion of the Bible to suit their own needs and circumstances and created a different theology from that of the Whites.[41] When they worshipped in secret bush arbors or in their cabins, they worshipped fully and freely in their own manner and interpreted the scripture and preached a liberating gospel.

Charles Joyner writes of slaves on plantations in the All Saints Parish area of South Carolina:

> Visitors to the Waccamaw rice plantations were struck by the religious fervor of the slave community—the slaves' active participation in church services, their ecstatic prayers and energetic shouts, and especially their

spirituals. Of the origins and beliefs of that religion, as well as its meaning to the slaves most of the visitors knew nothing. They never reflected that they were witnessing a remarkable cultural transformation: from a diversity of African beliefs and a multiplicity of African rites and practices to a distinctive Afro-Christianity that voiced the slaves' deepest ancestral values as they responded to a new and constricting environment.[42]

The African ways of religious worship and ritual that were endemic in them the slaves transmitted to their religious practices and combined them with the practices they encountered in the White Christian churches. Joyner goes so far as to assert of the South Carolina community,

> It was not God the judge of behavior—God the master or overseer—who was the object of worship in Afro-Christianity, but a God more like African deities: God the transcendent spirit. They worshipped this new Christian deity in traditional African ways, and they made European religious forms serve African religious functions.[43]

In like manner, we find among the churches pastored by Jack Graham the practice of what is called "getting religion," being saved, being converted. And we have the "mourner's bench," and certain patterns of behavior and tests of the group to determine whether or not one has truly gotten religion or whether or not Jesus has saved the person. Although such practices of relating a story of the conversion experience was common among the Puritans and in the revivals of the Great Awakening, I strongly maintain that the ways in which they were used in the Graham churches in the Meridian area contain genuine aspects of the African initiation rites, especially the puberty rites.

Taking a look at some of the practices and experiences of the people in the churches pastored by Jack Graham, we find that the families and community were held together, disciplined and mutually maintained by communal religious practices and relating of religious experiences that bound the people together in meaningful ways. Annie, Clara, and Gertrude explain how they were received into their grandfather's church in Enterprise, Zion Springs Baptist Church. They are the only children of Pearl and John Henry Graham, Jr., the third oldest child of his father. Their land adjoined the grandfather's land on one side, and Charlie, the oldest son's land adjoined the land of his father on the other side. And each of the two sons' family homes were situated on their land no more than about one twentieth of a mile from the father's home.

In describing the disciplined religious training and the family ties and influence within the extended family set-up, Clara presents an image of the grandfather that has strong resemblances to the African tradition of the clusters of families in a community or clan in which the oldest male member in the family was the authority over all as well as the religious leader.[44] She says the grandfather had as much influence on them as, or more than, the father did. They were brought up in a patterned church tradition in which attending all church activities was expected, such as Sunday School, worship services, training unions, special programs, and they were an integral and active part of all the activities. There was, however, a special ritual requirement before the young people were received into membership in the church society and could feel themselves a genuine member of the family grouping. This was the experience of being what they referred to as "truly converted."[45] And the process they usually underwent had interesting parallels to the puberty initiation rites in African societies.

First there was the age requirement of twelve years old, although there were some few exceptions wherein they could be younger or older. But when they reached the age of twelve, the mother or father or some older member of the family began to urge them toward the conversion process. Second was the context in which the conversion took place. There was a revival held at least once a year, in which a noted revivalist preacher would preach five weeknights, and all the people would be in attendance. The young people who were candidates or seekers that year would be asked to sit on a front row known as the "mourners" bench. They were to pray and fast and diligently seek God for their salvation.[46] At night they would attend the services, and during the day they were to be off to themselves, often in the woods, praying and fasting and petitioning God for their salvation. Family members, father, mother, older sisters and brothers played an active part in assisting the seekers in their search by giving counsel where needed, guiding and watching over them. They were carefully watched for any signs of change in them.

When the youngsters were convinced that they had been saved or had "gotten religion," they came up during a set time in the night service, the opening of the church doors, and gave the minister their hand. But this was no simple process, for there had to be a third requirement, which was a "retelling" of the conversion experience which convinced them of their salvation.[47] And if their story did not sound convincing to the pastor and church officials, they would have to go back and try again. Clara explained that the grandfather was very interested and concerned about their being "truly converted." He was aware, she said, that a lot of youngsters joined the church without knowing really what they were doing, without being "truly converted." But Jack Graham was "known by all the ministers in the neighborhood to thoroughly question a youngster when he [or she] would come to join the church" to determine if they were actually converted. And he had a "long line of questions he would ask them." "He not only went by what we said but he went by our looks, our reactions, and what have you." She said the people back then could look at persons and tell whether they were converted.[48]

Describing her own such experience, Clara stated that she and some others were slow to pick up on the process.

A bunch of cousins and I were reluctant about joining the church. He [the grandfather] would tell us all about how you would feel when you get religion and what have you. You would "feel as light as a feather," and you "would feel like you could step from the top of one house to the top of another one," all that. He really had it blown up in such a way that we didn't understand it, you know. And they believed, when it would come to the revival meeting, they would select the minister very carefully. And it was a type of minister they all believed could really, really preach. And this

type of preaching was to satisfy that particular group of people. They
believed in spiritual preaching, the shouting type of thing. And we as young
people didn't really understand it.[49]

Clara was sixteen years old when she joined the church, having been
waiting around for the prescribed feelings, which she could not have no
matter how hard she prayed. She recalled having yearned hard to
become a part of the church but was warned against it until she had that
"feeling."

> I recall times that I wanted to join the church so badly I would even have
> to hold to the back of the seat to keep from getting up. But yet, my
> grandfather told us that if we joined the church and really didn't have
> religion we'd be worse off than we were in the first place.[50]

Consequently, she and a group of cousins who were around the same age
as she just waited. She says she didn't exactly experience that type of
feeling. So she finally just decided that maybe the Lord didn't want her.
So she would go on and try to live the Christian life as best she could.
After she made this commitment she just stopped praying because she
had prayed all she knew how. And at that moment, she said, a change
came over her.

> And this change was just coming like a mighty rushing wind. It even
> frightened me at the time, and I didn't exactly know what to do. But then
> I caught myself singing some particular song that I would hear my oldest
> sister sing all the time that I would hate to hear her sing. "Praise God, I'm
> satisfied, saved and sanctified." and then I evidently had a different
> appearance. My father saw me, and he said, "Clara, don't you have
> religion?" I said, "No, Sir, I guess not." And he said, "Well, have you had
> any kind of feeling any different from what you had before?" I told him,
> "Yes, I thought one time maybe I had religion, but I just stopped." "Well,"
> he said, "then, you pray and ask God to make you believe you're converted
> if you have had this feeling. And if you continue to feel that way, then you
> go ahead and join the church tonight."[51]

Clara said she did as her father told her, and as they were going to church that evening, her grandfather stopped her on the road and asked also, "Daughter, don't you have religion?" She replied, "Well, I don't know. Sometime I feel like maybe I have." He said to her, "You look like you have religion." This gave her confidence, she said.

The family impact here was very crucial. Clara now felt the reassurance and reinforcement that she had not experienced two years earlier when her oldest sister got religion, and Clara also came home and told her parents that she too felt like she had religion. They looked at her then and didn't believe her. And they were right, she said, because she was only following her sister. But at the time when both her father and grandfather detected religion in her, she felt strongly that she did. And when she got to church that evening she discovered that her cousin Freddy had also gotten religion. Both of them, then, joined the church together.

The fourth stage in the initiation process was the baptism, which took place in a little creek just below the church. They would dig out the pool and "dam it up" and carry out the baptismal. Clara and Freddy and his sister Ejella, the three of the grandchildren around the same age were baptized together.

Clara recalled some of the questions asked in the interrogation of converts who came up during worship and declared that they had religion. She said the grandfather would

> actually ask you if you were converted. What makes you think this? How did you feel? You really had to tell. Had you been praying? Maybe, how long have you been praying? They would have you go off to yourself and pray, get away from everybody else.[52] They would ask you, "When you looked at your hands today did they look new? At your feet, did they look new?"[53]

Clara pointed out that if the youngsters could not talk very much and answer these questions satisfactorily, they would doubt that they had religion, and they would have to go back and try harder.[54]

From Charlie Graham's family, Timothy, Mittie, and Cleveland give similar accounts of the strict process of "religious initiation" of the young people in the family and church. Mittie used the expression "I found Christ." She had a more typical experience and remembers it vividly. It was in the church while the preacher was preaching that she was converted. She even remembers the name of the preacher after sixty years.

> I received Christ in my life at the age of twelve. And now I am seventy-seven years old. In the revival service he [the grandfather] had the Rev. Easeley from Meridian running the revival for him. And I never shall forget the text that Rev. Easeley took when I received Christ. He was preaching from the text, "As Moses lifted up the serpent in the wilderness, even so must the Son of Man be lifted up, and I'll draw all men unto me." And his subject was "Look and Live!" And from that time on until today, I've been looking and living. And as Rev. Easeley preached, it just seemed like something just touched my heart. I began to pay attention. All beforehand I would go to the mourner's bench and I would just look down, but something struck me that time, a Thursday evening, and he said, "Look up and live!" I began to hold my head up and look, and from that subject I'll never forget I often think about it. I often wake up at midnight, and I can tell you 'bout the subject and the time.[55]

Cleveland says he joined the church when he was eight years old, during a revival also on a Friday night. He remembers the name of the creek in which he was baptized, "They called it Double Branch Creek in Enterprise."[56] He says that even though he was very young, his grandfather was satisfied he was ready to join the church. He says the revival preacher helping his grandfather was Rev. A. J. Anderson, and he and his sister Ruth joined church the same night.

Timothy says he was converted at the age of fifteen and a year later was called to preach, although he delayed for several years before accepting the call. He had a somewhat typical conversion experience. It was during the usual revival, which at the Zion Springs Church of his grandfather's was always held during the first week in September. He says he "accepted Christ" on a Friday night. Throughout the week he had been on the mourner's bench listening to the preacher and praying and seeking his salvation. The family and church members told him a lot of things to do and he tried to do as they advised him. But he found out that what he needed to do was just accept Christ. He gave his life over into his hands, and as he was on his way to church that Friday evening, his conversion took place before he arrived at church. The way he describes it is that he had a feeling that came over him that made him know it was a change in his life, a supernatural change, a sudden change. When he told his story before the church they didn't question it. They could look at him and tell he had religion.[57]

Otis Brown and Dessie of the Lula Graham Brown family, at Savoy, Mississippi, and members of the Popular Springs Baptist Church, where their grandfather pastored for fifty-nine years, tell of similar types of experiences. Otis too was called to preach a year after his conversion.[58] Dessie said that the family and church community, as well as the grandfather, were very concerned that when they came up claiming to be converted they had to tell something to the church that convinced them that they were saved. They had to speak for themselves.[59]

Effie, whose family home is now Clarksdale, Mississippi, is the granddaughter of J. H. Graham, Sr. She was born in his house in Enterprise, to his daughter Odena Graham Blakeley (at the time, but later was married to a John Gordon). She too shared the rich religious background generated by her grandfather. She and her husband Bennett are strong in religious faith. Both were born in Mississippi and have never lived outside the state, as so many other Black people did, even her mother, after experiencing the racial difficulties and hardships. She and her husband raised their ten children there, most of whom moved out of the state when they became grown-up and finished school. They've moved to such places as Memphis, Chicago, Detroit, Milwaukee.

Effie's conversion experience took place in Starkville, Mississippi, in Oktibbaha County, about one hundred miles from Meridian. There was a revival going on in their church, Bethel Baptist Church. She was twelve years old, and her baptism was in a "fish pool." The setting was typical, only services during the revival were held twice a day, morning and evening. The evening service was held out in the yard of the church under a tree, the weather permitting. They would have prayer service for the seekers, and she says it was Thursday evening that she was converted and decided to join the church.

> It was an experience I never will forget. I had a little place I would go to pray when I would leave church, across the pasture. When I got to the pasture this particular evening (Thursday), as I started across the pasture, when I got to the pasture fence (barb wire) to go under it, then I heard a little voice say, "You got all you gonna get." So I didn't know what to do. I straightened up (from bending under the fence) and started to turn around; and then another voice said, "You go back to the house and they gonna laugh at you, they gonna make fun of you." And I was halted and started backward and forward for the third time. And the third time I just took off running to the house. And my mother was standing in the door of the kitchen, looking. She was just standing there watching me. And as I got to the door, she said, "Sister ..." I said, "I got that religion. I believe in Christ!" And one of the Deacons of the church was standing talking with Papa. When he looked and saw me, he ran to me and grabbed me and just pitched me up in the air two or three times. That's the feeling I will never forget. Every now and then that comes back to me just as fresh as on the day it happened.[60]

Religious restrictions were placed on the young people of the Graham families, stemming from their grandfather's teachings. Clara spoke of the teachings about dancing being wrong, "socializing parties," maybe some of their top interests they had as young people were strongly discouraged. Too much engaging in pleasures and good time was frowned on. They were never allowed to go to dances. Drinking, smoking, playing cards they never engaged in. They didn't forbid them to go to movies, which they did when older, but their parents never took them to places like that.

The Transformation of the Family Griot Tradition in the New African Setting in America

Pleasurable social activities did happen among the Graham family. Church suppers, picnics, barbecues, singing contests, hunting, fishing, sewing and quilting parties or sessions. Outdoor games and contests were common among the children. Numerous activities took place in the rural mecca of the hills of Clarke County. And of course, trips into town or to visit relatives distances away were fun too. These people enjoyed the simple pleasures of life. They enjoyed one another. They even enjoyed planting their fields, their gardens, and truck patches, tending them and watching them grow. In probably the last letter he wrote to his brother John H. Graham, Jr., on September 9, 1918, Ira W. Graham (1891–1918), who was a private in the U.S. military service stationed at Hattiesburg, Mississippi, sent his love and regard to his parents and all his brothers and sisters and expressed his desire to come home. Before the close of the two-page letter he inquired anxiously about his crops: "How is my crop getting along? Is my cotton open much? I sure does want some goobers to eat. Is they ripe?[61] Have you all pulled them up?" Ira probably never saw his crop, for within three months, before the year was out, he was shipped to France where he died in the influenza epidemic.[62] Nevertheless, we see how much he relished his crops, as was typical among the people.

Storytelling was a popular art among the Graham families, especially in the winter when they would gather around the fireplace, bake yams, make hominy, parch peanuts, and the like. There are persons in the families, as are in numerous other families of African Americans, to whom has been transmitted quite naturally the art of the African *griot*, a very important figure in African literary tradition, which was predominantly oral before the languages of Africa were written down. "Handed down principally through the kinship group, the oral literature was composed of supernatural tales, moral tales, proverbs, epic poems, satires, love songs, funeral pieces, and comic tales."[63] The function of the *griot* was to memorize the bits of oral literature and cite it at formal gatherings before kings or in informal gatherings of ordinary families. "They sang, told stories, and recited poetry. They kept in their memories the history, law, and traditions of their people and were themselves living dictionaries who occasionally performed invaluable services to their communities."[64]

In my research I encountered a number of persons who obviously inherited this skill among both the laity and the ministry. And the preaching style of certain African American clergy strongly exhibit this tradition.[65]

Among the laity of the Graham family Cleveland, son of Charlie Graham, Sr., proved to be the most outstanding bearer of the griot traits. He is a virtual reservoir of stories involving himself and members of his family, as well as the Jack Graham family. He is also full of the tales told by his people. I would like to cite a few of these in full just to demonstrate the trend and the style of Cleveland. In the first story he tells he sheds light on local histories and personalities, as well as on historical periods of the nation. In 1944, during the War, he and another young man were recruited from Meridian out to Mare Island Naval Shipyard in Vallejo, California as welders.

> So we went out there. When I left here I didn't have but $5.00. I had meal tickets and a train ticket, a pullman ticket. We went through the way of New Orleans. So when we got to Louisiana we went and played some pool. So we got back on the train on our way to California. My partner, he could play cards. He was kind of slick with cards. I let him have two or three dollars. And so when I got to Vallejo I had three cents. And the government furnished us more meal tickets. And they gave us a place to stay. We stayed there. This was in 1944, the last of 1944. And so they wasn't taking nobody, it was during the Japanese War (WWII), they weren't takin' nobody but experienced welders on Mare Island. And naturally they wuz giving that to the White people. So they had a few Black people who were tack welding. The White people were welding, the Black people were tack welding.
>
> They were only paying Black people $1.26 an hour. So they offered me burning which is a trade that goes with welding, cutting steel, they called

that burning. And I was angry, I wouldn't accept it. I used to work on the slab where they make, build frameworks for the ship. I worked there with the ship fetters. I didn't make but a dollar and twenty cents an hour, a dollar ten, that's what it was. I saved up $500 in six months. And so I stayed out there until the War ended.

And first report came out, that was a false alarm. They blew the sirens on the Island. They said, "The War is over!" Then we found out this was a false alarm. So we went back to work. And later on the final report came out. They laid most of us off then.

So I had gotten my foot broken when I was working under a cruiser scoot, on drydock four. Some man was taking some scaffling down out from under the cruiser. It was a painter, a two by twelve hit my foot and bounced up a little over a foot high, broke my foot across the arch. So the Navy came and picked me up and taken me to the Navy dispensary. It was a hour before I got waited on. So the Navy officer called me and said, "Get up and come over here." I stood up on one foot. I told 'im, "I can't walk." So they sent somebody over, and all they did was got some plaster pads and some cheese cloth and wrapped my foot up and sent me back to the barracks off the island. Some Waves taken me in a station wagon. They told me to come back the next day. They gave me some crutches.

So in about three weeks I could walk with these crutches, board the ferry and run down the gangplank with these crutches. So I was getting pretty good then. I was about eighteen years old.

I can tell you who was in charge of Mare Island. Admiral Chisadale was the admiral of the fleet at Mare Island. Admiral Lemmett was the main admiral of Mare Island. He was in the Pacific on a mission. So Admiral Chisadale was in charge of the fleet.

So I had quite a bit of experience at working; it used to be 40,000 people worked there day and night. They had three ships; they'd pull ships in from Pearl Harbor, floating drydocks, and we'd prepare 'em. I worked on USS Franklin D. Roosevelt, that was the aircraft carrier. We overhauled it and sent it back to combat duty. I worked on the USS Steelhead, that was a submarine, the USS Puffer. I used to work with Filipinos, different minorities of people. It was about 40,000 people working on that Island, day and night. So they'd have buses leaving every five minutes for the barracks, coming in from Oakland and Frisco and different places, going to that Island two and fro.[66]

When Cleveland returned to Meridian in 1947, he had some interesting experiences which he tells of in enlightening details regarding Piney Woods School up near Jackson, Mississippi, about ninety miles west of Meridian, where he attended a short while in 1949.

> It's a high school. It takes up 2000 acres of land about twenty miles on 39 highway south of Jackson. Dr. Lawrence C. Jones was the founder and Principal of that school. I can tell you how that school started out. Before Dr. Jones got to be a doctor in education, he bought forty acres of land out from Jackson. He's Black, yes. And so he saw some men working in the woods cutting down timber. He taken a newspaper and walked up to them and asked them could they read. They said, "No." So he offered to teach 'em the alphabets every day during their lunch hour. So he taught 'em the alphabets. Then he taken these men and cut down some logs and made a one-room log school. It was an old Black man there. He came over to see what they were trying to do. He donated them a piano for the school. Then the school started growing. Dr. Jones went about making speeches. He used to ride in a buggy. He didn't have a post office at that school during that time. He'd have to go to the post office in his buggy and get the mail.
>
> So White people got interested in what Dr. Jones was trying to do. They came from Iowa, and different places. Dr. Chandler came from Iowa, and so she, they came down and they started to donating money for the school. Somebody donated enough money to build a girl's dormitory. And somebody donated enough to make the boy's dormitory.[67]

He recounted that it was a private school then supported by the Lutheran Church.

> So people got interested in what Dr. Jones was doing. They came down to help him. They built a chapel and a dining hall, and they had a farm where the boys could work their way through school, raise cotton, corn, potatoes, and things. Chicago gave Piney Woods so many thousand heads of chicken. The state of Wisconsin gave them a boxcar load of cattle, and the school started growing. Today it takes up 2000 acres of land.[68]

Cleveland went on to relate the story of Mr. Plummer at Piney Woods school.

> They had a man named Plummer. He was from Africa, a tall Black man, wore a tam, wore a long beard. He used some of everything. He had diplomas all over the wall. I seen 'im one day. He worked there until he died. He was working with the boys. He'd go in the woods and dig rocks and bring 'em and smooth 'em out and build little bridges across ditches. He built all kinds of statues. Mr. Plummer taken these boys and built all kinds of statues on the side of the hills. He called that the "Outdoors Theater." And I said to 'im one day, I said, "Mr. Plummer, you the smartest man I ever saw. Where did you go to school?" He said, "I went to school in London, England, when I was a boy." I learned some of everything. And I never saw nobody in my life yet that could do what he did. He could do anything that he tried to do. He could take a mirror and set it in front of 'im, just like we sittin' here, and get 'im some paint and paint his picture. You couldn't tell to save your life that it wasn't taken with a camera. He was just that skilled.[69]

Cleveland told the story of his father's illness and death in 1941 at the age of 58 years. He was a diabetic.

> And he had a toothache, and he would have the toothache so bad until he would be sleeping a lot. And my brother Stanley was working for Dr. Larry Rush, Dr. Lesley Rush, and we found out Papa was sick, and Stanley decided he would take him to Rush's hospital and let the doctor see after 'im. And they X-rayed 'im and kept 'im there for a while, found out he had an abscess on his brain from the toothache. So the doctor gave him a spinal puncture to try to draw that off his brain. He took a stroke and lived eighteen days, never did speak no more.[70]

Cleveland had an interesting bit of history to share regarding the flight of Lindberg.

> I remember when Charles Augustus Lindberg flew from New York to Paris in the "Spirit of St. Louis." I was a little boy. My dad was out in the cornfield, and I heard 'im tell mama, I looked up in his face, he said, "You

know, they say Charles Augustus Lindberg flew from New York to Paris in thirty-three and a half hours in the 'Spirit of St. Louis.'" During that time Calvin Coolidge was president. He wouldn't let 'im fly back. He sent a ship over to bring 'im back. They have that plane hanging up in the museum today in Chicago, Chicago Museum of Science. I've had my hand on it, "The Spirit of St. Louis." He got his plane from St. Louis. That's why it's named "The Spirit of St. Louis."[71]

Cleveland related some interesting and exciting stories of his experiences in Chicago, where he went to look for work when all his searches proved useless in Meridian. Some of these involve humor. His oldest sister Vivian was living in Chicago and drove down for the summer, and he rode back with her and her husband.

So I went back with my sister and her husband. He had a old raggedy Pontiac. I don't see how we made it, but I worked my way back to Chicago fixing flats. We stopped in Southern Illinois, where they had a big stack of automobile tires, and went out there and got one. My brother-in-law asked him, say, "How much you want for this?" He said, "Gimme a nickel." He gave 'im a nickel, and that was the best tire on the car. So we went on to Chicago.[72]

Cleveland was shocked at the deplorable conditions he encountered in Chicago and gave a rather revealing account.

I never dreamed it was so bad. Paper was this deep (he indicated about a foot height or more with his hand). Mayor Conally was a Republican mayor in Chicago. And it was the filthiest place I ever went in. We stayed in a building, the owner of the building was named George Demerit. His father was a full-blooded Indian. He rode the horse from New Orleans to Chicago. So he was living. Their mother had passed. She was half French; the mother was half French; the mother was French an' the daddy was Creek Indian. So they wuz mixed up. George looked like a Puerto Rican. So Bobby had wooly hair. He looked more like regular Black people.

My brother-in-law had got a place in the basement. I'd see rats running 'cross the floor all through the day, and I didn't know what to do. I wanted to come back home, but I wanted to get a job to work. So it was a fella by the name of Gus Barnes went with us, my sister's husband's cousin. We had to sleep with the cover over our heads at night to keep the rats off us. So I began to make progress. It was two weeks before I could get a job.

So I found a job working at a box factory, where they tacked boxes. They had mail machines, you know, that you push a pedal an' turn the box around and tack it. I tacked a thousand boxes in eight hours. So I was making $1.10 an hour. I was doing pretty good, I thought. Prices wudn't as high then as they are now. So I kinda made it.[73]

He talked about the several jobs he worked on before he got work at General Motors, where he had a really good position from which he retired after twenty-three years. Some of the stories he tells about those earlier jobs are often amusing and sometimes striking.

I was working round with a Precinct Captain, and I didn't know about political work. So he told me I was his Assistant Precinct Captain. He had me going knocking on doors hustling votes, gettin' the people to come out and vote. I did pretty good until he told me, "I want you to go with me." I didn't know where he was going. So I went with him, and he went over to a Republican Precinct Captain, started a big fuss with 'im. And looked like they were gon' fight. He told 'im, "I don' never wanna catch you in my precinct no more! Stay outa there!" I walked off when they started to arguin.' He ain't seen me since.

Later I was asked did I want a job working at 26th and California.. That was a prisoner place, you know, where they carry these prisoners that had killed somebody. I told 'em, "No, I don't want that." He would've given me a gun to carry. So he said "I can get you a job working for the Bureau of Sanitation sweeping the streets and working on a truck." I said, "I'll take that." So this was '54. I taken that. Before then I had been working in East Chicago, Indiana, at Cast Arms Steel Mill. We built the M47 tanks, M48 tanks for the Korean War, just the bodies, and they put the motors in 'em somewhere else down in Missouri, Maryland, and different places. So we just built the framework. I was welding. So I got to be a welding instructor, at Cast Arms Steel Mill. [I noted that he had finally gotten a chance to do what he was trained to do.] Yeah, it was seven years before I got chance to do that. So I had five people working under me. I had three Black men and one White man and a Puerto Rican girl. So I would tell 'em what to do and where to weld at in the body of the tanks, you know, fighting tanks. So I worked there about eighteen months. I heard the place was gon' close. So I quit before they closed.

I came. back to Chicago and got this job working for the city. I worked there three years and three months.[74]

Cleveland had another bout with California working.

And I went to California and stayed out there a while, welded for the Los Angeles Steel Mill there. We built parts for the Colorado River, parts for oil wells. My job ran out and I had to come back to Chicago.[75]

So later I worked for Young Spring and Wire, where they built automobile seats and springs for the Studebaker. I worked there about four years. And the parts would be on assembly line, you know. I'd be welding while they'd be traveling. And so we built the framework where I worked. And they put the seats and springs in in the other department. So I got tired of working out there. I'd work seven days a week and wouldn't make but a hundred and fifty dollars.

So they wuz on strike at Elective Motors in La Grange, Illinois. It was two fellas came from there and wuz just working there just until they went back to work. So I asked did they think I could get a job there. Someone said, "Yeah, you can get a job." He told me he was gon' talk for me, told me when to come—a white fella from Kentucky. So I went and got hired shore 'nough. I quit Young Spring and Wire today. I went out there tomorrow and got a job.

But I got a good job. I worked myself up to $550.00 a week for forty hours at General Motors. I didn't work but three or four hours a day. It was like piece work that I was doing, but it wasn't called piece work. I was building gear casings for the traction motor. That's something like a oil pan that was put over and under the traction motors on trains. And so I'd make the company around $3,000 a day.[76]

One final bit of stored information Cleveland shared was concerning what his mother taught him when he was a child.

I can tell you some more. 'Bout when I was eight years old. I was younger than eight. We didn't have writing paper and mama taught me the Lord's Prayer before I went to school and alphabets. I'd get down on the ground and write the alphabets with my fingers. And she taught me how many chapters and verses wuz in the Bible when I was eight years old. I know now how many it is. I can quote it to you: 1,189 chapters, 31,173 verses in the Bible.[77]

Cleveland impressed me with his remarkable storehouse of information and incidents from the distant past and his ready recall of those things. It is truly a gift, an inherited gift.

Drawbacks in the Jack Graham Leadership Tradition

The superb leadership and purposeful direction and guidance Jack Graham provided for his people is highly commendable. He brought his relatives together and laid a strong family foundation based on both African and biblical principles. With the help of his mate, Sarah Ann Anderson Graham, he was able to train his children and instill them with strong and enduring values, as well as to provide a model for other families in the community. And in these and other efforts Graham influenced the establishment of a society that I refer to as the New Africa in America. The principles he instilled were agrarian ones. He taught them how to live well and control their environment, or how to interact with their agrarian circumstance and to make a comfortable living. They lived, as in Africa, in harmony with their natural environment. And they shaped a harmonious and cooperative community based on strong family ties.

The principles encouraged and instilled in family and church were industry (hard work); independence and self-reliance (they were not to be a burden to others but to achieve for themselves); courage and fortitude (a lack of fear of anyone, but to stand up for what was right); strong sense of self-possession; honesty, fairness, openness, frankness; and the most basic were love of God, love of land; love and respect for others, especially one's elders; and finally, respect for education and training of oneself both physically and spiritually in order to equip oneself for life in all its ramification.

Jack Graham did not seem to be concerned much about city life. He was content to maintain an agrarian existence in the New African bush of Clarke County. That style of life in all its possible riches and abundance, living off the land, seemed perfectly satisfactory. He seemed never to have weighed the possibility of moving away from the land. He rather made that existence peaceful, productive, and happy. He lived close enough to the city to enjoy its benefits and provisions. He would go into town to sell goods and purchase his needs. Some of his children and eventually most of his grandchildren moved to cities in the state and even outside the state, to Northern cities. He could not control that emigration, which was a general trend among Black people in the South at various periods of the twentieth century,[78] beginning in 1910. It is reported that by 1918 more than one million Black people had left the South. This meant for Jack Graham a watering down or erosion of his New African society of an agrarian paradise. Urbanization was taking hold among all peoples in America and with city life came a demand for different lifestyles and principles of living.

There were also some problems within his family of thirteen children that were beyond Jack Graham's control in spite of the moral and social restrictions and rigid requirements he demanded of his family and church. Although his children adhered to the religious and moral standards principally, there were some few deviations. One in particular involved some humor and shows that he was not always able to exercise complete control over his daughters. One of the grandsons told the story of how his mother and father got married. He said the relatives told him the story. His grandfather always wanted everything to be done right and in order, in a proper and respectful way. But in regard to his mother and father's marriage it didn't go according to expectations. He tells the story

My mother and my father were married at an early age. My father was about ten years older than her. And he wanted her for his wife some way or another. So my grandfather wudn't ready for her to marry. He was up preachin' one night. Now my father had an ole buggy, belonged to an old man called Willie Lugby, ain't that right, ...? And so he and my mother got married while my grandfather was preaching. My daddy caught the drops on 'im. She come out the door, and slipped off wid 'im. They hit the road, come over here to Savoy and got married. My daddy lost his license (marriage) he was runnin' so in the buggy. He had to get a flashlight and go back and look for it. My Aunt had just got married, and my grandfather wanted my mother to wait. So my daddy, after he got married, my grandfather told 'im he had wanted 'em to wait. But they went on and married. My mother was thirteen or fourteen, but my daddy was an experienced man. He knowed his way around.[79]

In a more serious vein, one of the weaknesses of J. H. Graham, Sr., seems to be in being at first too steeped in the Judeo-Christian and African patriarchal traditions. For in the true manner of these traditions he failed to accord his daughters equal status, especially where land was concerned. When his sons got married and started families he deeded them portions of his land (inheritance). And he instilled in the sons the love and respect for the land and possession of it. This he failed to do with and for his daughters before his death. Of course, after his death, in his will he had divided up his 363 acres among all the living children whom he had not given their portion of his estate previously. Each of these surviving children received approximately forty acres each. But living away from the homestead with their families in other towns in Mississippi and in large cities in the North, not a single one of the daughters held on to that inherited property. They either sold it for a small amount of money to one of their two living brothers or lost it to the conniving lawyer handling the property.

Seeing how fairly he distributed his land among his surviving children both male and female and his widow, one can assume that Jack Graham had overcome his patriarchal notions, but it was too late to save his daughters from being divested so easily of their divine inheritance. Most of his daughters outlived most of the sons and were widowed, some left with large families which they headed. It was not exactly like in Africa with some, where the next oldest male becomes head of the family when the father dies. Jack Graham must have become aware of a trend in

African America, whereby women have had to serve as family heads because of the endangerment of the male. Trying to make a living for their families in a society arrayed against them, the males have often overworked themselves and died an early death, leaving their wives to carry on the leadership of the family.

Two cases in the Graham family are outstanding. We have seen earlier that Jack Graham's oldest son Charlie died in 1941 at the age of fifty-eight, leaving his wife Maggie with their twelve children. She lived to be one hundred and four years old, having died in 1989. Yet she never married again but gave her life entirely to her family and church. Although the family was left with 160 acres of land on the homestead in Clarke County next to the grandfather's land, land which they retain even today, trying to survive through all the hard times with such a large family was a struggle. And most of the children joined the emigration of masses of Black children to the North in the first half of the twentieth century. Yet the mother remained in the area and kept the property intact with the help of others of the Graham family who remained.

The story of Odena, Jack Graham's tenth child, is somewhat different. But she faced a similar situation of being widowed and left with a family of twelve children. Odena was married twice, which circumstance in itself was not the best thing to happen. For according to scripture to have more than one husband, in the Baptist evangelical tradition, was biblically frowned upon. But apparently with her the family found it justified. She was accepted. Her first marriage produced two daughters, Hattie and Effie.

Odena met the man, John Thomas Gordon, who was to become her second husband, in Columbus, Mississippi, where one of her older sisters was living and only recently passed away in January, 1992. The two of them married and settled in Starkville, a city only about twenty miles from Columbus. John Gordon was a widower, also with two daughters by his first marriage, Laura and Sarah. With a family of four daughters they accumulated a large homestead and a farm consisting of a hundred acres of land. They prospered well until the Depression came and he lost his property. In the meantime their family was increasing; eventually they added nine children to the four they had brought together in their marriage, making a total of thirteen.[80]

John and Odena and their family were reduced from landowning farmers to sharecroppers, the poorest status of any farmers anywhere,[81] one step removed from slavery. Because of better farming opportunities they moved out of the Meridian area further North in the Delta. And it was there that John Gordon worked other people's land and got little remunerations from it for his own family. He lived on Brooks Planation in a place called Drew and labored, he and his large family, and struggled while other people got rich from the crops they produced. He died an early death in 1942, during the Second World War, leaving a family of ten living and unmarried children for Odena to head. He was only fifty-six years old when he died.

Odena was a remarkable woman, however. Had she been of a docile nature she may have succumbed before the overwhelming circumstances she faced as a widow. She could have taken her children and moved back to her grandfather's estate in Clarke County, requested her portion of the inheritance and built a strong agricultural existence like her father. But apparently she had learned too well the lessons her father and mother had taught of independence, self-reliance, courage, fortitude and faith, and the like.[82]

Instead of returning to her father's place,[83] Odena took her children who remained with her and sharecropped three more years and saved up enough money to go up to Memphis and make a down payment on a home and move them out of the state. She took her cow with her to the city[84] as an added means of survival. She herself did not work outside her home, but she had her children work and bring in money to help pay for the home and keep things going. She had a very difficult time, but she made it through without ever being on welfare or depending on other people outside the family. She planted gardens in her huge back property to her house and raised chickens in a small barnyard set up in the back yard. Effie believed it was Odena's religious faith, instilled by her father and mother, that saw her through those times.

> It was a struggle, but she kept the faith in Christ. She was a religious person and she just believed that God could do anything. And she just kept her faith in Christ and struggled and waited on God, tried to give her children the best education she could. She did a good job with her last three, which I'm proud to say.[85]

Odena survived the hardships of her life also because she maintained the principles instilled in the family by her father and mother. Like her sister-in-law Maggie, she never married again. But she believed that the family could maintain itself if it kept its ties with one another and cooperated and worked together in love. She promoted this among her children, as her parents had done. She set up the extended family arrangement and kept her grandchildren in her home, her younger brother and his wife at one time, and other relatives. She also maintained strong ties with her Graham relatives distances away. Not only that, Odena became a support for other families in the community who brought their children to her to keep. They soon saw that she had a strong love for children. She opened her arms to them. The small neighborhood in which Odena lived began to look upon her as its shining light of hope, love, and faith. The religious principles she had inherited from her father she began to exhibit among the people there.

Jack Graham had always cared deeply for Odena, as she had always loved and respected her father and his religious and social teachings. But when he saw what progress she had made in rearing her family and building a life for herself and her family in her own way just as well as any man could do, Jack Graham learned to respect her even more and obviously made a shift in his patriarchal stance toward women. As a tower of strength and endurance and unwavering religious faith, Jack Graham saw that here was a woman who, better than most of his sons, had drawn from and utilized his teachings to the benefit not only of her family but also for that of all people who made significant contact with her. In true African fashion and from the arts she had learned from her father and mother's practices, she used the herbs to cure most of the sicknesses in her family—colds, flu, pneumonia, and many others. Jack Graham was satisfied when he saw that his training had been transformed in Odena, who had created her own new Africa in America in an urban setting.

A third example which Jack Graham witnessed in his extended family that began to change his patriarchal thinking pattern was the case of his third oldest son and namesake, John Henry Graham, Jr. This man's land and homestead adjoined his father's on one side. He lived closest to his father psychologically, spiritually, and socially. He outlived all his father's sons except his youngest brother, as well as all his sisters except one. He was last of the patriarchs of the Graham family. He took up the ways and responsibilities of the father and became the source of strength, power, training and discipline. But he had no sons to whom to pass on the heritage of land, religion, and culture. Instead he had three daughters who were just as good as any son could be. They were strong, obedient, disciplined, respectful, intelligent, industrious, and dependable. To their father and to their grandfather Annie, Clara and Gertrude, proved themselves worthy of bearing the heritage.

Realizing this, both father and grandfather modified their patriarchal thinking and proceeded to prepare these girls for the kind of life's role they would have to play. They attended elementary school there in the area in Enterprise. But the nearest high school was in Meridian. There being no transportation system whereby they could commute the twenty miles to the city, the parents arranged for them to stay at a woman's house who lived near the school and kept boarders. They completed high school, college, and acquired post-graduate degrees in education. And then they also became educators, serving and advancing in roles of teacher, counselor, principal. They married men who were strong as educators and businessmen. As family members and professional people these women and their husbands became community leaders.[86]

Yet, they retained their strong love for the land they inherited from their father and mother. They maintain the homestead in Clarke County and the large acreage even to this day. So even though Jack Graham did not instill his daughters with the kind of regard for the land that his sons learned from him, these particular granddaughters did receive such a legacy from their father no doubt because he had no sons to whom he might bequeath it.

Jack Graham's youngest and only living son, Oscar, received the portion of Jack Graham's property (forty acres) on which the homestead of the Graham family exists, which adjoins the inherited property of Annie, Clara and Gertrude. He has built a newer brick home for himself and his wife, Annie Mae, next door to it and in 1988 was in the process of dismantling the old family home of his father. Much farther down the road lives Oscar's daughter and her family in a newer brick home located on the same land mass. These people and their families maintain the Graham inheritance. Oscar and his wife do much gardening, raising of vegetables and fruits and selling them to markets in nearby towns, in addition to marketing of timber on their lands.

Other Examples of the Interweaving of Land Possession, Religion, and Family Ties in the Meridian Area

We would find, if we did some searching, that most of the persons who prospered on their own land and became successful in maintaining it to pass it on as inheritances to their families, maintained a strong link between these three elements of land, family, and religion. One of the Figgers family members interviewed, Sarah, explained how her father happened to be one of the founders of the church to which she belongs today in Meridian, Mt. Olive Baptist Church. She says:

> It started out as a brush arbor, right here in the Meridian area. And my father was a native of Waynesboro [about 50 miles South of Meridian], Mississippi. And my mother was native of Louisiana. In their young days they met and got married and came to Meridian. After moving to Meridian, they attended this place where they wanted to put a church up, and they

had to have so many members to organize a church. They had to have some people who could get a letter. So my father and mother went back to Waynesboro and got a letter. And they came back to Meridian to help get the church started. They started a building campaign.[87]

If we looked more deeply into the background of the starting of this church we would find, without a doubt, that it was families who were interested in getting a church started. And certain ones donated the spot of land which they owned in order to facilitate the process.

Rev. Fred Jenkins's father owned 100 acres of land in Actibbaha County (Starkville, Mississippi), one hundred miles northwest of Meridian, which he maintained through the roughest economic periods. He willed it to his children at his death. Fred got twelve acres, upon which he has now settled after moving back to the area after his retirement from much travel and work for many years as a longshoreman in California and Washington states. He is a preacher now and raises livestock and farms this land, and he says that now for the first time in his life he has a sense of peace. His wife Sarah remains in California with one of their sons.[88]

One of the most interesting accounts is that of the community outside Philadelphia, Mississippi, Neshoba County, described by Florence Mars in her book entitled *Witness in Philadelphia*.

Mars's account brings out clearly the deep-rooted connection displayed among Blacks in east central Mississippi in the Post Civil War era between *religion, family ties, education* and *land possession*. She describes several communities of Black land owners that sprang up in Neshoba County (where the tragic Klan murders of three civil rights workers took place in 1964—Michael Schwerner, James Chaney, and Andrew Goodman) after the Civil War. Among these communities are Northbend, Stallo, Mickalusha, Hopewell, Poplar Springs, and Mt. Zion. The possession of land by these former slaves gave them a sense of place, pride, strength, and self-respect, among other things. It developed in them a "proud sense of history," as the author termed it. Mars focuses on one of those communities, Mt. Zion (note the deep religious

signification in the name of the place—Mt. Zion being the hill on which
the temple was built in Jerusalem and consequently, the name given the
People of God, most vividly depicted in Psalm 48). Mt. Zion was the
community in which Goodman, Chaney, and Schwerner centered much
of their organizing activities in Neshoba County a few days before they
were murdered. It is located about eight miles east of Philadelphia.[89]

One of the oldest Black communities in the county, Mt. Zion's proud
sense of history began with land acquisition:

> The first land in the community to be owned by [Black people] was bought
> in 1879 by former slaves Thomas and Harriet Jones. They bought sixty
> acres of land from Parson W. J. Seales, who had bought the land in the
> 1840's and 1850's from a Choctaw Indian named Oanawha.[90]

In the 1880's other Blacks moved in, also purchasing land from
Seales and other white and Black landowners, all of these new residents
having some kind of family ties. Citing such residents as Julius and Lou
Anderson, George W. Johnson, Burrell and Hannah Kirkland, J. C.
Clemons, Harry Cattenhead, Mary Snowden and her eleven children,
Mars declares:

> The families were closely related. Julius Anderson's wife was Burrell
> Kirkland's sister, and Kirkland's wife was Anderson's sister. Julius and Lou
> Anderson's daughter Dora married J. C. Clemons, and after he died, she
> married Harry Cattenhead. Mary Calloway came from Klondike community
> of Kemper County where Professor Essie Plez Calloway, her former
> husband, taught school. In 1907 one of his students, Arthur Cole, came to
> teach school in Mt. Zion, bought land on credit, and wrote to his brothers
> back in Klondike that there were good opportunities here. His brothers,
> Calloway Cole (named for Professor Calloway) and Threefoot Cole, moved
> to Mt. Zion several years later and became large landowners.[91]

The above account shows the definite link between landownership,
family ties, and education among former slaves. It is later pointed out
that the residents of this community were "deeply religious people, and

the first community building they constructed was a log church built in the early 1880's on Julius Anderson's land. Before that there was a 'brush arbor' church, constructed of pine poles that were covered with brush and pine straw."[92] Various temporary structures were subsequently built of rough hewn timbers, logs, etc., until a frame lap-board building was constructed that lasted for sixty-five years, when it was burned down by the Klan in 1964 during the time of the Goodman-Chaney-Schwerner tragedy.

Having to go to cities such as Meridian or Philadelphia to get a high school education, the residents of Poplar Springs and Mt. Zion joined together to borrow and raise enough money to build Longdale High School and a nearby home for teachers in 1948.[93]

It was the Mt. Zion Methodist Church described above that was the center of the organizing efforts of Schwerner and Chaney, who were chased out of town for their activities there in early June, 1964. Subsequently, on June 16th of the same year, the Klan interrupted the members leaving an evening meeting and bludgeoned Bud Cole and burned the church to the ground. Of course, this was around the same time as the incident where the three young freedom workers were killed.

But after the case of their murders were solved, the members of the Mt. Zion Church displayed the same strength, courage, fortitude, fearlessness, determination, and resiliency of those of New Hope in Meridian in working to rebuild the church, which was completed in February, 1966, less than two years later. A plaque in memory of the civil rights workers was placed just inside the door, whose words express the people's theological understanding and interpretation of the incident. It reads:

Out of one blood hath God made all men.
This plaque is dedicated to the memory of Michael Schwerner, James Chaney and Andrew Goodman whose concern for others, and particularly those of this community led to their early martyrdom. Their death quickened men's consciences and more firmly established justice, liberty, and brotherhood in our land.[94]

The Two Basic Meanings of Land Among Black People in the New Africa in America.

In closing this chapter it is fitting to reflect on why land was and is so important among African Americans. Fundamentally, the reason is a religious one. We have seen that in both the African religious and social background and the Judaic religious context to which they were exposed in America land was of primary importance. The African ancestral lands were a gift from God to the people to be distributed and used by the various family groups, but never to be permanently and selfishly owned. Though land was not purchased, it was every family's right to possess it so long as they needed or desired it. When it was no longer used by them, then it reverted back to the communal ownership. Essentially, access to the land meant in Africa openness to God, to the ancestors, to nature, the validation of one's human and divine connections. In the communal nature of life in Africa, there was an unbroken bond between the living, the dead, and the yet unborn. And access to the ancestral lands was an integral part of that connectedness.[95] This kind of thinking was retained in the blood, in the genes of African Americans. Therefore, when Emancipation came the Africans in America strongly expected to be granted some land on which to settle and re-establish their sense of being in the world.[96]

The Judaic heritage depicted in the Old Testament strongly reinforced this African thinking regarding land possession. The establishment or founding of the Jewish people was based on God's gift of the land of Canaan to Abraham and his seed.[97] And the promised land becomes a divine image that permeates the whole of the people's history. When Israel was enslaved in Egypt for four hundred years, they never lost sight of the promise. They were called out of Egypt to go from their enslavement to possess the land as God's covenanted people. And this story of enslavement and deliverance from bondage, this particular meaning of salvation did not escape the African slaves in America. They readily saw themselves as a "new Israel" or as God's chosen people whom he would and did free from their bondage.[98] Therefore, when their deliverance came the African former slaves expected and demanded access to the land. It was their right, their natural, God-given privilege. According to the Bible, possession of land was the next step to freedom. Dvorak summarizes the situation well: "Rumors that land would be given or sold cheaply to former slaves fanned eschatalogical hopes that blacks' economic relationships to society would be transformed in the new order. The Old Testament promise of land to a people liberated from bondage spoke eloquently to and magnified these hopes."[99]

As the promise of land to the ex-slaves did not materialize those relatively few who were able or fortunate enough to acquire land treasured it highly. Jack Graham was one of those. He went after it eagerly and constantly continued to accumulate it. And so did his sons, especially John Henry Graham, Jr. And when his father died in 1956, he struggled to hold on to the land inherited by the other siblings who readily sold their portions of the land willed to them by Jack Graham. To Jack Graham the land meant freedom, independence, family stability and togetherness. It meant that they would never be enslaved again, but it also meant closeness to God. It had that higher religious symbolism. It was significant as the earthly home, the new Africa in America, and it also served as a symbolic link to the spiritual "promised land" the heavenly home that runs through biblical theology.[100]

Endnotes

1. Walter Brueggemann, *The Land* (Phila: Fortress Press, 1977), pp. 14 & 134; Genesis 15:7–8 and 18.

2. Interview, Columbus, July 12, 1988.

3. *Ibid.*

4. Ruth Polk Patterson tells of the disappointments and frustrations among Blacks in Arkansas because of the false hopes raised by the Southern Homestead Act of 1866. She mentioned their anxiousness to homestead land but were unable to do so because "By 1866 most former slaves had hired themselves out to employers in order to survive." She says there were requirements they could not meet, such as the five-dollar registration fee, the price of the land, etc.;*The Seed of Sally Gooden: A Black Family of Arkansas 1833–1953* (University Press of Kentucky: Lexington, 1985), pp. 31–33.

5. Buford Satcher, *Blacks in Mississippi Politics 1865–1900* (New York: University Press of America, 1978), p. 17. See also James Garner, *Reconstruction in Mississippi* (Gloucester, Mass.: Peter Smith, 1901), p. 134; John Hope Franklin, *From Slavery to Freedom* (New York: Vintage Books, 1947), pp. 311–12: "This impression stemmed from the Confederate apprehension during the War that the Union government planned to seize their land and convey it to ex-slaves, and from the bill creating the Freedmen's Bureau which gave tacit encouragement to such a plan. Although nothing came of it, the federal government sought to encourage the dispersion of population from congested centers by opening public lands in Alabama, Mississippi, Louisiana, Arkansas, and Florida to all settlers regardless of race. Eighty acres were available for the head of each family. Within a year freedmen secured homesteads in Florida covering 160,960 acres of land. 'Forty acres and a mule' as a gift of the government had not been realized, but wherever possible the [Blacks] were acquiring land. . . ." p. 312.

6. Barksdale, p. 1. John Hope Franklin cited the fact of 350,000 acres of land owned by Blacks in Georgia by 1874, *From Slavery to Freedom* (New York: Vintage Books, 1947), p. 312.

7. Ruth Polk Patterson, p. 33.

8. Hortense Powdermaker, *After Freedom: A Cultural Study in the Deep South* (New York: Russell & Russell, 1939) pp. 75–94. See also James W. Garner, *Reconstruction in Mississippi*, pp. 261–63, and Buford Satcher, p. 17.

9. Powdermaker, pp. 57–58 & 99; Patterson, p. 33.

10. *Ibid.*, pp. 95–99.

11. *Ibid.*, pp. 99–104.

12. *Ibid.*, pp. 99–100.

13. See Powdermaker, pp. 102–107; Florence Mars, *Witness in Philadelphia*, pp. 153–54.

14. John Hope Franklin, *From Slavery to Freedom* (New York: Vintage Books, 1947) p. 26.

15. *Ibid.*

16. James Ngugi, *Weep Not Child* (New York: Collier Books, 1964), pp. 45–46; See also chapter 3, "African Religions," in Richard C. Bush, et al. *The Religious World: Communities of Faith* (New York: Macmillan Pub. Co., 1982), pp. 34–35.

17. Ngugi, p. 47.

18. Joseph Owens, *Dread: The Rastafarians of Jamaica* (Kingston: Sangster Books, 1976), pp. 219 & 220.

19. Melville J. Herskowits, *The Myth of the Negro Past* (Boston: Beacon Hill, 1941).

20. E. Franklin Frazier, *The Negro Church in America* (New York: Schocken Books, 1963).

21. Charles Joyner, *Down By the Riverside: A South Carolina Slave Community* (Ubana, Ill.: University of Illinois Press, 1984), p. xx.

22. Franklin, p. 40.

23. *Ibid.*

24. James W. Garner, *Reconstruction in Mississippi*, states that there was no uniform system of public education prior to the War but rather some private schools for Whites only. But, "with the occupation of the state by Federal armies, the work of teaching [Blacks] began." Agencies which established schools were the American Missionary Association, the Freedmen's Aid Society, and the Society of Friends. When the Freedmen's Bureau was established beginning in 1865 a more comprehensive and systematic plan of education for Blacks was begun. The schools were under military supervision, with Joseph Warren, Chaplain of a Black regiment serving as superintendent and the benevolent associations supplying books and, in many cases, clothing for the students. The teachers were supported by charity groups for the most part, namely, the Northwest Freedmen's Commission, the Friend's Society, the United Brethren, the American Baptist Home Missionary Society, the National Freedmen's Relief Association, the American Missionary Association, and the Reformed Presbyterian Board, pp. 354–55.

25. Fairley and Dawson reported the following information regarding the progress: The lofty, sturdy yellow pines of the Piney Woods area became popular and highly profitable during the 1870's "bringing boom times to Lauderdale county and its neighbors." "By 1883 trains were running from Meridian to Hattiesburg." "As

Meridian became a key point on the mail route from Cincinnati to New Orleans, boom times arrived that would not cease for decades to come." By 1886 news reports were comparing Meridian to Atlanta, the "greatest rail center in the south." "By 1907, forty passenger trains were passing through Meridian" daily. "Eventually, the long-leaf pines were tapped for all they were worth as nationwide demand for products grew and timbermen discovered there was nothing valueless about the towering trees," including a substance coming from them to make turpentine, main stem used as material for bridges, car-sills, lumber for export, sawdust for tar products, fuel, turpentine, etc. "Meridian became a lumber industry center" when the railroads provided access to the extensive pine region extending to the South and West of the city. The impact of the timber trade was said to be even greater in the outlying area. Lumber and cotton mills sprang up overnight along the rails, prompting development of churches and schools for the workers, pp. 78, 79, 80, 81, and 82.

26. Fairley and Dawson, pp. 81 and 88.

27. Franklin, p. 32.

28. This is highly reminiscent of the similar patriarchal role of Abraham in the Jewish religion, which, of course, was also a source of Graham's actions in establishing the family.

29. Theodore H. Gaster, ed., *The New Golden Bough* (New York: New American Library, 1959), pp. 89–90.

30. See Introduction.

31. The Churches pastored by Jack Graham were: Spring Hill Baptist Church, Zion Spring B. C., and Zion Hill B. C., all in Clarke County; Poplar Springs B. C. in Lauderdale County (in Savoy), First Baptist also in Clarke County in Enterprise, and another church at Hickory (Mittie, Interview, May 23, 1988, Meridian); also Lula Graham Brown's son Otis gave additional ones: Good Hope B. C. in Newton County, Bartholomew B. C. in Jasper County, New Prospect B. C. in Jasper County, and Mount Pleasant B. C. in Newton County, Interview, Savory, July 14, 1988.

32. The fact that when his first wife died after fifty-nine years of marriage to him, he sought a new wife within the kinship group (marrying his deceased wife's cousin's widow) indicates another link with African practices wherein a relative is expected to marry a woman widowed by a kin. (Compare also Boaz's marriage to Ruth, the widow of Naomi's son, Boaz being a kin of Naomi's husband (Ruth 2 & 4).)

33. Interview, Columbus, July 12, 1988.

34. Interview, Meridian, May 23, 1988.

35. "Hooping" is a dramatic display in which folk preachers would sing and grunt their sermons in rhythmic patterns after having given the bulk of the message.

36. Interview, May 23, 1988.

37. *Ibid.*

38. Interview, May 23, 1988, Meridian. Here is echoed the shamanic type of trait Jack Graham possessed for his family and community.

39. *Ibid.*

40. See Charles Joyner, *Down By the Riverside*, pp. 141–71; also Katherine L. Dvorak, "After Apocalypse, Moses" in John B. Boles, Ed., *Masters and Slaves in the House of the Lord: Race and Religion in the American South 1740–1870* (Lexington, KY: University Press of Kentucky, 1988), pp. 173–191; C. Eric Lincoln, *Race, Religion, and the Continuing American Dilemma* (Hill and Wang: New York, 1984), pp. 60–86; Albert Raboteau, *Slave Religion*; and Hortense Powdermaker, *After Freedom*, p. 232 and 246.

41. See Albert Raboteau, *Slave Religion*, and John B. Boles, Ed., *Masters and Slaves in the House of the Lord*.

42. Charles Joyner, p. 141.

43. Joyner, p. 141.

44. John S. Mbiti, *New Testament Eschatology in an African Background: A Study of the Encounter Between New Testament Theology and African Traditional Concepts* (New York: Oxford Universities Press, 1971), p. 6.

45. Clara, interview, Meridian, May 20, 1988.

46. This process also has some resemblances to the vision quest among some Native Americans, such as the Sioux and others. But the requirements are certainly different.

47. Certainly the evangelical tradition among Christians in America used the same basic requirements as described here, and Black people exposed to the revivals that spread across the South and the Nation as a whole adopted this basic pattern. But the most interesting theory is the ways in which they adapted and transformed this basic pattern into their African-oriented practices.

48. Interview, Meridian, May 20, 1988.

49. *Ibid.*

50. *Ibid.*

51. *Ibid.*

52. This practice seems to be a holdover from the initiation rites in Africa when the initiates were taken away from the village out into the bush for an extended period. Only in the African tribal situation they were taken in groups and subjected to a systematic process of trials and feats, etc. Individuals were not sent off to themselves in quest of something. However, as mentioned earlier, such was the case

in the vision quest among native Americans. For a description of the initiation rites among Africans, see John S. Mbiti, *New Testament Eschatology in an African Background*, pp. 7–8. The Native American vision quest was performed in ritualistic fashion under the guidance of a shaman. The youngster left the camp and spent time on a hilltop, exposed naked to the elements without food or water, praying and lamenting for a vision, a guardian angel as a life's companion, a messenger from the divine realm (See Kenneth Dollarhide, "Native American Religions" in Richard C. Bush et al. *The Religious World: Communities of Faith*, pp. 19–21.

53. Interview, May 20, 1988, Meridian.

54. Hortense Powdermaker in *After Freedom* has a chapter devoted to this process she observed closely and discussed with her informants in the Black community of Indianola, Mississippi, "Getting Religion," pp. 253–73. She describes the process and quotes the personal experiences in which there were reported seeing of visions, hearing of voices (also true of some of the converts under Jack Graham). Some spoke of sins falling off and their feeling light as a feather. Inner experience as well as external signs were needed by some. For example, one seeker asked the Lord to make a cloud pass over the sun and it was done (pp. 260–65).

55. Interview, Meridian, May 23, 1988.

56. *Ibid.*

57. Interview, Meridian, May 23, 1988.

58. This rapid call to preach after a conversion seemed to be typical among the people. Rev. Pack, in chapter three tells of the same type of calling.

59. Interview, Savoy, May 25, 1988. Otis's brother Charlie told of being baptized in a hollow. "It was way up there in the mountain. But I'll never forget, when I knowed anything I was standing up. I was down on my knees praying, and when I knowed anything I was standing up."

60. Interview, Clarksdale, May 20, 1988.

61. *Goober* is an African term for peanut, derived from the Kongo people, a Bantu tribe of North Angola and Southwest Zaire. In the Kongo language the term is spelled *Nguba*. The word is used chiefly in the South U.S.

62. See appendix for the complete letter.

63. John Hope Franklin, *From Slavery to Freedom*, p. 37.

64. *Ibid.*

65. See Chapter 3.

66. Interview, Meridian, May 23, 1988.

67. *Ibid.*

68. *Ibid.*

69. *Ibid.*

70. *Ibid.*

71. *Ibid.*

72. *Ibid.*

73. *Ibid.*

74. *Ibid.*

75. *Ibid.*

76. *Ibid.*

77. *Ibid.*

78. See John Hope Franklin, pp. 399, 434–35, 471–75.

79. Interview, May 25, 1988. He said her sister who was a year older than his mother was the last to get married. She married a preacher who grew up in one of Jack Graham's churches and was ordained to preach by him. His conclusion was that his grandfather tried to maintain control but he couldn't handle that situation with the girls all the time. "No, no, them gals jumped the fence and got out from under 'im."

80. One, Laura, died while they remained in Starkville. The rest are still living today in various parts of the country. Odena often spoke of this marriage as divinely ordained, "made in heaven," as contrasted with her first. She believed God had shown it to her. The other children are Sarah, Hattie, Effie, John, Albert, Alice, Elnora, Paul, Ira, James, Chinelo, and Palmer.

81. See Section One of this chapter.

82. I asked Odena's daughter Effie why her mother didn't return home to her father's estate. She replied: "I believe things would have been better for her if she had went back home. But I don't think she wanted to live down there in Meridian. One reason, this is just my idea, because she never have said why, but I just always thought that after her and my father didn't get along, she didn't wanna be down there. She just didn't wanna live down in that area." (Effie's father is named Allen Blakeley. He died in 1987 at the age of ninety-six.) Interview, Clarksdale, May 20, 1988.

83. Odena's mother had died in 1941, Jack Graham's first wife.

84. At that time Memphis did not have a law against having livestock in the city.

85. Interview, Clarksdale, May 20, 1988. She spoke of the fact that the last three were able to pursue their education to obtain college degrees and professional positions.

86. See Chapter One, section five.

87. Interview, Meridian, May 23, 1988.

88. Interview, Starkville, July 10, 1988.

89. Florence Mars, *Witness in Philadelphia*, p. 153.

90. *Ibid.*

91. *Ibid.*, pp. 153–54.

92. *Ibid.*, p. 154.

93. *Ibid.*, p. 155.

94. *Ibid.*, pp. 175–81.

95. See Ngugi, *Weep Not Child*, pp. 53–64; Mbiti, *New Testament Eschatology*, pp. 75–81; Azim Nanji, "African Religions," *The Religious World*, pp. 37–40.

96. See W. E. B. DuBois, *Black Reconstruction*, pp. 368–69, 434; Buford Satcher, *Blacks in Mississippi Politics 1865–1900*, p. 17.

97. See Genesis 12.

98. See Katharine L. Dvorak, "After Apocalypse, Moses" in John B. Boles, *Masters and Slaves in the House of the Lord*, pp. 173–191; Walter Brueggemann, *The Land*, p. 134.

99. Dvorak, p. 180.

100. For a similar interpretation among Africans in Africa see Mbiti, pp. 78–81.

Theologies and Preaching Styles of Black Ministers of the Meridian Area

The General Picture of Black Preaching and Theology: Images of the New Africa

The most pervasive area of life in which we find the establishment of the New Africa in America is the religious domain, the Black Church. The communal nature of it and the all-inclusive function of it, is a direct throw-back to African society. And the African American preacher is directly modeled on the African prototype of the priest, the shaman, medicine man, rainmaker, chief, combined with characteristics of the Euro-American ministry and features of Old Testament prophets. Many people acknowledge the transmission of African chieftaincy and priesthood traits to African American preachers. C. Eric Lincoln says, for example, that "By the end of the Civil War the role of the Black preacher included the offices of educator, liberator, political leader, and sometimes that of physician (or healer) as well as that of advocate and spiritual leader."[1] Lincoln acknowledges the Great Awakening as providing the first significant public exposure for Black preachers and the first opportunity for Whites and Blacks to learn from each other. "But," he says, "the Black preacher's style, his spirituals, and his long colorful narrative prayers had already been developed in the swamps and bayous of the Invisible Church."[2]

Felicia Kessel sees a direct connection between the African priest and the African American preacher. She says,

> The priests of African religion were considered sacred specialists with the office of priesthood often being hereditary. As those who are called to the ministry today by God, so, too, were priests called to service through spirit possession.
>
> During the early days of slavery, those who became leaders of the slaves were people who had close knowledge of African priesthood. There were also those who claimed to have special ability, not only to lead, but to have special contact with the divine and to be able to perform African religious ceremonies. Most of these leaders were children or relatives of the African priests. Like that of the African priests these leaders had unlimited power over their fellow slaves.[3]

Noting that there was no separation of church and state in African religion, she sees African heritage continuity in the African American ministers' "playing a holistically significant and crucial role in the political, economic, social and cultural development of the African-American community."[4]

Gerald L. Davis characterizes the African American preacher's style as unique, as derived from an "African ethos." He refutes those scholars who attribute the affective African American preaching style to the "slaves' mimicking of White Baptist and Calvinist itinerant preachers who moved from plantation to plantation during the years of slavery." He points to sources that strongly indicate that the African American sermon style, if not the theology, has "historic precedent in the affective religious and secular narrative systems of several West, Central, East, and southern African groups."[5]

Henry Mitchell asserts that the "basic culture/religion continuum from Africa was never broken," and he grounds his position in psychological understanding.

> Whether by means of a Jungian "collective unconscious" or the "primitive" transmission system known as "mother's milk," no folk culture, worldview, religion can be stamped out unless its bearers are massacred *in toto* or denied all forms of association, including the rearing of any of their children.[6]

He believes that "African religion is still alive and doing well in the Black Church and even the Black street culture of today."[7] Yet he does not claim that it exists in a pure form, unmixed. In fact, his position regarding Black preaching as well as Black religion, is that they are the product of the convergence of "two streams of culture, one West African and the other Euro-American."[8] In connection with this cultural blending, Charles Joyner makes the significant observation that "African American continuities with African religion are found not so much in static and archaic retentions, but in distinctive modes of expression that were the product of the slaves' creative response to a new environment in which they had to adapt to both Christianity and slavery."[9]

A number of scholars, including Joyner and Katherine Dvorak, also maintain that Black theology has rather unique African orientations. Cecil Cone is probably the most vocal proponent of this position. He proclaims that the slaves encountered not the God of White missionaries but rather the God of their lost African heritage. Their innate understanding of the divine was rooted in the African religions, according to Cone. As in Africa, African Americans, he says, see God as a part of all reality and all life as sacred. Life is not "chopped up into categories" as he sees in the "Greco-Roman and the Westernized" views, so that there is a dichotomy between the sacred and the secular. The religious view permeates the whole of life, rather.[10]

C. Eric Lincoln expresses firmly the distinctiveness of Black religion and says that it "begins by affirming both the righteousness of God and the relevance of Black people within the context of Divine righteousness." He refers to the "informal theology of itinerant preachers carrying on the traditions of the oral historians of the Old Country [Africa, the tradition of the griot]." Some of these, he says, were "illiterate and unschooled, but they had somewhere, somehow caught a vision of the majesty of a God in whose bosom the black man could rest with equanimity and assurance. That vision sustained the Black Church until it could, in effect, raise up its own theologians to make God and His black children more relevant to each other."[11] In these statements

Lincoln summarizes the transition that has taken place in Black preaching and theology over the past one hundred years or so, from the end of the Civil War to the present. And this period includes the time of Jack Graham and other ministers to be dealt with in this present chapter. We will take a look at the earlier and later ones, the informal and formal, the less educated and the educated in the Meridian area to get a picture of their preaching styles and theologies and how they have influenced Black life and life in general in the area.

The Jack Graham Legacy

In summary, some key elements of the theological perspectives of Black People of the Southeast Mississippi area are the following:

1. The interface between African religious and societal traits (embedded in the collective memory of the people and jogged into consciousness by the Judaic culture, religion and history explored in the Old Testament—for it was an archaic religion like African religions of the time) and the American religious experience.
2. A strong emphasis on family ties, land possession, moral development, and social improvement.
3. A strong emphasis on freedom and equality, liberation as seen in the Bible (the Exodus, the Shadrack, Meshack and Abednigo incident, the story of Daniel and the lion's den) and the bold assertion of rights and liberties, and a constant resiliency when thwarted by violent acts of opposition, an overall fearlessness.

Theologies and preaching styles of Black ministers of the areas helped extensively to set the tone and tenor of the peoples' religious, social, economic, and political lives. The preachers consulted and interviewed for this study range in status from that of the Reverend Elijah Jackson, Pastor of the prestigious New Hope Baptist Church and President of the Baptist Convention of East Mississippi[12] (representing some 200,000 members, residing mostly in the Meridian area) who is a native of Winston-Salem, North Carolina, educated at the Morehouse School of Religion of the Interdenominational Theological Center in

Atlanta, Georgia; to what one might call the circuit preachers who serve several small rural churches at the same time, in the traditions of the Reverends Jack Graham and Richard Pack, whose roots lie deep in the soil of the area.

The preaching and pastoring style of Jack Graham were intricately related to his great concerns for building a strong family and community that dwelt on land that belonged to them. He was a devoted spiritual preacher, steeped in the Baptist tradition. One of the most thoroughly used books in his library is the 1885 edition of Thomas Arthritage's book *A History of the Baptists* autographed by the author underneath a picture of him. One can see that the book was read over and over again. Jack Graham was a strict disciplinarian, requiring adherence to strict religious rules and practices on the part of his children and grandchildren, as well as the members of his church. There were the typical rules regarding the diligent seeking of salvation and the "signs" of one's having been redeemed, converted, etc. There were the "mourners bench" traditions where those "seeking" religion would sit during revivals, and whenever one would truly "get religion" and walk up and take the preacher's hand, the whole church would break out in praises, singing, and hallelujahs. Jack Graham could always tell whether the seeker truly had "gotten religion" or was faking it.[13] And the "two streams of culture," West African and Euro-American, described by Henry Mitchell (See above) are definitely present in both Graham's preaching and pastoring style.

As a preacher, Jack Graham was a powerful speaker in the folk tradition. He was a tall, dark, stately man, with a deeply serious and devout countenance. He was educated and used good language. And once he took his text and expounded upon it he would eventually become filled with spiritual animation and would use dramatic portrayal and retelling of the stories of the Bible with strong emotiveness and descriptive intonations that would re-enact and recreate the moods and meanings of the stories. His style was very much that which Davis refers to as the "performed African-American Sermon."[14]

The single most used book in his library, aside from the family Bible is the 1902 edition of *Bible Characters*, edited by Richard S. Rhodes (Chicago: Hodes & McClure Pub. Co.). Dog-eared with faded, yellowing pages, all coming loose from the hard cover, having been patched up with tapings and the like, this book contains some of the most descriptive, interesting, informative, and exciting retelling of stories of Bible characters by some of the world's most prominent, influential, and effective evangelist preachers and orators of the 19th century: Dwight L. Moody, T. DeWitt Talmage, Joseph Parker, Henry Ward Beecher, Thomas Guthrie, and Charles H. Spurgeon. Stories of Abraham, Barabbas, Gideon, Elijah, David, Deborah, Paul, Pontius Pilate, Zaccharius, Jesus, Moses, Job, Sarah, Hagar and Ishmael, John, Queen Esther, abound in these pages with wit and wisdom and enthusiasm and contemporary meaning and elaboration that are moving and enlightening. Pages are folded back and pencil markings appear here and there to indicate that Jack Graham must have used these stories extensively to enliven and embellish his own sermons.

One of the places in the book where the page remains folded back is where Dwight L. Moody is relating the story of Abraham in offering his son Isaac and commenting on it in contrast to Jesus on the cross.

> After they have sent up a petition to God, Abraham lays Isaac on the altar and kisses him for the last time. He lifts the knife to drive it into his son's heart, when all at once he hears a voice: 'Abraham! Abraham! Spare thine only son.'
>
> Ah! there was no voice heard on Calvary to save the Son of Man. God showed mercy on the son of Abraham. You fathers and mothers, just picture to yourselves how you would suffer if you had to sacrifice your only son. And think what it must have caused God to give up His only Son. We are told that Abraham was glad. This manifestation of Abraham's faith so pleased God that he showed him the grace of heaven and lifted the curtain of time to let him look down into the future to see the Son of God offered, bearing the sins of the world (p. 20).

This book also has numerous paintings depicting Biblical scenes by such artists as Gustave Dore (his "The Trial of Abraham" opposite page 24), Raphael, Bourgereau, and others, which make the Biblical incidents even more vivid.

Another place in the book where the pages remain folded back indicating frequent use is Moody's story of Arab, which includes the taking of the garden of Naboth. It begins (and it must have been preached to former slaves):

> There is a familiar saying: "Every man has his own price." Ahab had his, and he sold himself for a garden; Judas sold himself for thirty pieces of silver, and Esau for a mess of pottage. Ahab sold himself just to please a fallen woman. And so we might go on—citing men who have sold themselves. It is easy for us to condemn these men, but let us see if there are not men and women doing the same thing today. How many are selling themselves tonight for naught? It is easy to condemn Judas, Herod and Ahab, but in doing this do we not condemn ourselves?
>
> We thought that slavery was hard. We thought it hard that those poor Black people should be put upon the block, in the market, and sold to the highest bidder; but what do you think of those men who sell themselves today to evil? (p. 21)

He continues later in the story with increased drama and feeling:

> Well, when Ahab goes down to take possession of that vineyard there is a message that had come from the throne of Heaven. God has been watching him. He notices all of us, and there is not a hellish act that has been, or is going to be, committed but God knows about it. Elijah stood before Ahab as the latter went down to the garden, and Ahab got out of his chariot and met him. He knew that Elijah knew all, and he did not like to be reproved. Ill-gotten gains do not bring peace. If you get anything at the cost of the truth or honor, it will be peace lost for time, and perhaps for eternity. (p. 24).

The most turned back leaves in the book are the ones in the stories of Jesus, especially the ones by Thomas Guthrie, pp. 640-75; Charles H.

Spurgeon, pp. 746–824, where phrases are underlined and notations written in the margins; and Henry Ward Beecher, pp. 478–98. On page 479 of Beecher's account he represents Christ as (and many of these words are underscored by Jack Graham):

> Therefore, it is as *Teacher, Guide, Brother,* and *Savior—it is as Shepherd, Physician* and *Deliverer—*it is as *Mediator,* a *Forerunner* and *solicitor in court—*that Christ is familiarly represented. He is sometimes, also—though seldom as compared with other representations—represented as a *Judge* or *Vindicator.* The force of the representations of the Gospels, and of the laws which have sprung from the Gospels, is to present Christ as so seeking the highest ends of human life and so aiming at the noblest developments of character in men that every man who feels degraded, bound or overcome by evil shall also feel: "Here is my *Succor;* here is my *Remedy* for that which is wrong; here is my *Guide* toward that which is *right;* here is my *Help* in those great emergencies for which human strength is vain. Living or dying, we are the Lord's." This is the spirit that was meant to be inculcated (pp. 479–80).

The theological meaning instilled by Jack Graham's preaching and teaching and leadership training may be seen in the welcome address to the Union Meeting held at one of his churches, written and delivered by his son John Henry Graham, Jr., who was a Deacon in the church. The son preserved this speech between the pages of his own family Bible down through the years.

Welcome

Bro. President, Union and Friends.

I am indeed glad to meet you all once more in life. I am glad that the Good Lord has waken us from our deep slumber, and has enabled us to stand before you, to make you perfectly welcome to our church and its affairs.

You have left your several different homes, and did not know as to whether or not you was welcome.

So I am up here to let you know that the doors are open and we welcome you on the inside of our temple that you may come in and transact such business that God may smile upon you.

We welcome you because we feel that you are a progressive class of people striving for the lifting of falling humanity. We welcome you because we feel that it's our Christian duty to welcome our Shepherd among the flock that they may lead us in the footstep of our Lord and Savior Jesus Christ.

We welcome you to our several different homes to such which are prepared for you, for we look to you as a leader, a progressive class of people to lead the flock that they may follow and say something that will be meat to the soul. We take the physical body, lots of us if we can not get meat for it, our strength feel unworthy to the health. And if we cannot get meat to feed the soul to strengthen it, God cannot get any glory out of us, and therefore we are simply good for nothing to our soul. So we make you welcome to all the departments of this church so that you can feel yourselves among your best friends. And the word Welcome means consolation, joy, happiness. You know when you are made welcome to a place you can feel consolated, joyful, and happy.

For the Lord wants a band of faithful working soldiers. And you cannot do the work well unless you feel you are welcome.

So we truly make you welcome to the betterments of this church so that you can come in and do such work that God can get glory out of it and make us feel that we are on the right road.

Those words and expressions appear to have been written and given in the early years of the church in Clarke County, either the 20's or 30's when John Graham, Jr., was a young man in his father's church. And the "union" referred to was either the Baptist Training Union or some other type of inter-church organization.

Finally, as to Jack Graham's theological and social character, he was an astute and exact businessman. He handled the affairs of his estate carefully and sagaciously. When the Depression years came and so many families lost their lands and were forced to become sharecroppers, not so with Jack Graham. He maintained his wealth and position.[15] He left a precise and equitable will that divided up his real and tangible property between his second wife and nine children who remained living, which was made in 1954, about two years before his death.

On the local levels, ministers like Jack Graham and Richard Pack (below) represent the small town and rural counterpart to the movement leaders and political activists such as Martin Luther King, Jr., Jesse Jackson, Leon Sullivan, Andrew Young, Hosea Williams, Joseph Lowery, Fred Shuttlesworth, and many more described by Jerry Guess in his article, "Freedom's Warriors, The Fighting Black Clergy: An Historical Overview," [16] and those Felicia Kessel points to in "The Evolution of Black Ministry in America."[17] Such men as Graham and Pack were the foot soldiers who prepared the way, nurtured and nourished the people. They came closer to what Lincoln describes as the "peculiar genius" of the Black preachers deriving from the fact that they have never been far from the people. Having risen "from among them as someone they knew and trusted—someone God raised up in their midst," whose "credentials" were their "gifts," when they "made good as a preacher, the community shared in" the accomplishments. And the awards they received from that community, acknowledging their faithfulness, enabled the people to express vicariously the satisfaction they themselves felt with their own attainments. The preacher, he continues,

> was more than leader and pastor, he was the projection of the people themselves, coping with adversity, symbolizing their success, denouncing their oppressors in clever metaphor and scriptural selection, and moving them on toward that day of Jubilee which would be their liberation.[18]

Richard H. Pack: An African American Griot

Theologies and preaching styles of other ministers of the areas consist of (1) those in the style of Jack Graham, (2) some which inculcate facets of that style and variants of it, (3) as well as some new breeds of ministers who have received advanced degrees in college and seminary training. I want to focus on a few of these, one or two from each category. Two ministers I would like to contrast from categories one and three. Of the first category is the Reverend Richard H. Pack.

Initially, let me relate how I became interested in this man and the kind of background he possessed. In May of 1986 I attended the funeral of John Henry Graham, Jr., who was one hundred years old at his death. The funeral was held at New Prospect Baptist Church in Little Savoy, Mississippi, a few miles outside Meridian; and the burial was at the All Day Cemetery about 20 or 25 miles from Meridian in Clarke County, where most of his deceased relatives and many other friends of the community are buried. I was highly impressed by a number of things that captured my interest and enthusiasm and remained in my mind for months to come. First there was the enormous amount of respect and reverence for this man among the members of his church and the ministers and other people of the communities in and around Meridian. Second was the massive numbers of relatives; children, grandchildren, great-grandchildren, nieces and nephews, cousins. One remaining sister (Sarah Graham Gregory, ninety-eight years old) and a brother (Oscar Graham, eighty-four years old) and others who came from all across the state of Mississippi and the United States, from such places as Memphis, Tennessee; Chicago, Illinois; Detroit, Michigan; and from as far away as Portland, Oregon. And the mood among them was as though the "sun" had fallen from their sky or had shifted its position and all their hopes and dreams and sense of stability in orbit around it had been shaken or dislocated. It was as though they came to mark the passing of one of the last living witnesses to a tradition that had shaped and shielded them and their families and their history.

A third thing that impressed me was the incredible mixture, even blending, of extreme age and youth of all ages, of rural and urban character and personality, of Northerners and Southerners stemming from the same family roots, of simplicity and sophistication, and of "saints and sinners," so to speak, all with a similar aura of ritual solemnity, awe and reverence as the funeral and burial ceremonies proceeded. The mystery of the religious tone of that occasion was haunting. I sensed then that there was something in the background and setting of these people that was a root cause of this momentary harmonious blending.

Attending the funeral was one minister named Allen Blakely, who was ninety-three years old. One year later, I was back in Meridian attending his funeral (He was also buried at the All Day Cemetery). And the audience of mourners was almost as huge, and some of the same people, as well as a similar mixture were present. But what impressed me most this time was the sermon preached (the eulogy) by a man 83 years old, who looked to me at that time to be even older. When he rose and came to the pulpit lectern it occurred to me that we were going to hear not much of a sermon. He had neither Bible nor manuscript. This was the Rev. Richard H. Pack.

Being somewhat thoroughly familiar with the New Testament, its content, history, and composition, as well as other books or writings concerning the stories of Jesus and the persons and events of his time—writings that did not get into the New Testament canon but have been collected and published in a book titled, *The Lost Books of the Bible*, often referred to as the New Testament Apocrypha; I was stunned as this preacher commenced to deliver a completely engrossing, dignified, and enlightening, and invigorating sermon in the mixed style of a somewhat learned biblical exegesis and the intriguing and beguiling folk tradition of chanting, biblical story-telling, and dramatic re-enactment of biblical incidents. And most astonishing in his delivery was an incredible blending of incidents in the life of Jesus, from his birth to his death, resurrection, and parousia (second coming) drawn from all of the four canonical Gospels and from the New Testament Apocrypha without the slightest bit of offensiveness to the audience. There was also his own reaction or editorializing and theologizing to embellish the stories and make them suit his own and the people's social and religious context.

After this occasion it became my determination to return to this Southeast Mississippi area and investigate the religious roots of Black people there. I was convinced that there was something there worthy to be explored that I had encountered nowhere else, a uniqueness that stood out in spite of the common Black religious and social features that were also evident. And one of the main persons I intended to find and interview, among others, was this Rev. Richard H. Pack.

In this small town of about 48,000 people, Pack was not hard to locate. It was not easy, however, to get him to submit to an interview. After the initial resistance, though, he finally did. It was a little awkward getting him started talking. I had to entice him with true praise of his "beautiful, dynamic, well-put-together funeral sermon, reflecting a rich religious heritage, a great mind; a great preacher and religious leader blessed with talents and abilities and a long life (He was eighty-four years old)." With this introduction he got started, and when he did begin with slow, measured, deliberate tones, I realized that I was really in the presence of a neo-African griot (The griot is a person from the West African oral history and literature tradition, when there were no written languages or records, who, somewhat like the minstrel of the European Middle Ages (only he was a genuine historian), kept in his memory the history and literature—stories, poems, proverbs, etc.—of his ethnic group and recited it on special occasions.)[19]

In this manner Rev. Pack related the following facts about himself. He was converted at the age of seventeen years and called to preach on that day out in the woods near his home in Lauderdale, Mississippi. He was ordained and called to his first church a year later at age 18, and has been pastoring ever since. He could not remember how many churches he has pastored, but he only missed six months out of the pulpit in his sixty-six-year preaching and pastoring history. He served four churches in the city of Meridian: One for seven and a half years, one for nine, one for thirteen, and one for two years.

In his late thirties he pastored out of the state for five years in Decatur, Illinois. When he returned to Meridian, six churches in Macomb, Mississippi, were eager for his pastorage. He tried to pastor five for a while, alternating from one to the other on successive Sundays, but finally settled for four (five were too many).[20] One of those churches he served eighteen years, where the membership reached 1100. When his wife took ill, he resigned the church in Macomb and returned to Meridian, where she passed in the hospital in 1977.

Three months after her death he was called to what is locally referred to as an "All-Time" Church (meaning one that meets every Sunday), Elizabeth Baptist Church, in Lauderdale, Mississippi, his home church where he was born and reared, converted, baptized, and ordained. He has been there ever since. In addition he pastors a church in Alabama, Mt. Pleasant Baptist Church between Cuba and York, Alabama, where he's been for seven years. These two churches are the only ones he is pastoring now. He exclaimed, "And that's all I want. I done got up in age now. During my ministerial career, I done some tough preaching. I'd run some eight to ten revivals a year, each running ten nights in a row. I done stopped accepting so many revivals."

But at his age he still does revivals. He had just come out of one the first week of April (1988), running five nights, beginning Easter Sunday night. He is still in great demand either to pastor or run revivals in churches he has pastored in Meridian and elsewhere. (He ran revivals for Rev. Jack Graham before he passed in 1956). He mentioned he had accepted two more to do in the remainder of 1988.

I questioned Rev. Pack regarding his educational background. He related that he finished high school at the Meridian Baptist Seminary (then and for a long time the only place Blacks could get a high school education in the area). Afterward, he took "four years in theology there." He says he "never tells it" because he doesn't "like to boast like some ministers." There were eleven preachers in the class when they finished the four-years' training and were issued their diplomas. He said, "The other ten were grabbin their's," and when the Dean handed him his he said, "No Sir, I don't want it." The Dean said, "Well, Brother Pack, you were about the brightest student I had these four years. So, why you don't want it?"

He replied, "Well, Dr. Rivers, I been here at your feet for four years. I've never asked you a direct question, but I'm gonna ask you now." he said Dean Rivers called all the other ten ministers up to hear what Pack was going to ask. Pack resumed his question: "I say, I refuse that diploma, and I wanna ask *you*, 'would you hire me to build a house when you haven't seen one I built?'" The Dean answered, "No." Pack said he replied, "That's why I don't want that piece of paper. Gimme the job and let me do the job, and it will speak for itself. That paper won't accomplish nothing."

He said the Dean then said to the other preachers, "You know, Brother Pack got more sense than all of you put together."

Rev. Pack said these men have all died now. But they would "get up on Sunday and holler 'bout my diploma this and my diploma that." He added, "I don't care how large a congregation is or how small, if you go on and do the job, somebody will know you been at work somewhere. You don't have to get up and brag about what you know and where you've been."

I had expected him to tell me something about where he got the material he had preached about in that memorable funeral oration, and the stories he told about when Mary and Joseph were in Egypt, and the like. But since he didn't, I asked him the direct question. He pointed out that it came from *The Lost Books of the Bible*, which he had acquired apart from his seminary training and after he had left seminary. He said, "I didn't get *The Lost Books of the Bible* from the *Seminary*. I bought it extra." Laughingly, he said, "I don't know as they knew anything about *that*! But I was just fortunate to get hold of that book, *You* know it! I was buying books and ordering books, and I saw a paper once with *The Lost Books of the Bible* in it. So I ordered me one."

He said he "always wanted to get as much knowledge and learn as much" as he could. "I tell you what, I have where I was reared up there in the country, back pine. I'd throw a piece of pine on the fire, and I'd lay on my stomach before that fire all night long reading the Bible and different books. I'd have books scattered all around me. And many times, my mother'd say, 'Rick, get up from there and get in the bed.' Very seldom now, when I get ready to preach, I don't hardly open the Bible." It was evident that he had a powerful memory. He said preachers often sit around a church on a Friday night when he preaches, and they comment, "I ain't never *heard* a preacher preach like Pack before and never open a book!"

As I was sitting there talking with Rev. Pack and asking him about that memorable sermon and what he drew from *The Lost Books*, he started to get back into that sermon, and soon he was fully into it and re-preached it in almost the exact manner as he did at the funeral a year earlier. The following is that story exactly as he preached it to me in slow measured speech that afternoon (May 24th, 1988):

> That's why so many preachers get animated over that about when Joseph and Mary and Jesus was in Egypt, and old Herod, when he issued a decree, when the wise men came to see Jesus at his birth, and they went by Herod's and said "We've seen his star, and we wanna know where to find him," and Herod said, "When you go find him bring me word that I'll go worship him too." But Herod didn't wanna worship the Christ. He wanted to kill him. and the wise men when they saw Jesus they presented him gifts of various kind. Frankincense, Myrrh and gold and, ah, when those wise men, the Lord went to them in a dream and said, "Don't go back by Herod's. Depart to your own country another way." And when they didn't go back by there, then Herod issued a command and had all the boy children killed from 2-year old down in order that he might get a chance to kill Jesus, but Joseph and Mary were gone to Egypt. And the Lord directed Joseph and Mary to go to Egypt, and they were down there until the Christ child was around, well, 12 years old,[21] something like that, but anyhow, they stayed down there in Egypt and, ah, the Lord has Joseph to stay there until "I bring thee word Herod is dead."
>
> And during the time he was in Egypt, the Christ child Jesus was a little boy, a little lad, and one day he and some more boys were making some mud-birds. And an old man came along and told Joseph, "That boy of yours is down there making mud-birds on the Sabbath." Joseph went down to reprimand him. You know about it. And Jesus had 12 little mud-birds in a row. And when Joseph reprimanded him, he clapped his hands together and those mud-birds flew away. And you could hear the humming of the wings. And he said, "Good-bye, I'll see you again someday. Now, you're going to be my twelve disciple, 12 apostles." And he named those 12 birds

his 12 apostles.[22] Then when Herod died and he came out of Egypt, they heard about Herod was dead all right, but his son was serving in his stead, his son Archalaus, and they thought Archalaus had blood in his eyes against Jesus as his father did. And they turned and went down to Nazareth at Galilee. And when Jesus was 12 years old, Ah, the world was taxed, and they all had to go up to Jerusalem and register.[23] And when they went up there to register, Jesus, when they got ready to go back home they couldn't find Jesus. Joseph and Mary, they looked for 'im 'bout three days, and when they found 'im, he was in the Temple in the midst of what you call educated men. He was in the midst of 15 educated men.[24] And every question they would ask him, he would answer it just right off the top of his head. And an educator looked at him and said, "Boy, whose son are you?" and he said, "Well, I tell ya, my mother's name is Mary, but my Father, I'm as old as He is. I was there when He said, 'Let there be light.' I'm old as creation." They all were surprised at 'im, and when Mary and Joseph found him, he was talking with those educated men, and he said to them (Mary reprimanded him; they scolded him) and he said, "Well, it 'bout time I be about my Father's business." But he said, "I'm going back home with you." And when he went back home with them, he was there in Nazareth 18 years in seclusion. And when 18 years expired, he was 30 years old. And he got up one morning and put on his robe and his sandals, and he told Mary his mother, "Well, woman," he never did say mother, he called her woman, he said, "I've got to leave you now."[25] And he walked seventy-two furlongs, and some people call 'em miles, but it weren't seventy-two miles, seventy-two furlongs. It takes eight furlongs to make one mile. And ah, he walked nine miles, eight into seventy-two'll go nine times. He walked nine miles and came up on the east side of the Jordan,[26] where John, his first cousin was baptizing, and uh, when John was baptizing, and Jesus came walking up, he said, "Behold, the Lamb of God!" Everybody looked, and here come Jesus. And he told John, "Baptize me." And John said, "No, I'm not even worthy to unloose your shoes, let lone baptize you." He said, "Yes, John, but suffer it, it becomes us to fulfill all righteousness."

And that when he said for "us" to fulfill all righteousness, he meant his Father and the Holy Spirit. And John taken him and walked two hundred feet out into the rippling waters of the Jordan and they stopped out there where two streams of water crossed each other, and he baptized Jesus in the fork of those two streams.[27] And when he came straightway up, the Holy Spirit came and lighted on his brow, and God spoke in heaven and said, "This is my beloved Son, in whom I'm well pleased."

Then he was caught up by the Spirit and went out into the wilderness, and there he fasted 40 days and nights. And that's when Satan tried his uttermost to get him to bow to him. But first he tried 'im from three viewpoints, the Devil did, appetite, praise, and wealth. He was tempting Jesus. And the first thing he said, from appetite, "Now, you say you're the Son of God, and if you want me to recognize you as the Son of God, you turn this stone into bread." And Jesus said, "Man shall not live by bread alone."

And then he couldn't get 'im there, then he taken him on the pinnacle of the temple, and said, "You say, you're the Son of God, just jump off and God will let his angels take procedence of you, and they'll just ease you down lest you dash your foot against a stone."

And Jesus wouldn't do that. And then he showed 'im all the beauties of the world, silver and gold and everything.

He said, "If you just worship me, bow down, and everything you see, I'll give it to you." And the Devil didn't know that Jesus knew all about it before he was. And Jesus told 'im, then "Get behind me, you shall not tempt the Lord thy God, Him only shall thou serve."

Then when he left, he wrought many miracles. He healed the sick, and cleansed the leprosies, and even raised the dead. He raised Lazarus, who'd been dead 4 days. And ah, when his time came, gettin' close now, he said to a man one day. He said, "Go down there and you'll find a man, a pitcher of water, a man buying a pitcher of water. And you follow him to the guest chamber and make ready for the Passover." And he made ready for the Passover, that was the communion service, upstairs. And when he got there to the communion service he had his 12 apostles with him. And it was 13 at the table, the 12 apostles, and he made the 13.[28] And he said, "One of you all gonna deny me, and the other one gonna betray me." and they all said, "Lord, is it I?" and Judas Iscariot, he said, "Lord, who is going to betray you?" And he said, "The one I give this sop to is the one gonna betray me." And he gave it to Judas. And Judas said very slowly, "Lord... is...it...I?" And Jesus said, "Thou's said." And Judas, then, he sneaked away. He went out the side door of that upper room. Went down one of the filthiest streets it was. And he went and got him a garrison of men, that's between five and six hundred men to go to arrest Jesus.[29] The men didn't know 'im. And when the communion was over, Jesus left and went to the

Garden and left the others outside, taking three inside, Peter, James, and John, and said "Watch with me while I go yonder and pray."

And the book say, "And he went a little farther and fell on his face." And that "little farther" means, I don't care how you suffer or how I suffer, Jesus, when you tell him, "Lord, I'm burdened, I'm just downcast." Now Jesus says, "I know it," because he went further than you ever will go. He bore more pains and sorrow than you or I ever will bear. That's why it says he went a little farther.

And then when he came back, he found them asleep. He went the third time and found 'em asleep. And he said, "Wake up, now," say "Your heart is willing but your flesh is weak. Get up, my time is at hand. It's time to go." And when he walked out of the gate of the Garden of Gethsemane, there was Judas with his mob crowd. They didn't know Jesus. Judas knew 'im because he had been with 'im, and he'd told the men, "Now the one I kiss, that's Jesus." He walked up and kissed Jesus.

Then the mob crowd rushed in on 'im, and they fell like dead men. And Peter cut off the High Priest's servant's ear with his sword. Jesus reached down and got the ear and put it back just like it had never been severed. And he said, "Put up the sword, Peter. He that fight with the sword shall perish." And he told those men, he said, "Don't come to me with staves, rushing in on me like I'm a murderer of some kind." He said, "No man takes my life. I will lay down my life, and I'll take it up again."[30]

He said, "You can tie me, I'll go on with you."

They taken him before Pilate. That was on Thursday when they arrested 'im. They dealt with 'im all night Thursday night, and Friday morning, they put the cross on his shoulder, and he began to wag his way to Calvary with that cross. And the cross was heavy. And the sins of the world was on that cross. And, ah, I say sometimes when I'm preaching, "Jesus was lugging, and they were whipping and knocking 'im about, he was on his knees sometimes, waggin under that cross." I say sometime that I thank God that I'm a Black man, because a Black man helped Jesus carry the cross to Calvary. A Black man was standing there with a little boy by his side,[31] he was named Simeon of Cyrene, I think, and they made him, that "Nigger," they called 'im, get under that cross and help Jesus carry it to Calvary. And that was the first beginning of slavery. The white man made that "Nigger," as they called 'im, get under that cross. And when they nailed 'im to the cross, he was between two thieves. And those two thieves, when Mary was pregnant with Jesus, she left Nazareth and went to a little

old place called Anzane. That's where her cousin Elizabeth was. And
Elizabeth was Zachariah wife. And, ah, she was with child. And when Mary
was on her way there, she passed thru a robber's den. And all the robbers
was sleep but two. And one was named Damon, and the other was named
Titus.[32] And one of them said, "What a pretty, beautiful girl that is." And
he said, "Nobody ever passes through here but what we don't attack 'em."
The other one said, "Let her alone! I never seen a girl look that beautiful
before." That was Mary, and she was pregnant with Jesus. And he said to
'im "You let her alone, I'll give you my coat to let her pass on by." And
they let her pass on by. And them two thieves were the two crucified with
Jesus. And the one that spoke up for Mary the mother of Jesus to pass
through, he was on the right. And the other that wanted to do something
dirty to Mary was on the left. And the one on the left said to Christ, "You
call yourself the Son of God, Come down and save yourself and us." Jesus
didn't say a word. And the thief on the right hand said, he said, "We're the
ones deserve to die. Jesus haven't done any wrong." And he said to Jesus,
"Lord, when thou cometh into thy kingdom, remember me." And Jesus
stopped dying, and looked at 'im and said, "This day, thou shall be with me
in Paradise." And the *Lost Books of the Bible* say, when Jesus told 'im that,
he said, "But wait, before you get to Paradise, I'm gonna put a sign of the
cross on you. And when you get there, you tell 'em you come by way of the
cross." And that's why Dr. Watts wrote one day and said, "Must Jesus bear
the cross alone and all the world go free, no, there's a cross for everyone,
and there's a cross for me." We've got to bear our cross.

And Jesus, when he said the last words, "Father, why has thou
forsaken me?" He said, "Forgive them, for they don't know what they
doing." And the last word, he said, "It's finished!"[33]

When he reached spiritually and got man by his hand, reached in
heaven and got his Father God by his hand, and joined God's hand and
man's hand together. And he said, "I've finished my job now. Well done,
it's finished." Then he give up the ghost.

On the third day morning he got up out of the grave. He was around
here about twelve days, and one day he got an apostle and went to Mt.
Olive, the cloud swung down, and he stepped on the cloud. And they stood
there looking at 'im. And he said, "Just like you see me going on a cloud,
I'm coming back one day," and they stood there gazing. Said, "Why gaze
ye into the heavens? In like manner as you see me go, I'm coming again."
And when the last day come now, when the day of judgment, when God

raps his judgment gavel, and calls the world to order, Gabriel gonna sound his alarm, say "Time that has been won't be no more!" And Jesus is there now, sittin' down by his Father. He have on his robe. And his robe have "mercy" written all over it. And every way he turns, he's mercy, mercy, but when God declares, judgment, raps his judgment gavel and Gabriel blows his horn, he gonna pull off that robe, he gonna put on another robe. And that robe he put on then is going to have judgment and justice written on it all over it, every way he turns, gonna be judgment and justice. And no more have mercy now.[34] You got to go (he laughs), stand the trial in judgment. And sometimes I think now, I reads my paper and I see how people are going now, sometime I think that that time ain't long. But none of us know. And, listen, you remember Sodom and Gomorrah? When God burnt up Sodom and Gomorrah it wudn't but three people saved, Lot and his two daughters. His wife looked back and turnt into a pillow of salt. And when the flood was, it rained 40 days and 40 nights. And it wudn't but eight folks saved. And I think sometimes, when the master comes back now, I wonder, how many gonna be saved! But I know one thing, I'm gonna be one that'll be saved. Yes, I'm gonna be in that number when the Master says, "Well done, thou good and faithful servant." And since I been in the ministry, I've had my ups and downs. I've come up on the rough side of the mountain. I been out preaching, and I was away from home, had money in my pocket, couldn't get nothing to eat, three days and nights. And I been away, and I've heard people say, "Naw, you won't sleep in my bed." but the Lord, well, the man said that one night, I preached his funeral.

Pack stated that there were twelve children in his family, two girls and ten boys. They're all gone but him. As I questioned further back into his origins, social, religious, political, and the like, Rev. Pack stated that his mother and father were named Mary and Monroe Pack. His maternal grandparents were Smart Bell (grandfather, who was blind) and Ellen Bell. They were slaves. His paternal grandfather's name was Harry Bronson. The name "Pack" came from the overseer of the slaves, all of whom had to bear his name. By birth, he said, he was a Bronson. His father died at the early age of 47 years, but his mother lived to be nearly a hundred.

Asked about the religious background of his ancestors, he related what his mother had told him. She said, "Slaves, weren't allowed to go to no church, and when they prayed they had to put their heads in a washpot or something so their voices wouldn't be heard." She say, "They had a hard time trying to serve the Lord. But the Lord heard their prayer."

He continued, "They'd go to one another's houses, shut the doors and have their praying and singing. The Lord has been good to us, brought us a mighty long way!" He commented on how times have changed. Revivals don't have the "Mourner's Bench" anymore. He said, "Education has spoiled the preachers, too popular, got that high falutin' stuff and the folks don't know what they talking about."

Rev. Pack had a lot of interesting and revealing stories and information and personal experiences to relate about the social and political situations of his lifetime. He was pastoring in Philadelphia, Mississippi, at the time of the three Civil Rights workers' murders in 1964 (Andrew Goodman, James Chaney, and Michael Schmerner). He pastored two churches there, one six years and the other ten years. He left there and went North.

One experience he relates was during the time the "KuKlux " [Klan] were burning down so many of the Black churches in Mississippi and attacking people. He was a fearless preacher and often carried a pistol for protection. When he was living in Macomb, his wife had had surgery, and he had just gotten her out of the hospital and taken her home. He was conducting a revival. When he got ready to leave that evening, going to church, she stopped him and said, "Rev. Pack, you'd better put your gun in your car." He said, "Well, give me the 38, and you keep the 22." She gave him the gun and he went on and preached that night. It was quite a way from where he lived. When ready to return home he put on his top coat, got in the car and was headed home. He had a jug of water in the trunk in case the car ran hot. As he started out the sheriff's patrol started following him, and when he was nearly home, he pulled him over and said, "Get out of the car." "I did, and he searched me," he said.

Then he ordered him to open the trunk, but Pack replied, "You open it." "He did," Pack continued, "and the jug of water was in there, and he fell in there up to his stomach, thought it was whiskey, you know. I said, 'Help yourself.' He said, 'Aw, this water.' I said, 'Well, take a drink of it. I'm a preacher, I don't have whiskey.'"

As the gun was lying on the seat, the deputy saw it and said, "Well, you got a gun, so you gotta go to jail. Who are you anyway?" Pack replied, "I'm a minister." The deputy said, "Well, you gotta go to jail, with this gun in your car."

Pack answered, "Well, I just got my wife out the hospital, cost me $500 a day. And I wanna go by and see her and let her know where I am." The sheriff replied, "Naw, you can't go by there!"

Pack: "I say, 'what you say?' He said, 'You can't go by there!' I said 'You got a gun' (and the fella that was wid 'im had reached over and got mine.) I said 'Both of y'all got guns, and I ain't got nair'n.' I said, 'Either one of 'em won't shoot me.' I said, 'I'm goin' by my house and see 'bout my wife.' And they carried me on by there."

They then took him to jail, the Justice of the Peace charged him $119. He asked for his check book to write them a check. They replied, "Naw, you can't pay your own fine!" So, they locked him up, and he told the jailer to call his deacon and get him to come and get him out so he could go see about his wife. The deacons came (two of them) and paid his fine. They let him out and he asked for his belongings. The jailer gave him his car keys, wallet, pocket knife, but deliberately dropped his watch on the concrete floor, trying to break it. Pack was furious and went to grab the fellow and break his neck, he said. But the deacons held him back and pleaded, "Don't do it, Rev. Pack, don't do it." He said, "I'll kill 'em!" Then he said to the fellow, "If that watch ain't running when you hand it to me, I'm gonna kill you right here in your jail house!" The fellow picked up the watch, shaking all over, and said, "It's running, it's running!" Pack looked him in the eye and said, "You know one thing? I haven't done anything wrong. That gun was my protection, and I'm a minister." "If it weren't for my deacons standing here," he continued,

"You or I one would go to hell tonight!" The deacon said, "Come on, Rev. Pack." He got in his car and drove off and saw a woman walking down the road. It was his wife coming to see about him.

They went home. He got there and got his shotgun and other pistol and started out the door. His wife asked, "Where you goin'?" He said, "I'm going back down there and kill everything white!" She screamed, and he cooled down and laughed, and she knew he was all right. The next day the High Sheriff saw him and wanted to know the names of those deputies who had mistreated him, so he could "put them under the jail." But he couldn't remember their names. But the sheriff apologized and gave him a permit to carry a gun.

Another incident occurred when the Klan went to bomb his church one night. Some of the deacons got wind of the plot and hid inside the church. And when the men came with the gasoline cans full, the deacons popped out and exclaimed, "All right, what you want?" "Those guys took off running," Pack said.

The New Breed of African American Ministers

In contrast to Richard A. Pack is the new breed of ministers in category three above, who have received advanced degrees in college and seminary training. Contrary to what Pack says about education having "spoiled the preachers," I found the ones I consulted to be quite sincere religiously and socially. And they do not seem to have lost their spiritual depth, in my estimation. Rev. Alphonso D. Lewis, a minister in his thirties, is pastor of Mt. Olive Baptist Church in Meridian, a relatively large brick church situated in a middle income neighborhood. It is a beautiful church with all necessary space for worship, offices, classroom and facilities. The congregation is of good size and socially mixed with upper-, middle- and lower middle-classes. And the style of worship and programming reflects the interests and needs of such a mixture.

I visited the church on July 10, 1988, and recorded the service and interviewed Rev. and Mrs. Lewis in the Pastor's study. Neither is a native of Meridian but came from areas within a one hundred mile radius of the Meridian area. Lewis was born and raised in Jackson and his wife, in Hattiesburg. They met when both were in attendance in college in Hattiesburg. Rev. Lewis did quite a bit of traveling and service outside the state while in the Air Force, which he entered after high school graduation. During stays in New Hampshire and Tennessee, he attended consecutively the University of New Hampshire and the University of Tennessee. Upon his discharge he accepted the call to the ministry and enrolled at William Carey College and afterwards the University of Southern Mississippi, both in Hattiesburg. After graduation he did further study at the Baptist Seminary. He and his wife both are graduates of USM. They have been in Meridian five years. She is a teacher in the Head Start Center. Having pastored first in Prentice, Mississippi, he accepted the call to the pastorate of Mt. Olive in 1983.

Both the Lewises come from a very religious background. His father is also a minister; he pastored in Ann Arbor, Michigan. Out of a family of seven four are ministers—his youngest brother and two of his sisters. One of the sisters serves in Ann Arbor, the other in Hampton, Virginia, where her husband is an Air Force Chaplain. He has other relatives and in-laws in the ministry also. Mrs. Lewis's father and mother are very active in the church in Hattiesburg, the father serving as a deacon. And Mrs. Lewis's sister and her husband both serve in the ministry in Hattiesburg.

I found Rev. Lewis as a pastor to be spiritually strong and forceful as well as politically and socially active both in the local church organizations and the civic and political community. He is well-versed on the local government and political affairs of the area and participates actively in these. His concerns and activities reflect a good balance and integration of the religious and community affairs. In the church agencies he serves as Executive Secretary of the Foreign Mission Board of the East Mississippi Baptist Convention and is an active participant in the local Interdenominational Alliance, which cooperates with the NAACP and other groups in helping to shape the political life of the community. And he is an active member of the Chamber of Commerce. Yet, none of his community involvement seems to detract from his forcefulness as a spiritual leader and pastor.

On the Sunday I visited his church it was filled to capacity and a large inspirational choir was serving. In the rear balcony one of the men was video-taping the service, as was usually the case every Sunday, I was told. The choir processed on the song, "Let Us Walk With Jesus Each and Every Day." After the Doxology, Responsive Reading, the Opening Hymn was sung, "When We All Get to Heaven." One of the deacons then prayed a relatively short pastoral prayer, which the choir closed out with the chant "Hear Our Prayer, O Lord." Then followed a choir selection, "'Tis so Sweet to Trust in Jesus." Though the service was obviously more structured and stylized than in some churches with more laboring class members, there remained a sense of warmth and feeling and friendliness in the atmosphere.

As preparations were made for the Mission offering the pastor made appeals for one of the member's sister who was burned out. During the offering the Pastor read from the Beatitudes, "Blessed are the poor in spirit, etc." At the offering's end the choir led in the chant of the Lord's Prayer, beginning with, "Let the Words of My Mouth." There followed a pause in the sacredness of the service for the hearing of announcements.

In this period much was revealed about the character of the church, the ministry, and its programmatic make-up. The announcements concerned meetings, programs for that Sunday and during the week. From these it could be seen that the church interacted well with other churches in the community. One of the announcements, for instance, was an invitation from New Prospect Baptist Church to a fellowship program and king and queen contest. The announcer asked the visitors to stand and have words. Quite a number did so, most of whom were from out-of-state from such places as far away as Los Angeles, Chicago, and other places. They were attendants at the Figgers Family Reunion which was in process during that weekend. A number of hefty "amens" were heard among the people as the visitors identified themselves and gave expressions. The pastor welcomed all, including me, and encouraged the congregation to share freely with me as a researcher and investigator.

I found the pastor's words regarding the upcoming revival later in the month reflective of a sincere concern for the spiritual growth of the people, as well as the upbuilding of families in the church. He announced three pre-revival prayer meetings for the week prior to revival. One of these was to be a family revival prayer meeting. And they strongly urged every family of the church to be represented in that prayer service.

After the collection of tithes and pledges the choir sang two selections: "Be Very Sure Your Anchor Holds" and "Search Me, Lord." Then came the "Sermon Hymn" or hymn of preparation, "Close to Thee."

In his sermon, titled "God is Our Keeper," the Pastor used as text Psalm 121:1, "I will lift up my eyes to the hills, from whence comes my help." The sermon was exactly in the African American performed sermon style analyzed by Gerald L. Davis.[35] In a brief exegesis Rev. Lewis gave the historical and liturgical background of the Psalm, its original uses in ancient Jewish worship practices. In the modern Christian context he interpreted it in terms of looking to Jesus and not other persons or things for help or consolation. I observed in the development of the sermon a balance between what Davis referred to as the "weighted secular" factor and an "abstracted sacred" emphasis.[36] Thus, he began by pointing to Jesus as the only one who can provide that for which the heart hungers. Therefore, one cannot look to things of the world or technology for such satisfaction. He stressed the benefits of gaining strength for worship, and looking to Jesus for help in times of sickness and for overcoming the temptations of sin. The preacher then transferred the sermon emphasis to the more "concretized secular," in Davis's terminology. He asserted God's power to "keep us from the temptation to live a self-centered life." Specifically, he pointed to responsibilities as citizens. His words were: "We must live up to our responsibilities as citizens. We live *in* the world but are not *of* this world.

But while in the world, we have to meet our obligations as citizens, political and social."

The preaching style became more and more powerful and animated as Lewis progressed in his development, accompanied by much hand clapping and verbal responses of "Amen," "Yeah," and the like from the deacons and other members of the congregation. As the sermon stressed points of contact with their daily lives the congregation became more responsive. The preacher went on to emphasize Jesus' commitment to giving abundant life as stated in John 10:10. Accepting Christ, he said, is "being set free to do what God wants you to do." He said, "Christianity is not a prison house as so many present it. Once you're in Jesus your life becomes better; not that there will be no hardships, but you can bear them better, you have help." "God is our keeper. Let us look to God for hope."

In the final portion of the sermon the preacher began to "raise the spirit"[37] by various means, such as direct references to needs of life situations, personal testimony, and by singing the sermon, accompanied by responsive sounds from the congregation such as "yeah," "uh huh," "my, my," "well, well." Examples of some of his expressions are: "God has never broken a promise!" "We have assurance our sins have been forgiven." "If you don't feel your sins have been forgiven, you have the burden of unresolved guilt. Jesus took the guilt. He died for your sins." "Living in a world with dangers all around, you will find help." "Your needs can be met. Jesus can answer all our needs." As he began to sing the sermon, the expressions came somewhat like this:

> He will...take care, God has supernatural healing. He will...come to your rescue. E-v-e-r-y now and then...I call 'im without opening my mouth. He will..., yes He will, yes He will...answer *all* my needs! The psalmist told us where *his* help comes from. My help...come from the Lord. Every...now... and then, I'm *so* glad, I'm *glad*. I hear the Psalmist say, "Behold...He that keepest Israel *will* not *sleep* or *slumber*." He is...He is...He is...[The preacher would state a protective or helpful function or role of Jesus to him after each repeated "He is..." And with the following forceful repetitious

phrasing he brought the sermon to a dynamic close]: "*Try* 'im, *try* 'im, try 'im, He *will*, he will, I *know* He will. You may be *up*, *hold* God's hand! You may be *down*, *hold* God's hand. He's *all right*! He's *all right*! He's *all right*."

And the sermon came to a close with, "Look to the hills, from whence cometh your help!" A repetition in the imperative mood of the scriptural text given at the beginning.

In interview after the close of the worship service, Rev. Lewis gave interesting and revealing information regarding, among other things, the interrelatedness for of church life with all other facets of life in Meridian, and particularly regarding Mt. Olive Baptist Church's community involvement. One thing he noted was that most of the Black Baptist churches in the city originated from New Hope Baptist Church, the oldest in the city. And of course, New Hope came about as a result of former slaves, after emancipation, withdrawing from the White First Baptist Church. In his estimation the church life in Meridian is interrelated with just about all other events and processes in the city. He stated,

> Some of your most influential Blacks, practically all of them are active in the Church. And their active support and the way they were able to get into the positions they're in came from the support of the churches they are members of. In the political arena, and educationally too, most or our educators are active church participants. And their support comes from basically church members.[38]

He gave an example of one of his own members, who is an associate pastor of the church there and also serves as Deputy Superintendent of Schools for the city. Lewis pointed out that most of the Blacks that are contributing to the welfare of the community, educationally, politically, and socially, are active church members.

In reference to Mt. Olive, the pastor stated that it is one of the oldest churches in the city, having been founded in the early 1920's. The church, he said, was very active in the community. Even the two previous pastors were active in the community, such as in the Chamber of Commerce. And the church has always been supportive of the pastors and their community involvement. As stated earlier the congregation has a social class mixture of upper, middle, and lower. Among the professional members are an assistant principal, a number of teachers (one was just voted "Teacher of the Year."), and a medical doctor. But the pastor asserted that there is "a commonality among the members when they come to church. You don't see necessarily the differences; it's more of a unity when they're at the church." [39]

In answer to a question concerning ways in which the religious community has been unified in its efforts to deal with the societal problems, Rev. Lewis replied that there is one agency which serves as the voice and forum of the Black religious community—the Interdenominational Ministers' Alliance. He stated,

> Whenever they have candidates running for election it's usually decided in church meetings, with the mixture of various churches, who will be the best candidate for the position, Black or White. And it's usually the Ministers' Alliance that is consulted. An opinion from the Alliance represents all the ministers and all denominations here in the city. The Ministers usually get the input from their congregations.[40]

He also reported that issues of social, racial, economic, or of any nature are usually brought to the Alliance. And they discuss it and try to come up with a unified suggestion as to how to deal with it. And their positions are respected in the city. Numerous press conferences have been called by the Alliance, and the spokesperson would address the issues on behalf of the ministers and churches. Two specific involvements he mentioned are the NAACP, to which the churches render strong support both financially and programmatically; and the Love Kitchen, which is an interracial and interdenominational project or agency that feed the hungry, the homeless, the aged, or whatever. They have meals every day which are free and open to all. All the churches involved contribute funds and food for the agency.

Ministers in the Style of Jack Graham and Richard Pack—and Variants from It

Three ministers seem to fall into category two mentioned above—those who inculcate facets of Jack Graham and Richard Pack with various differences. Two of those are Rev. Otis Brown and Rev. Timothy Graham, both grandsons of Jack Graham. Brown pastors two rural churches, which he has served for many years. He is matter-of-fact, plain-spoken, and his preaching style is that of rural folk-preaching, with a number of the characteristics of Jack Graham and Richard Pack, such as story-telling, singing the sermon, and whooping. Timothy Graham pastors two churches, which he too has held for many years, one in the city of Meridian and the other in the rural area. He tends to blend the rural characteristics of honesty, sincerity, and unpretentiousness with the refinements of a more urban and educated ministry.[41]

Most outstanding in this second category is Dr. Marcellus C. Thompson, Pastor of New Olivet Baptist Church of Meridian. The theology and style of the pastor is reflected throughout the worship service. In fact, the pastor asserts himself very smoothly and naturally but forcefully in every facet of the worship. One sees that he is always completely in control of the worship situation no matter what group or individual is functioning any given moment. For instance, if the choir is singing a special selection, the pastor exercises influence by breaking into the singing at intervals to take over the lead, hum, groan or say "go ahead," "uh huh," "Sing, Child." If the deacons are taking up a collection the pastor exercises his influence by interrupting and injecting information and giving direction.

I visited the church on May 22, 1988, for the Sunday morning worship. It is not a large church but small, cozy, less elaborate than Mt. Olive. The pastor's style was very plain, matter-of-fact, unpretentious in language, unrefined in tone, although he is a man of excellent education. He created an atmosphere of simplicity, sincerity and warmth. He was the only pastor who invited me into the pulpit to share in the leadership of the worship. The choir processed on "Since I Laid My Burdens

Down." From this moment it was clear that this would be a less formal, less structured service. The congregation was more of the laboring class, a mixture of rural simplicity and urban character. One of the deacons led the consecration prayer at the altar, a longer and more fervent one than the one heard at Mt. Olive, more a pastoral prayer. "Yes," "Yes," "Yes, Lord" were frequently heard during the prayer, seeming to come from one female voice. The choir then proceeded to the choir stand on "We've Come This Far by Faith Leaning on the Lord." The morning hymn was "Alas, and Did My Savior Bleed," followed by the Responsive Reading from Jeremiah 31 on the "New Covenant." After the Mission Offering the choir selection was "Lord, Bless Me." The pastor responded all during the song with expressions such as "All Right!" "All Right!" "Lord, Yes!" in loud tones, lending affirmation to the choir and stimulating spirit in the congregation and choir. The singing was in high-spirited mood, forceful, a call and response type of situation, followed by many "Amens" and Hallelujahs at the close.

The announcements and welcome to visitors revealed much regarding the character and style of the church and pastor. The woman read invitations from various churches requesting fellowship services with them, invitations to the choir to come and serve in the Choir Day Program, and to come share in the pastor's thirty-eighth anniversary at Galilee Baptist Church, who was, by the way, Marcellus C. Thompson. This was the second church he served as pastor there in the city. Another announcement was an invitation from the Deacons' wives of the East Mississippi State Women's Auxiliary to participate in a Gospel Song Festival. The request was for participation and donations, a portion of which would be earmarked for the Meridian Baptist Seminary's Renewal Fund.[42] Finally, the New Olivet Men and Women's Day Program was announced for the following Sunday. The announcer gave warm welcome remarks to all visitors, whom she had asked to stand.

After the announcements came the Pastor's Remarks as listed on the program. From his lengthy, unhurried, relaxed style, one could sense that Dr. Thompson was a prominent citizen of the area, a well-respected, seasoned preacher. And his manner and demeanor were of the African chieftaincy type common among many African American preachers. He was paternal, patriarchal, supportive, mildly domineering, in complete control of his people, flock, tribe. He was the head, totally in charge. Everything would naturally go as he directed it. It appeared that few if any would dare cross him, but he did not appear mean-spirited, autocratic and completely dictatorial. The truth was that through long years of service he knew his flock and how best to steer them, and they apparently trusted him as their leader.[43] He seemed to be one who has always been gently persuasive.

The woman who accompanied me to the church was one of John Henry Graham, Sr.'s, daughters. She greatly revered Dr. Thompson, and so did all her family. This pastor had preached all the Graham funerals except Jack Graham's. And in his remarks the pastor made this plain, among other things involved in that relationship. He opened his remarks with expressions of welcome to all visitors and declared, "We're more than happy to have our friend in Christ, Dr. Mitchell, who is pastoring in Tampa, Florida." He then cut in to express gratitude for one of the members who was out of the hospital and back in church that morning. Loud applause and vigorous "Amens" came from the congregation.

As he proceeded in his remarks, the pastor hit upon a number of things which are quite revealing about himself, the people, and the community. I am therefore quoting the rest of his remarks in full. He continued,

> Anyway, we're happy to have Dr. Mitchell. She was invited here today. She's here visiting. Has gone on and studied in the ministry and has her doctorate degree from the book (the people responded with "Oh, wonderful," "uh huh"). I appreciated gettin' it from the book.[44] My baby last Saturday marched in Baton Rouge and got her Doctorate in Law degree. And I like it when it comes from the book. Honorary is all right, but as Rev. Harvey always used to say, "I want somethin' to show for it." When I learned she was in our city, I really asked them to come.[45] She didn't come up here on her own,[46] I asked her up here as pastor of this

church. You know, I have gone as far as New York City to conduct revivals for a lady. And that lady there is fortunately a Missionary Baptist. So then we don't worry about whether you be a holy roller or whether you be a whatever you are. If it's not in the heart, it's not there! So we're just happy to have her come and share with us today in these services. She said, "Well, I wanna record it." I said, "Well, do anything you wanna. If you wanna make pictures, you do that." You see, you have to be flexible. You got to be open-minded. You just can't stand out and say, "This is my thing!" This is "usses thing." I always say that. That's how I get through the world.[47] You know, a man said the other day, "Oh, they moved him from the Council on the Aging" [an agency to which the previous governor of the state appointed Dr. Thompson]. I said, "No, they didn't move me. I went in with Bill Allayne. When Bill Allayne went out, I went out. And I didn't ask Mabus [the present governor] to let me stay on 'cause I didn't want to." Four years of that voluntary stuff is enough. Pay enough money as it is. All that running up and down the road, you get tired of that. Let somebody else do it. But people don't know any better. They don't know, when that man's administration goes out, his men go out.

So we're happy to have her here and [our neighbor]. We know her. This is our florist. And I've known her from a girl up. In fact, all of the Grahams, all that set of folks are my folks. Yeah, I been in that family, I married some and buried all of 'em. Yeah, cause they're my friends. And so we will formally introduce her, a little later on. I believe I'll do it now. I believe I'll ask her [my companion] to stand. If there're some more of you out there, we're happy to have you too.

When I saw Bridge's little niece there this morning I thought about how her grandmother used to lead those beautiful girls around up here on the hill. When I saw two little children coming up there, my mind went right back to her. And she would bring those children to church. And they wouldn't move. They'd just sit there. And if one acted like she wanted to move, all she had to do was jes' look around. That was it! She had law and order. So, we jes' happy to have all of you here. This lady's husband is here, and may God bless you. And so at this time we want Mrs. [my companion] to stand. Okay, God Bless you. And she also teach in out city school. You our special guest, stand, [speaking to me], and if you wanna say a word you can. We're happy to have you.

The congregation gave general "amens," and the pastor, throughout my words. And when I finished he said, "All right, all right, let the church say amen. She's searching up the roots of the family. That Graham family goes way back there. Way back there. And she's searching them. And that's what we need to know about where we came from. A lot of you don't even know about the times we had Black postmen here. You had men in all fields of government, Black. We fooled around here during the days of carpetbagging and lost it, and we're losing now, fooling around with a few votes. God bless you. Now, can stand."

The pianist had begun to play softly, "Jesus, Keep Me Near the Cross," the Sermon Hymn or Hymn of Meditation. The pastor joined in in loud voice, "Near the cross," and at intervals hummed, and moaned at others; he began to lead the tune over the voices of the choir and people. The pastor added at the close of the hymn that the member who lost everything in the burning down of her house would be thought of in a sizable way at a later date. In preparing for his message, the pastor announced two verses as his text, one was Matthew 22:11 and the other, John 3:3. The Matthew text read thus: "When the king came to see the guests, he saw there a man which had not on a wedding garment." John 3:3 read: "And Jesus answered and said unto him, 'Verily, verily, I say, except a man be born again he cannot see the kingdom of God.'"

In a surprising way, Thompson took these passages, one from a synoptic Gospel and the other from the Fourth Gospel, each seemingly having no relation to the other, and combined them into a new and unique significance. He performed his own harmonizing of the two gospel traditions at this point. He gave the title of his sermon as "Dressing Up for the Wedding." And he related putting on the "wedding gown" to being born again, being cleansed and renewed on the inside. He spoke of David's saying in the fifty-first Psalm, "Wash me whiter than snow," and asserted, "Can't nobody do that but the Lord." "Renew a right spirit within me." On the application the preacher spoke of a lot of people in these times who "have their name on the church roll but their spirit is wrong." "Here is a man sitting around here," he said, "without a uniform on, my brother, how did you get in here?" He continued, "There are some people with their names on some church rolls and they haven't been born again, and so it says, 'how did you get in here?' In order to walk the King's highway you've got to have on God's walking shoes. The blood of Jesus must cleanse us from our sins. It's dressing up time! We don' know when the wedding gon' take place." These were the central points of the message. Nearing the close, in the climax, the preacher began to moan and sing the sermon and to use slight whooping, by way of "raising the spirit." The spirit reached a high pitch.

The Invitational Hymn was "Precious Lord, Take My Hand," and the pastor in high spirits began to take over the lead of the song, humming and moaning loud, intoning the lyrics above the choir and injecting words and expressions about the meaning of the song in his life. In personal testimony, he spoke of his daughter's marching in the graduation to get her Doctor of Laws; and said it took eight long years and a lot of money, but "God can provide all your needs! Ain't God all right? Oh, have you tried 'im? I tried 'im a long time ago! I *know* He's all right." He called the deacons forward for the offering, and the choir sang, appropriately, "Oh, it is Jesus in My Soul."

Before closing the service, Dr. Thompson made another reference to me and explained that he has a "lot of ladies preaching." He doesn't question them, he said, because he doesn't know what God told them to do. He has Rev. W. C. Clark's daughter. She's pastoring a United Methodist Church, he said. "And you leave that to God. That's just like trying to run another man's house. Leave it to Him. And whatever is right, it will be God. So, we're happy to have Dr. Mitchell."

He then asked me to give the Benediction.

African American Preaching and Ministry Near the Apex

Rev. Elijah Jackson, Pastor of the historic and prestigious New Hope Baptist Church,[48] and President of the East Mississippi Baptist Convention, represents and exhibits the rich characteristics of the African

American preaching style and tradition carried to or near the highest or deepest level of understanding, function, and expression. His training, style and demeanor place him among some of the finest African American pulpit orators nationwide, on the order of Dr. Gardner Taylor, Dr. Sandy Ray, Dr. Howard Thurman, Dr. Martin Luther King, Jr., and the like. In 1988 he had been appointed only recently to the presidency of the nearly 200,000 member organization of the East Mississippi Baptists, which was ninety-five years old at the time. Being its president made Rev. Jackson automatically a vice-president of the National Baptist Convention USA, Inc., led by Dr. T. J. Jemison. Jackson is a native of Winston Salem, North Carolina, having been trained in the ministry at Morehouse School of Religion of the Interdenominational Theological Center in Atlanta, Georgia.[49]

I visited New Hope on Sunday morning, May 22, 1988 and shared in the worship service. The sermon Rev. Jackson preached was of a different style from any of the others I heard during my investigation in the area. But it contained most of the same basic components as the others. The sermon was well adapted, however, to the make-up of his congregation, which accounts for the variations. Miss Faye Inge, member of the church and daughter of the previous pastor, Rev. Inge, spoke with pride about the church's history.

> It pulled out of First Baptist, the White church, where the ex-slaves resented the way they were treated, seated in the balcony, and formed their own church not far from the White church. It began as a brush arbor. When the first brick structure was built, the first Black school in the state of Mississippi started in the basement of this church.[50]

Inge was one of the first Blacks to integrate Meridian high schools in 1965. She cited a number of things about the church that helped to characterize it. So many of its members are business and professional people, as well as political figures. She pointed to the fact that a number of firsts among Blacks in the area are among the membership: the first Black to participate in the Junior Miss Pageant, the first Black state corrections officer, the first Black to serve on boards and commissions.[51] Of course the former resident of the NAACP, Mr. Darden, was also a member, among other dignitaries of the city.

Certainly, such a church with so many prominent citizens as members would of necessity be a class-conscious church, no matter how its members strive to overcome the tendency. Also, the worship services and styles of preaching would have to be geared to meeting the needs of people whose professions and roles make them public servants and business executives who have tight schedules to meet, as well as numerous problems facing them at home, on the job, and in the community. They are sought after as speakers and leaders in various organizations and establishments.

It is in light of this context that Rev. Jackson's sermon on May 22, 1988, must be understood. When I entered the church, the devotional, offerings, and preliminaries had already occurred and the choir was singing the Preparation Hymn, "This Little Light of Mine." The atmosphere seemed dignified, formalized. When the preacher began his sermon, which was also very formal in tone, deep, probing, there were no "amens," only silence, listening, because it was a thought-provoking message, but near the end the climax was very much like that of the traditional African American sermon, which inspired numerous "amens," "yeses," and "uh huhs" throughout the congregation.

The text of Jackson's sermon was Matthew 5:13[a], "Ye are the salt of the earth, but if the salt has lost its savor, with what shall it be salted?" The sermon topic was "Spiritual Calluses," seemingly unrelated to the text. And there was no direct exegesis of the scriptural passage, nor even any further mention of it. But as the preacher proceeded to develop the topic throughout, it was clear that one who was perceptive could easily make the connections between the text and the content of the message. In other words it was left to the imagination of the congregation to make the obvious connection. It was a challenging and dynamic sermon, much of which I want to quote here.

He began by stating and explaining the exemplum or the analogy which he was using. "Those of us who work with our hands, and understand from experience what calluses are, we've had all kinds of lotions to try to soften the calluses. You have to be doing something in order for calluses to develop. A callus is a thick, hard layer of skin which, through constant use, has become insensitive to feeling. You can rub a callus all you want, there's no feeling involved." The imagery was quite vivid, and the expressions on the faces I noticed showed understanding and approval, as well as expectation as to the next movement of the sermon. After mentioning the different types of calluses experienced by people of different occupations, the preacher shifted to the spiritual and mental realm.

> Those of us who deal with what you call intangibles, things of the mind and
> things of the spirit, should there be calluses? In the realm of education, for
> example, should there be mental calluses? Spiritual insensitivity? The more
> I look at this, and the more I think about it, those of us who handle things
> that are holy, are there calluses?

Persons who are familiar with the style of preaching of Howard Thurman, with its silences, long pauses, slow and emphatic movement, deep, serious tones, etc. could easily recognize his influence on Jackson's style, as one finds on so many other preachers coming out of the Morehouse School of Religion and the Interdenominational Theological Center in Atlanta, as well as many other places served and frequented by Thurman.[52]

Jackson proceeded further with a quotation from scripture: "The day when you hear my voice, harden not your heart, Jesus said." Then he explained "spiritual calluses."

> Hardness of the heart does not bring about spiritual calluses. Spiritual
> calluses are caused by sincere, dedicated individuals trying to be religious.
> Many times we mistake the forms of religion for the religious itself; we go
> through the motion of religion, but missing the meaning of religion. There

is absolutely no awareness of the values brought about as a result of religion.

The preacher all along was speaking in slow, measured tones, with intervals of silence, pauses, great stress on words. He then gave an example of those who had been coming to classes during the week where they had been studying the Church Covenant and heard him speak often of reading it without understanding the foundation and other facets of the meaning.

> To read it means nothing if you're not familiar with the foundation. How can we tell if the religion we are going through is suffering from spiritual calluses?

He asked frequent questions such as this and elaborated on the answer. He would also repeat statements slowly with emphasis. He answered the above question with the examples of "growing insensitive to God in our worship services as well as in our private lives is developing calluses. Also, growing insensitive to God." He then asserted,

> This doesn't happen overnight, constant use, not yesterday, but constant use [citing from his definition earlier of physical calluses]. Now, test yourself this morning, see if you have spiritual calluses. Are you at this very moment as conscious of God's presence as you are of your own? We are creatures of habit. We can repeat from memory the Lord's Prayer, and sing a hymn without even being aware of the singing of the words or of anything we've said. We are creatures of habit. We can go through these things without being aware of what we're doing.
>
> We become so wrapped up in what we do in worship services that we forget to be sensitive to what God might be trying to say, trying to do for us. We're wrapped up in the service itself so that God is not able to get through. Many are insensitive to the word of God, the thing we are to live by.
>
> We get the idea that the Bible is not a book for us to live by but for the ignorant, those who don't know any better, the Bible is for them and

not for us. We are insensitive to the word of God in our own individual
lives.

He went on to mention "Our insensitiveness to people, to their
sufferings, sins, needs, their humanity." Also, "those who practice
religion on the one hand and on the other they treat people like they're
dirt under their feet." There are people, he said,

> who practice religion and don't care what they say to anybody. Those who
> will talk to you like you're a dog right here in God's house, and will leave
> and go outside and laugh about it, insensitive. People just don't care, in the
> church practicing religion. There is no such thing as respect, only a sharp,
> unbridled tongue in the house of the Lord. Insensitive to the feelings of
> others.
>
> Spiritual calluses! But you know, I've learned over the years that such
> people are basically cowards, who will insult you here in the house of the
> Lord. You don't catch them doing that out there in the streets because out
> there they know what will happen to them.
>
> Those who profess to love God without concern for their sisters or
> brothers are merely rationalizing a high level of self-love. It has nothing at
> all to do with the love of God. Jesus was sensitive and concerned for the
> feelings and conditions of others [He gave examples]. We too ought to be
> sensitive and concerned with others and their needs.

He went on to carry this need for sensitivity over into opportunities
for service, stressing those who are going through the motion of carrying
on a church program, doing just enough to get by; failing to see the
opportunity to do something for God and for the church. He declared,

> When we're blessed with success in the church or in personal life, we
> ought to become more sensitive to the blessing of God in our lives. The
> biggest hindrance in our lives is we become satisfied with doing nothing,
> nothing for God, nothing for the kingdom of God, nothing for the church,
> just satisfied!

Many times we become one of yesterdays and used-to-bes, the doers
of yesterday. "To serve this *present* age, my calling to fulfill." We have to
find our place in the church and the world here and now!

Up to this point the sermon has been a diagnosis, one might say of
the spiritual problems or ills that appear to be besetting people. And one
might say with Gerald Davis, the preacher here is "intimately attuned to
the daily secular needs of his congregation and to the social and political
environment in which their lives are acted out."[53] Jackson is not
preaching a general sermon, although people in general can get much
from it, but he is speaking directly to the problems and ills of his
particular congregation. No doubt, the kinds of very active, busy lives
that most of them lead as professional and business people render them
more susceptible to the "spiritual calluses" or insensitivity of which the
pastor spoke. Although the message was designed to speak to people on
any social level in the congregation, most of the examples given were
reflective of people whose daily lives can easily drift away from the
spiritual into completely secular matters and involvements, and whose
church attendance becomes ceremonious. Certainly this can happen to
anyone on any social level, but Jackson spoke with the assurance of
having encountered the maladies of which he spoke right there among
his flock, and he was challenging them.

The preacher moved on from this point to press for solutions or
cures of the problems. He declared,

There are no quick ways to cure our insensitivities. but there are common
sense ways we can begin to work on our calluses. It took work for 'em to
come into existence, and there's no quick way to get rid of them. There are
some common sense ways.

He mentioned a number of ways such as 1) considering, after realizing
the calluses, how best to treat other people. He said, "All of us from top
to bottom, everybody wants to be treated right." 2) A good dose of
honesty, he gave as a second thing. "Everybody ought to be honest with

him/herself. You know if you have spiritual calluses hanging around."
3) Another he mentioned was a "good dose of heart-searching." "We
have to learn how to be bigger than the next *fella.* You have to be bigger
than folks who mistreat you." 4) His final suggestion was "to open our
hearts to God, ask Him to come in and be with you, help you out, raise
you higher than you are."

From this point the preacher moved to climax his message. And he
pointed directly to Jesus and the power that is available. Becoming
animated and high-spirited, he aroused the heretofore silent
congregation to eager responsiveness as we heard general "amens,"
"yeses," and "uh huhs" throughout the pews. The pastor intoned such
words as "There's power in the blood this morning, there's forgiveness
power, all you have to do is accept it." The music began to play the
song, "There's power in the blood." And the preacher continued
"There's power if you want it this morning. All you have to do is reach
out, as sinful as you are, God will accept you." The choir and
congregation picked up the lyrics of the song as the preacher issued the
invitation to Christian Discipleship.

The Benediction was followed by the four-fold Amen.

One basic difference noticeable in the New Hope service that was
not present in either of the other services attended was the brevity of the
worship period. Everything in the program had moved along as
scheduled. There had been no belabored occurrence such as in the case
of New Olivet, where Dr. Thompson's "Pastoral Words" took as much
time as the sermon, and there was no expressed discontent among the
people. They did not seem fidgety during his long talk nor in a hurry to
leave the church after service was over. But the service at New Hope
began at 11:00 a.m. and was out before 12:30 p.m. This was what the
congregation expected and they would have accepted no less for they
were people who had many other obligations during the week, as well as
on Sunday afternoons. Their counterpart in churches of more laboring
class status would have criticized their hurriedness style of the "Spirit,"
but their service was suitable to their lifestyle. They were public servants

as well as servants of God, and the two go together in their minds, which is the way it usually is in Black life (no dichotomy between the sacred and the secular), and they had myriads of duties and obligations to meet besides spending extended periods in Sunday morning worship. Perhaps there is a need to accept a variety of Black worship, as well as Black religion as asserted by Hans A. Baer.[54]

On the Recent Development of Female Ministerial Presence and Functions in the Area

Although they have been around a long time,[55] not much has been written about the African American woman preacher when the Black preaching tradition has been discussed. Reflecting on Charles V. Hamilton's book, *The Black Preacher in America* (1972), which she says was the first full length work ever published on the Black preacher, Leontine T. C. Kelly, a bishop in the United Methodist Church, says, "This provocative study is authentic in its presentation and its conceptual exclusivity—the traditional Black preacher is male."[56] She read the book while in seminary and realized that though Black women ministers did exist in some denominations and women hold positions of authority in apostolic circles, such a definitive study as late as 1972 saw no need to include them in a look at Black Ministry.[57] The situation remains much the same today. Whatever writing about Black women in the ministry, with few exceptions, is done by African American women themselves.[58]

Whereas women in the mainline African American church tradition have previously had to confine their ministry to musical, missionary, religious educational, and evangelistic services, a revolutionary event has taken place in recent years in the situation. Black women are answering the call to the preaching and pastoring ministries in greater and greater numbers. The seminaries are filled with women seeking degrees in ministry. And mainline Protestant denominations are gradually becoming accustomed to women pastors of major churches. Of the twenty-nine women preachers included in Ella Pearson Mitchell's two volumes of sermons by Black women,[59] a number of them are pastors of major churches, mainly in the Baptist and Methodist traditions.

Although I did not do extensive research on the theologies and preaching styles of women in the Meridian area, I did encounter in my general investigation some interesting and revealing situations regarding the Black women preachers. I learned, for instance, that one woman was pastoring on A.M.E. Zion Church within Meridian. And Dr. M. C. Thompson mentioned the fact that he had a number of women preachers, one who was pastoring a United Methodist Church.[60] Rev. and Mrs. Alphonso Lewis spoke of the women ministers in their families. Two of Rev. Lewis's sisters are in the ministry, one in Ann Arbor, Michigan, and the other in Hampton, Virginia. Mrs. Lewis's sister and the sister's husband are in the ministry and are still in Hattiesburg, Mississippi. It was apparent that even though women are a small presence in ministerial roles in the Meridian area they are not numerous enough to make their presence felt in any influential way. People appear to be getting adjusted to women in the pulpit, yet out of the several Baptist churches I visited during my investigation, only one of the pastors invited me as a minister to serve in the pulpit. No one mentioned a woman's serving as pastor of any Baptist church in Meridian. Yet, there are some women in Southern cities further North, such as in Atlanta and Richmond, Virginia, who are pastoring Baptist churches. But most Black women pastors are in the North, such as New York City, New Jersey, or out West in places such as Los Angeles nd San Francisco.[61]

One of the great-granddaughters of Jack Graham, Maxine Hall, described the problems she faces in attempting to exercise her calling to the ministry in the Baptist tradition. In 1986 at her great-Uncle's funeral, John Henry Graham, Sr., she expressed her hesitations and fears. But she was encouraged by a second cousin, a granddaughter of Jack Graham, Chinelo Gordon, who was a pastor of an A.M.E. Zion Church in another Southern state. Hearing this woman bring words of greeting at the funeral, Hall said God spoke to her through the woman's words. She said,

I had struggled with that, and I said, now, you know how Satan whips us
outta ignorance, and I told my mother, I said, "Mama, now, why didn't you
tell me there was a lady in our family that was a minister?" She said, "I
forgot about it." I said, "Well, you know, I wasn't gonna go to that funeral.
And something said, 'Go on, go!'" And I came back and I said to Mama,
"You know, I went," I said, "Because it was something that I needed to
know! Yeah," I said, "I had a second cousin there, was struttin' in the
ministry." I said, "I knew that just give me a boost!"[62]

Hall's experience is exemplary of the difficulties faced by many
women trying to accept and exercise their ministerial calling in the
Baptist tradition of the area. As she expressed it, there is just no support
group for what they feel compelled to do. She had consulted one of her
male cousins in the ministry who came through on an evangelistic
mission, Chinelo's brother, in fact. He was no help at all. Asked how the
Baptist church of which she was a member had taken to her ministry, she
replied:

Oh, my pastor *did not* at first. But he knew that's what I was doing all the
time. Every time I would get up I would preach, preach up a storm! And
when I went to him and told him, he said, "I, I, I knew, but I know it's
something God wants you to do, but God hasn't told me yet." I said, "But
you got it all messed up. He called *me*, He told *me*!" I told him, "You
know what? God ain't told me He called you either, but you did!" I said,
"Just like I believed you, you got to accept what I say!"[63]

Apparently, her pastor was greatly threatened. But she set him at ease
with her candid forthright manner.

I told him, I said, "God didn't ask me to go sit up in your pulpit, but this
is something God has told me to do, and you're an authority over me and
I got to tell you. Now, it's up to you whatever, but God is dealing with it."
I said, "I just *got* to do this." And you, know, God's just making a way! God
is opening up his heart. Some Tuesday nights when I get up, he say, "Teach
Bible study." I break right out and preach![64]

Hall said she had not brought her official message yet, so far as the people were concerned, and she did not even speak of being ordained, simply of being used by God.

> But the Sunday night of my calling, I was on program out there for some words of inspiration. I brought the word *then*, just tried to clean up! I went from Isaiah 35:8. You know that scripture 'bout a "highway will be there...," I preached that sermon![65]

She began to give expressions from one message she had given regarding the eye as the lamp of the body. What she said surely revealed essential features of her belief.

> I said, "The eye is the lamp of the body. If that eye sees gardens, then that garden's in the body. If that eye sees the light, that's light that's in the body. And Jesus is the light. So if you see things of the Spirit, then Jesus is in the body. And he controls that body. It's no longer you that lives, its Jesus that lives in you. Then, if it sees sin. Satan dwells in that body. He controls it, and we commit sin. We have a sinful nature. So it depends on what the eye sees that determines the actions of the flesh."[66]

Hall came from a ministering family. Her father, James Moore, was a minister. She talked of how her calling came to her. All her life God had been dealing with her, she said. When she was first converted she was a youth. She backslid later and then returned to the church. While in a state of backsliding, she said she was always in turmoil, at no peace.

> I would be sittin' up in cafes and places, trying to party, and something would be saying, "Get outta here, you ain' enjoying yourself. Get...just a rage, you know!"[67]

She said that after she returned to the faith she started seeking God.

> I said, "God, you know, I remember when I was thirteen years old, I was sittin' right out there in the church I'm a member of now. And I watched

this preacher's wife, and she was such an inspiration to me. And she would just be right with her husband, mourning and praying for 'im as he was preachin.' Oh God," I said, "that's what I wanna be when I get grown. I just wanna be like that. And I want me a preacher for a husband."[68]

She went on to describe how God started dealing with her.

I didn't know what it was. I used to wake up at night just preachin' *down*, just preachin.' And I can tell, I can almost remember every sermon that I was preaching, the scripture and all. And I'd say "What am I doin' preachin'?" And it would be just crowds of people there. I'd say, "Why am I doin' this?" I never would tell nobody. But I'd like to be by myself, you know. Cause I know I would be actin' strange.[69]

Later, she said she started seeking God for a husband. Her first marriage had ended in divorce because their lives were not compatible religiously. And one Sunday God showed her her husband. It was an A.M.E. preacher by the name of Hall, who came to their church one Sunday. He was pastoring an A.M.E. Church in town. And as she was sitting in church that day, she heard a voice say, "That's your husband." She got very nervous, broke out in a cold sweat. She got up, went out into the foyer and got some water. She was really troubled, but as it turned out, she did marry this man eventually.

However, her husband got into trouble with the law because of something his nephew got involved in while living with them. He was sent to the state penitentiary at Parchman. And it is there that she sees that God is dealing with her husband.

But let me *tell* you now, the blessing is in it. After he went down there, God restored 'im, dealing with the Holy Ghost. And let me tell you, he's working under a government program in Parchman, preachin' the word, teachin' a class every Tuesday and Thursday night in the free world. That's what he's doin', God's plan and purpose was to allow this to come upon him where he could get 'im to himself like He did John when He put 'im on the Island of Patmos, and deal with 'im and make 'im and mold 'im.[70]

Hall said she was undergoing all these trials regarding her husband's troubles, and God came to her with that scripture about the potter molding a bowl of clay and had to destroy it and make it over again. "That's what God did for 'im." She said it's beautiful how God has made the two of them one in the ministry.

> Let me tell you, you know, God'll give him something to tell me to do, and he'll call me on the phone and say, "Honey, God told me to tell you to go do this." And honey, the blessing will be right there for somebody. I was out at the hospital when my brother died 'bout a couple of weeks ago. And my husband had called me on a Tuesday and told me, "Honey, when you go see your brother, you walk up and down the hospital corridor. There's somebody out there that God wants you to pray for. And He's gon' show you who they are."[71]

As she did this she encountered a woman in great pain, for whom she prayed, and the woman was healed. There was great rejoicing over this healing. Hall has discovered that her ministry is one involving a number of spiritual gifts such as healing, discerning, knowledge, etc. This was very similar to her father's ministry, which largely involved healing and discerning. She has an interesting story to tell about her father's discovery that she was going to be a preacher. He is no longer living, but he told her husband before they were married as he would visit the house,

> He said, "You know, Reverend, all my life I been sayin' that God didn't call a woman to preach, but guess what? God done showed me, He gon' call my own daughter. She gon' preach the word." He said, he was telling him, "If you don't wanna be married to a woman that's gonna preach, you better back off!" And he told 'im, "I got something else to tell you, God showed me that you and Maxine gonna be husband and wife."[72]

She and the friend laughed about it, but all the father's predictions came to pass.

Endnotes

1. C. Eric Lincoln, ed. *The Black Experience in Religion* (Garden City, N.Y.: Anchor Books, 1974), p. 66.

2. *Ibid.*

3. Felicia Kessel, "The Evolution of the black Ministry in America," *Crisis Magazine* (June/July 1990 vol. 98, no. 6), p. 56. See also David T. Adamo, *Black American Heritage* (1985) for a description of the extensive role of the priest in African society.

4. *Ibid.*; See also Charles Joyner, *Down by the Riverside*, pp. 141–44; Gerald L. Davis, *I Got the Word in Me and I Can Sing It, You Know: A Study of the Performed African-American Sermon* (Phila.: University of Pennsylvania Press, 1985), pp. 9–10.

5. Gerald Davis, p. 10.

6. Henry Mitchell, "Two Streams of Tradition," in C. Eric Lincoln, Ed. *The Black Experience in Religion* (Garden City, N.Y.: Anchor Books, 1974), p. 70.

7. *Ibid.*

8. *Ibid.*, pp. 70–75. See also Joyner, p. 142.

9. Joyner, p. 143.

10. Cecil W. Cone, *The Identity Crisis in Black Theology* (Nashville: A.M.E.C., 1975), pp. 26–39; Also quoted in Dwight N. Hopkins, *Black Theology USA and South Africa* (Maryknoll, N.Y.: Orbis Books, 1989), pp. 78–80. See also Joyner, pp. 142–43, 159–62; Dvorak, pp. 175–76; and Albert Raboteau, *Slave Religion*, pp. 57–60 & 65.

11. Lincoln, p. 68.

12. The Baptist Convention of East Mississippi was in its 95th year in 1988, and it operates the historic Meridian Baptist Seminary, now an extension of Natchez College, but for years provided the only place where Black people could get a high school education in the area.

13. See chapter two for a fuller discussion and exemplification of the conversion process and practices in Jack Graham's churches. Charles Joyner relates the process to practices in African religion in discussing spirit possession among the slaves of All Saints Parish in South Carolina.

> The necessity of experiencing spirit possession for conversion marked the continuation in Afro-Christianity of one of the most persistent features of African religion (especially pronounced among the Bantu, the Yoruba, and the Fante-Ashanti) in the New World. Conversion was characterized by a spiritual journey, or retreat, called "seeking." The seeker's prolonged

praying and meditating during this period induced an ecstatic trance without which conversion was not considered authentic (Joyner, p. 162).

14. Gerald L. Davis, *I Got the Word in Me*, pp. 10-13, 49-64, and 65-70. According to this noted folklorist the African-American performed sermon is unique and has a definite formulaic structure consisting of four or more narrative units (pp.65 ff.) and performed in a rich and complex environment, involving numerous visual elements and considerable interaction between a preacher and the congregation (p. 11). Also, of utmost importance is a "weighted secular factor" along with the "generalized sacred elements of a sermon formulaic unit" (pp. 61-64).

15. See chapter two.

16. Included in *Crisis Magazine* (June/July 1990, vol. 98, no. 6), pp. 13-14.

17. *Ibid.*, pp. 52-58.

18. Lincoln, p. 67.

19. See chapter two for further explanation and a view of the lay counterpart to the ministerial griot.

20. Hortense Powdermaker summarizes the typical process of the multiple pastorage. In the community of Indianola, Mississippi, in which she did her study, she says: "Only one congregation, the Methodist-Episcopal, meets every week. The others have their pastoral Sundays, either the first and third or the second and fourth Sunday of the month. The preacher has several congregations and visits them on alternate weeks. Sunday school classes for children and adults meet every week, although the largest attendance is on the pastoral Sundays. On these days services are held twice, in the morning and in the evening. Baptism and revivals come once a year, during the summer," p. 233.

21. Pack does a lot of what is called "redacting" in Biblical scholarship. He adds his own facts and details to the stories to make them more relevant and understandable to the audience. Notice here his insertion of the age of Jesus at the time, which was not given in the source used.

22. Notice the considerable liberty taken here with the facts of the story. In the first place the material here about Jesus' life in Egypt is not from the accepted New Testament canon but rather from the New Testament apocrypha known as *The Lost Books of the Bible*. And in the story of the sparrows there is no mention of the boy's parents being told about the incident, nor of the twelve disciples or the naming of them. These emendations probably may be attributed to imaginative and creative minds at work in the oral traditions of the African American experience.

23. Once again, Pack gets his facts confused. There is inconsistency, of course, in the age of Jesus he gives upon his return from Egypt and the age at which he was taken to Jerusalem, both being given as twelve in spite of the time lapse. Then Pack gets the nativity story mixed up with the trip to Jerusalem for the Passover in the Biblical account. It was in the birth story that they went to Bethlehem to be taxed,

not Jerusalem. But the mix-up of these details does not detract from the preaching occasion for his audience. For the essential meaning and the preacher's interpretation of the events are what count at this particular point. Facts can be straightened out later.

24. Another added dimension to make the story more exciting, along with the dialogue that follows.

25. This incident is an embellishment which may be accounted for by looking at the male/female relations current in the present society.

26. The exact distance and location are added details.

27. Other added features here for effect.

28. It is not clear why Pack emphasizes the number thirteen here.

29. The added details about Judas's action and an exact number of men are also embellishments. But scholars do estimate that the arresting soldiers numbered in the hundreds.

30. This represents Pack's own harmonizing of the Gospel, wherein he has taken a statement from the Gospel of John and blended it in with the details from the Synoptic Gospels.

31. An added dimension.

32. Nicodemus VI:23 of *The Lost Books of the Bible* gives the names of the thieves as Dimas and Gestus. In Infancy VIII of *The Lost Books* the story is told of Mary and Joseph and the baby Jesus traveling around in the desert country in Egypt and had to go through a country infested with robbers. The two thieves, Titus, the humane one, and Dumachus, his companion, struggled with each other over the prospect of robbing them. And seeing this kindness, Jesus prophesied that he would be crucified at Jerusalem and these two thieves with him and that Titus would go before him into Paradise. Pack tells a story considerably modified. I am not sure whether he has made these changes or he has gotten it from the oral tradition.

33. Here too is a harmonizing of the Fourth Gospel with the Synoptic Gospels' accounts.

34. These details represent considerable redactions either in the oral tradition or in Pack's own interpretation and dramatization of the story.

35. See Davis, pp. 49–64. Davis summarizes them thus: "An African-American sermon is a verbal mold readily recognized as such by African-Americans in performance; it usually has three or more units structured formulaically, is organized serially in performance, and is given cohesion through the use of thematic and formulaic phrases. Each part or unit of the verbal mold and the narrative system itself must be subordinated to a larger religious intent. The larger intent must embrace a concretized secular and an abstracted sacred polemic tension," p. 46.

36. Davis, in spite of evidence found by Frazier and others that Black preachers have helped African Americans to become "accommodated to an inferior status," maintains that "whatever the political views and sentiments of the African-American preacher, he is intimately attuned to the daily secular needs of his congregation and to the social and political environment in which Black life in the United States is lived and acted out." I believe he is right in this assessment, as well as in the belief that the secular emphasis in African American performed sermons is "a key concept in distinguishing the African-American sermon from sermons of other cultural groups," pp. 63–64.

37. This method is referred to as affective or emotive preaching, a necessary facet of African American sermons, especially in the climax of the message. See Henry Mitchell, *Black Preaching* (New York: J. B. Lippincott Co., 1970), pp. 188–89 and 194–95. Mitchell describes the climax as the point at which, "The bearer is permitted to relax a bit from reaching after new spiritual insight, and to lift up in confirmation and gratitude what he has already received." "In order to accomplish this, the Black preacher has shifted from objective fact to subjective testimony—from 'he said' and 'it happened,' to 'I feel' and 'I believe,'" pp. 188–89. In the climax, Mitchell asserts, the point that has been made is "burned into the consciousness of the hearer. Embrace and celebration are emotional. And a good Black climax will appeal to the highest and noblest emotions..." pp. 194–95. See also Gerald Davis, who explains that affective or emotive worship is "enjoying a radically ascending popularity" today: "Even those congregations which count among their members well-educated, professional and middle-level management African-Americans are insisting on preachers who are both learned and affective in their preaching," p. 41.

38. Interview, Meridian, Mt. Olive Baptist Church, July 10, 1988.

39. *Ibid.*

40. *Ibid.*

41. See Chapter Two for more extensive treatment of Brown and Timothy Graham from interviews.

42. See below in Interview with Faye Inge later that afternoon, May 22, 1988, New Hope Baptist Church. Efforts were underway to restore the Historic Seminary Building and make it a national landmark.

43. See Chapter Two for more details on the African Chieftaincy role of the Black preacher.

44. He had reference to the academic doctorate in contrast to the honorary one.

45. Speaking of me and the lady who accompanied me.

46. He had reference to my being in the pulpit.

47. All during his talk members of the congregation were expressing sounds of agreement and affirmation such as "Amen," "Uh huh," "Yes."

48. See Chapter One on the founding, community involvement, and development of this church.

49. Laura Nan Fairley, "New Hope Church Pastor Appointed to Lead Group," *The Meridian Star*, May 21, 1988, p. 8C.

50. Interview, New Hope, Meridian, May 22, 1988.

51. *Ibid.*

52. See Mozella G. Mitchell, *Spiritual Dynamics of Howard Thurman's Theology* (Bristol, Inc: Wyndham Hall Press, 1985), also Elizabeth Yates, *Howard Thurman: Portrait of a Practical Dream* (New York: The John Day Co., 1964).

53. Davis, p. 64.

54. In *The Black Spiritual Movement* (Knoxville: The University of Tennessee Press, 1984), p. 12, Baer states that it is misleading to speak of the religious experience among Blacks as uniform and monolithic, for it is characterized by considerable variability.

55. See William L. Andrews, *Sisters of the Spirit: Three Black Women's Autobiographies of the Nineteenth Century* (Bloomington: Indiana University Press, 1986.

56. Leontine T. C. Kelly, "Preaching in the Black Tradition" in Judith L. Weidman, Ed., *Women Ministers: How Women are Redefining Traditional Roles* (New York: Harper and Row Pub., 1981), p. 71.

57. *Ibid.*, pp. 71–72.

58. See Ella P. Mitchell, *Those Preachin' Women: Sermons by Black Women Preachers* (Valley Forge: Judson Press, 1985); also Ella L. Mitchell, *Those Preaching Women: More Sermons by Black Women Preachers* volume 2 (Valley Forge: Judson Press, 1988); Also Renita J. Weems, *Just a Sister Away: A Womanist Vision of Women's Relationship in the Bible* (San Diego: Lura Media, 1988; and Jacquelyn Grant, *White Women's Christ and Black Women's Jesus: A Feminist Christology and Womanist Response* (Atlanta: Scholars Press, 1989). Two exceptions are William L. Andrews's *Sisters of the Spirit* and Hans A. Baer's *The Black Spiritual Movement*, which presents a balanced view of male and female ministers in the movement.

59. See note 58.

60. Worship service at New Olivet Baptist Church, Meridian, May 22, 1988.

61. See Ella P. Mitchell's two volumes, *Those Preaching Women*.

62. Interview, Columbus, Mississippi, July 12, 1988.

63. *Ibid.*

64. *Ibid.*

65. *Ibid.*

66. *Ibid.*

67. *Ibid.*

68. *Ibid.*

69. *Ibid.*

70. *Ibid.*

71. *Ibid.*

72. *Ibid.*

CHAPTER 5

The Contemporary Landscape: Religious, Cultural, Educational, Political Blending in the Meridian Area

The Spiritual Heritage Maintained

Music is often an excellent barometer of the times. It certainly seemed so in Poplar Springs Baptist Church's Choir Day celebration May 22, 1988. Dessie Ree Wilson was the Mistress of Ceremonies that Sunday afternoon in Lauderdale County. This church was 115 years old at the time, having been founded in 1873. It is the church where Reverend John Henry (Jack) Graham was funeralized in 1956, and which he pastored for 55 years. The music and the style of the celebration reflected the strong religious roots of the people. It reflected the character of their spiritual and social journey from the latter 19th century to the present time. One notable trait or characteristic that stood out in the people's music and attitudes was the refusal to let go of spiritual verities and values learned from their earliest history in this country. In spite of modernity, in spite of the technological, social, educational, and economic advancements they have experienced, they tended to maintain in this semi-rural setting spiritual values and truths passed on to them from their ancestors such as the Reverend John Henry Graham.

Choirs had come from many different churches in the surrounding area to celebrate with the Poplar Springs Baptist Church Choir their anniversary. One outstanding theme that reverberated through the various songs is one that is common to African American religion in general—the commitment to Jesus and the way of life and witness he requires. Mt. Pleasant Baptist Church Choir sang, "I got a Mind to Live for Jesus All My Days." Another church choir sang songs concentrating on the goodness of Jesus and witnessing to it: "If the Lord's Been Good to You, You Ought Tell It. I'll Tell It Everywhere I Go," and "Oh, It is Jesus in My Soul." Like others, they sang as though they really enjoyed the singing and spoke in sincere expressions, as though they also really enjoyed the fellowship of that program.

The first Apostolic Church of West Meridian's Choir sang about the possession of Jesus and celebration of freedom in Heaven: "When I Get to Heaven, Gonna Sing and Shout, Gonna Walk Around Heaven All Day," and "Jesus Is Mine." The Golden Grove Baptist Church Junior Choir sang two songs that reflected the mutual commitment to Jesus and his commitment to the believer: "I'm Climbing Higher Mountains Trying to Get Home" and "I Know Jesus Will Not Let Go." Rev. Richard McDay, Pastor of Bethel Baptist Church, sang a solo to represent his choir, which was not present. He concentrated on another important theme in African American religion—keeping the faith through all kinds of troubles and hardships. He sang "Keep the Faith Through the Night." He said it was his father's song. He really moved the congregation with such lines as, "If you jest hold out till tomorrow, everything will be all right. In my life I've had my share of troubles. Somebody told me that the darkest hour is just before day. In my life, you know, I've had my share of troubles...So many nights I have to lay down and face tomorrow, believing that the Lord will make a way..."

All of the singers were unpretentious, bold, plain, sincere, spiritually strong, and exhibited no showiness or artiness. The Poplar Springs Church Choir, the honorees, sand at the closing, as they had done at the opening of the program. Their songs were strongly pleas to Jesus.

Walk with me, Lord
Walk with me.

All along this tedious journey,
Walk with me.
You walked with my mother,
Walk with me.
You walked with my father,
Walk with me.
Hold my hand, Lord,
Hold my hand.

Brother Norman Coleman sang a solo, "Because He Lives," and Sister Fields sang "Precious Lord, Take My Hand.

The Pastor of the host church, Rev. Bennie J. Hopkins, Sr., gave frank expressions in his remarks concerning the character of the program: "We thank God for all that our eyes have seen and our ears have heard and our hearts have felt."

Spiritual Losses

In another context, within the urban setting of Meridian, Sarah Graham reflected on changes that have occurred in attitudes and religious practices of African Americans of this area as a result of social and political innovations and reforms. To her, the post-civil rights era during which advances have been made socially and economically, has brought on a decline in religious commitment.

As the people prospered after integration, they began to fall away from the church. The older people started getting checks and everything, and they just stopped goin' to church, don't wanna pay any money in church. And they don't wanna go and listen to the gospel being preached. And we talk with 'em, and we have some say, "I'm just as good as those who go to church every Sunday."[1]

Sarah Graham spoke as the wife of Pastor Timothy Graham. These people, she felt, didn't seem to realize that it was the church that helped them to get where they are.

Because everything about civil rights started in the church. But some now
have all kind of excuses, to keep from goin' to church.[2]

Mrs. Graham here was bringing to light what is a national trend in
African American post-civil rights religious attitudes. And it is more
complex than most churches in the community tend to realize. Many
have become more religiously sophisticated, for instance. They have
come to realize that religion and spirituality is not maintained solely in
the church as a geographical location and gathered spiritual community.
They see also that the church does lag behind the new social and
psychological awareness of the people in so many ways. So often the
church does not satisfy the newer social sensitivities people now have.
Furthermore, the fellowship and gratifications of T.V., sports, and other
social affairs lure the people away from the church and satisfy many of
their needs that were once met by the church.

The people retain their membership in the churches and hold to the
old African American adage, "You can't die outside the church." But as
Mrs. Graham pointed out, they will not attend night services or
afternoon programs, except for a faithful few. They tend to reserve the
church for emergencies and catastrophes.

If something comes up they look for the church people to come to their
rescue. "I'm a member here," they say. "We have had people call at death
and say, Rev. Graham, such and such a person is dead, and they're a
member of Pilgrim Church" or "they're a member of Pleasant Hill
Church," and Rev. Graham hasn't ever seen 'em before. But still they want
to bring the body to the church. [Rev. Graham has pastored these churches
for 20 or 30 years and hasn't seen these members, she said.] And yet they
claim to be members. And this kind a makes you wonder, where are we
going? Now if you have a singing, they'll come to that. But not to hear the
word of God.[3]

Other trends that are a part of the general African American
religious character today Mrs. Graham observed among church
communicants in Meridian. Those are adaptation of Euro-American or

what they consider White attitudes or general American styles, and social class stratification in the churches that cause division and decline in attendance and in regard for the religious life of the churches. She stated, "Black people have had a lot of progress, and they've stopped going to church. You know, we try to imitate Whites too much." She noted a relaxing of the spiritual times and goals and activities in favor of what may be termed secular pursuits. She seemed to feel that they have paused in their religious enthusiasm in order to enjoy some of the leisure life they had previously observed on the part of Whites. She said, "We've started goin' fishing' on Sunday, playin' ball, washing our cars, anything to keep from goin' to church. We've started making these things little gods for us."[4] Commenting on the ways different social classes among Black people in Meridian view the church, Mrs. Graham stated:

> You have the professional people, you have the middle class, and then you have the very poor. The professional people think nobody is good enough to preach to them. The middle class people are the social people. They have their clubs and little social things or groups. The poor people can't afford what it takes to go to church. They don't have the clothing, they don't have the money. Some say, "Every time you go to church, all you can hear is money."[5]

Asked about what class of people tended to go to church, Graham declared: "The poor. Not the poor poor, like people who're living kinda like on fixed income, like social security and retired people, something like that. Very few professional people you find in church, very few. And if they're there they're there to criticize."[6]

Graham, of course, was reflecting on the make-up of her own particular church, more or less. Her view would be different if she were thinking in terms of New Hope Baptist Church and some of the other more middle class or professional class Black churches in Meridian.

Blending of the Religious, the Political, the Social, and the Economic

Interviews earlier with Clara Butler, Gertrude Darden, and Annie Kent, the daughters of John Henry Graham, Jr., middle class professional Black people of the Meridian area, have shown how professional and business class Black people have been able to blend the religious, the social, the cultural, the educational, and the economic within their total perspective of life. The same is true of middle class Black preachers such as Rev. A.D. Lewis, Rev. M.C. Thompson, and Rev. Elijah Jackson, all of whom in their leadership roles may be compared to the African chieftain, guru, shaman, or medicine man, in dealing with the spiritual, social and cultural needs and ills of the people.

In this section, we would like to take a close-up look at two of the top political figures in Meridian and the ways in which they have been able to blend the various religious, political, economic, and cultural facets of life within their total life perspective. As stated in an earlier chapter, Mississippi has the largest number of Black elected officials of any state in the nation. In 1988, there were 18 Black people in the Mississippi House of Representatives and two state senators. Meridian had one Black city councilman out of a total of five, Dr. Hobert Kornegay. And the Representative to the state House from Meridian was an African American by the name of Mr. Charles Young. Both of these men were active church members and strong advocates of religion in their careers and in their daily lives. Their history and background were reflective of strong religious training and values.

Dr. Hobert Kornegay, born August 28, 1923, is a dentist by profession, who grew up in Meridian, was educated in the public schools there, received his undergraduate education at Morehouse College in Atlanta, and his medical training at Meharry in Nashville, Tennessee. Unlike most persons previously interviewed who stemmed from a rural background of landowning, farming foreparents, both Kornegay and Charles Young grew up in an urban setting. Their progenitors were city property owners but not landowners, per se. Kornegay's father, Hobert Kornegay, Sr., came from an area in Alabama and settled in Meridian,

50 miles from his Alabama home. His grandmother, Mrs. Clemmy Gaines, was one of the mattress makers at the Meridian Mattress Company, now Coutre Manufacturing. She used to hand stitch the ticks that were filled with cotton. His mother, Mary Louise Ganes Kornegay, did some mattress work also, but she was mostly an independent domestic who took in washing and ironing in her home to help finance Kornegay's education (he was an only child). His father was a laborer at United Ice Company. The family owned their own home.[7]

Kornegay did not appear to be a great religious enthusiast, but to him religion seemed a natural component of life and society, a given, along with all the other facets of existence. To him it blended with the social, cultural, economic, and psychological make-up of the universe of human existence. He recalled that there were no ministers in his family, but he grew up in an extended family set-up where cousins often lived with him and the family. The neighborhood was made up of "nice persons whose children attend church, and everybody was very congenial and got along in a neighborly fashion."[8]

Kornegay tended to have a penchant for education and culture and the way religion stimulated or enhanced these areas of life. Having graduated from Morehouse College in 1945, he noted at the beginning of the interview that he admired Dr. Howard Thurman (a prominent Black religious scholar, preacher, and philosopher of the 20th century). He said he had had the "great opportunity" to hear him speak at Morehouse about three times. Kornegay still remembered words from Thurman's address on the College's anniversary, from which he quoted the following: "For those of us who have survived and those of us who are living now, we must do a greater thing than dying was. For we must live and accomplish equally as much if not more than those who have passed on before."[9]

Kornegay grew up in church, but he remembered and cherished most the combined effects of education and religion on his training. He was baptized at El Bethel Baptist church, two blocks away from New Hope Baptist Church, where his membership is now and where he serves on the trustee board. It was one of his "professors," who had become a minister, who baptized him at the age of eleven. He appreciated the fact that he was exposed to the type of ministers and professors who gave him exposure to the history and culture as well as to the religion. "At Meharry," he said, "professors taught you the classics, the arts, as well as the sciences."[10]

Of all the persons interviewed in the area of Meridian Kornegay appeared to be the only one who was individualistic in perspective. He admired and aspired to great personal achievement. Having been on the Meridian City Council 12 years, he expressed appreciation for the fact that he commanded the respect of his colleagues on the council. And he admired those ministers and other leaders who were achievers. He spoke of those preachers who were proud of their leadership roles in the community who had choirs that would sing "beautiful" music and have vesper services where musicians would play instruments such as harps, etc. "They introduced you to something kids don't get now." In his high school he said religious training was good, a number of students became outstanding ministers. He mentioned the name of Lemuel Allen, a bishop, he said, in the Methodist Church. He talked of numerous young men he named who have gone on to great positions in the country, the military, in music and other fields after finishing school in Meridian.

Kornegay is married to Mrs. Ernestine Price Kornegay, and they have four children. As a dentist he has done private practice (1948–53), worked for Myricks Meridian Nursing Home, served as dental surgeon for Volt Tech Corp, and on the staff of Riley and St. Joseph's Hospital, and as a consultant in preventive dentistry for Mississippi Head Start University P.R. Dental School. He has also served on various government boards and commissions, such as being chairman of the Lauderdale Economic Opportunity Program, 1971–75, director of the Meridian Redevelopment Authority Urban Renewal, 1971–75, and the board of directors of the St. Francis Homes.[11] Without a doubt he has distinguished himself and made valuable contributions in the community.

Charles Lemuel Young, Sr. (born August 27, 1931) is a third generation Lauderdale Countian. A diversified business executive, he was educated at Tennessee State Agricultural and Technical University with a degree in Business Administration. He also received training at the University of Denver in Public Relations. Serving as vice president of TV–3, WLBT, President of Royal Oak Development Company, and president of E.F. Young, Jr. Manufacturing Company, he is a member of the Mississippi State House of Representatives from the Meridian Area. He has distinguished himself in the Meridian community as a life member of the NAACP, executive and co-founder of Mississippi Action for Progress, past director of the Meridian Chamber of Commerce, and past director of Mutual Federal Savings and Loan.[12]

Young stems from a family background that from the beginning merged ministerial, religious, and business functions within their total lifestyle, and used their talents and expertise to enhance the community of their day. His maternal grandfather, John S. Beal, was a businessman, operating a cafe, a pool room, and other business establishments in Meridian, Jackson, Hattiesburg, and other places. His paternal grandfather, Eugene Fred (E.F.) Young, Senior, was a minister and a semi-businessman in Lauderdale County. His two sons, Eugene Fred Young, Jr. and Roy L. Young were both business men and strong churchmen in the area. Eugene Fred, Charles Young's father, and his mother, Mrs. Velma Beal Young, established the E.F. Young Manufacturing Company and kept to the business industry predominantly. But his uncle, Roy L. Young, a businessman/minister, became a bishop in the Christian (*colored*, then) Methodist Episcopal Church and was over the Alabama District.[13]

Young cited the combined way that business and ministry worked in his paternal grandfather's experience. Rev. E.F. Young, Sr. "saw the need, because in the olden days Blacks couldn't be buried, to start the H.B.A. (Holbrook Benevolent Association) as an organization that would see to it that Black people could be properly buried, and that they could have some insurance and health benefits." His mother and father were versatile business functionaries in the community. His mother, who is principally the founder of the beauty products manufacturing company that bears the family name, was trained as a beautician and as a home demonstration agent. She worked as a trainer with the 4-H Club (Future Homemakers of America). But the beauty industry attracted her the most. Young says that the E.F. Young Manufacturing Company, one of the oldest Black Manufacturing companies in America, came about because his mother was a beautician and his father was a barber. His father was driving a taxi and cutting hair. The E.F. Young Barber Shop is still in existence. There was also an E.F. Young Hotel which is now closed, but the building still stands as a landmark with the name still attached. But out of the building Young's brother operates one of the family construction businesses.[14]

As would be expected there is a strong sense of family history and tradition among the Young family. For instance, they allow the signs to stay on the hotel building because of the historical significance. "At one time," he said, "those were the largest signs in Meridian." [15]

This family history belies the stereotype of Black people's being basically consumer-minded rather than producers. "Quite a few Black southerners," Young pointed out, "ventured to go in business because they had no alternative." They didn't have opportunities to get good jobs. If they wanted to make a living they had to go into business of some sort. His parents and grandparents were "survivors," he said. He too, is a survivor, he declared. Other than working in the civil rights movement of the 1960s, he proudly asserted that he has never worked for anyone but himself. Their family were never landowners so far as acreage was concerned, but real estate owners for business properties. Through their construction businesses, they have approximately 200 apartments in the Meridian area.[16]

Interestingly, none of the business, zeal and ambition has diminished the religious character Charles Young and his family, who are all in the Christian Methodist Episcopal Church. Rather, the strong religious character and foundation has contributed to the business and social structure of the family and its relations and functions in the community. Young, who is chairman of the trustee board of his church, Newell Chapel C.M.E. Church in Meridian, states:

> I've found that religion and business go hand in hand. A lot of people have reached the assumption that they do not. I find that to operate a business, the best way to get my guidelines is from the religious works that I actually do. I make it a practice of not doing a thing in my business to you that I wouldn't want you to do to me. I find it pays off very much. I find that the bread that I cast upon the water gon' come back to me fourfold. The basic foundation of religion works for me, and the people I associate with and work with every day, I treat in that same fashion. If they're doing a good job, I wanna reward 'em. If they jump up and make a mistake then...Moses never reached the Promised Land.[17]

Charles L. Young and his family tradition represent another aspect of the African American character that combines both African and American (new world) traits within their total make-up; they retain the best of the African religious, social, economic, and political character within the *urban* setting of an American environment. While the Grahams and other families discussed represent the New African character developing in the rural setting as landowners and farmers, the picture we get with the Youngs is that of the new world African in the urban situation. Some differences exist in the two settings, such as the greater amount of individualism and sophistication on the part of city dwellers. But it is quite significant that on the part of both urban and rural dwellers, religion remains a strong element, a vital part of the total perspective. It is the glue that holds families and community together and it is the foundation upon which all else in the society is built.

Meridian Today: The Queen City at the Crossroads

As stated before, Meridian was once the key city in the state of Mississippi, the largest until Jackson took the lead in growth and population. Now Jackson is the most progressive city, the capital and the largest, about four times the size of Meridian. Meridian, however, is a beautiful city, quiet, stately, with not much traffic anytime of day. It is an industrial center but it has not expanded technologically or industrially. One of the real disadvantages is that the city has a tiny airport that lands only commuter airplanes and very few of those. There appears to be a resistance to expansion of the airport and to the city's growth. One of the first reasons for such a reluctance that one would probably think of is the fear of the loss of old values and an increase in crime. But among the several persons interviewed none saw this as a major fear. All saw the hindrance to growth as that of a conservative municipal leadership who wanted to maintain power and control.

Sarah Graham and her husband, Rev. Timothy Graham, had some thoughts on the subject. Mrs. Graham was concerned about the need for growth in the population that would take place with the increase in industry and opening up of jobs for people. She said, "There's no work around here, and a lot of people have left here." She recalled the roadblocks to growth caused by the former mayor, Al Rosenbaum, who served under the previous councilmanic form of city government. He was a councilman, elevated to mayorship by his colleagues. "Everything good that wanted to come in here he would fight it," Mrs. Graham stated. She remembered one case wherein Delta Airlines was serving the city airport and they wanted to expand the airport for larger planes to land there, but the mayor opposed it. "And so Delta pulled out. And everybody who wanted to ride Delta had to go to Jackson or even to Memphis to catch a plane. He prevented the growth of Meridian, he and the City Council."[18]

Rosenbaum was a part of the controlling rich Jewish component of the city. The NAACP was among the groups who fought for a change in the city form of government to one with a mayor elected by city-wide vote and the city manager hired by the council. Hobert Kornegay, the only Black member of the present Council, was elected in 1972 and served as Vice-Mayor with Mayor Rosenbaum for a term. He saw the problem of growth in a similar way to that of Mrs. Graham. He said, there were:

> Some narrow-minded persons who didn't wanna see the city grow. Sometimes there're persons who think you can get too big and outgrow them. So the public blamed it on the Chamber of Commerce, and the Chamber blamed it on others. Actually, when Meridian decided that it was losing ground and should grow, it was almost too late to do too much because they had too little to do anything with.[19]

Kornegay feels that now, with the new form of government in place with a new generally elected mayor, the city is now in the process of "trying to reach some type of growth potential, to expand the city limits, etc."[20] He spelled out why for a long time the "more progressive [meaning richer] Whites" held the city back:

> A long time they didn't want industry to come because it would pay higher wages. And other people would lose their help [employees] that they were paying maybe $175 or $200 a week. They didn't want somebody to come in and pay 'em almost twice as much.[21]

Kornegay expressed appreciation for the new form of city government now. He says the mayor is elected now and is a strong mayor who selects committees and has a veto. He also seemed happy that growth for the city appears to be possible. But there still remains a major handicap to growth—a divided City Council. With a council of five members Kornegay noted that he himself held a swing vote, and he has to be very careful how he votes. There is also evidence of contention between the mayor and the council. Kornegay mentioned the recent lawsuit brought by the mayor, who charged that the council couldn't be trusted, that they told him one thing and did something else. "When they went to court they found this wasn't true. They [the Council] won the lawsuit. It was a historic case in the Supreme Court."[22]

Sarah Graham believed the new mayor was trying to do all he could to grow the city and was being prevented by conservative council members. She relented the fighting in city government.

> They're fighting him badly, the City Council. We have three councilmen that worked with Rosenbaum, and they are fighting the mayor we have now. So somehow it's a sad case here in Meridian. It's very sad to see our people who operate the city fighting among themselves.[23]

She felt that having a Black councilman didn't help the situation. She said he always sided with the conservative ones: "Whatever Frazer and Williams [councilmen] say, he goes along with it. He sticks right with them. He served once as Vice-Mayor under Rosenbaum."[24] In her estimation, Kornegay still holds to conservative thinking stemming from Rosenbaum's influence. "He's not for the colored. He's just a Black face there."[25]

Rev. Timothy Graham, Mrs. Graham's husband, was more explicit in his description of the city's problems with growth. He highlighted the issue of racism.

> The city of Meridian for years was run by rich Jews. All right, these rich Jews lived out in the Northwood section, around like that. And they did not pay Negroes good salaries for what they had. They had a chauffeur, a housemaid, a yardboy, and all these people worked out there at their home. And they did not wanna support jobs where it would take their labor away from them, 'cause they knowed they would have to raise their salaries. And that for *years* has been in Meridian. Rich Jews ran this town. That's the reason why we don't have as much industry in here, because they kept it away. They were afraid Blacks would be able to be paid more salary.[26]

Charles L. Young, the Representative to State House from Meridian, could not shed much light on the local situation. And he was very cautious about what he said. For the previous nine years he had been in the state legislature and managed to stay out of the affairs of the city politics. He has his hands full at the state level, although he stays in contact with his constituents in Meridian and tries to minister to their needs at the state level. He stated that what might have hurt Meridian was that it was always classified as a railroad town, which made it become more transient. He said "it's hard to say now what stopped it from growing. It may have been a combination of things." He did indicate that the "attitude now toward growth depends upon the leadership." Young's cautiousness in expressing his thoughts too freely regarding the local situation was due largely to the fact that he headed one of the major committees in the House—the Municipalities Committee, which would deal with any new laws or anything affecting the cities throughout the state. They would have to come before that committee before becoming law. He did not want to prejudice his position.[27]

Both Kornegay and Young had some interesting points as to why Black people in Mississippi have such a vibrant interest in getting elected to political office. Kornegay declared that interest is stimulated among them when "they see what is possible through the balloting process, what can be accomplished when they recognize that you are not considered unless you get out there and voice your opinion about things, see what needs to be done and what you can do to help the situation."[28] Young gave a similar reflection: "When you look at this and see that these people are all doing very well in dealing with the political arena, all are very astute in doing this, it encourages others to seek out offices and lets them know that 'I can win!'"

However, I don't think either office holder gets at the heart of the issue. If they had looked more deeply into the Black/White situation in Mississippi today, I believe they would have noted some more profound developments that contribute to the phenomena of more numerous Black elected officials in the state. It is my belief that the state of Mississippi, especially in some areas like Central Mississippi, is more conducive to the "New Africa in America" model I point to in this work. I see this as being true because it has remained less developed commercially and industrially overall. I do not wish to laud backwardness and lack of progress, but simply to note a fact. Black people in Mississippi have been very smart and industrious, that is, those who have taken leadership roles in their families and in their communities. They have shown an eagerness to purchase land and build farms, to set up businesses, to improve themselves and their people, to get an education and get involved in teaching and social programs to rebuild families and communities. And where conservative-thinking, racist White people have held the line and prevented growth and progress, the Black leadership have kept on growing and helping to prepare themselves and their people for the change they were sure would come one day. Therefore, as opportunities opened up and changes gradually came about, we have seen that same eager spirit among Black people in running for political office and getting elected so that they could become involved in effecting changes and building a better society.

It is instructive to note Melany Neilson's portrayal of Mississippi at the crossroads of progress in race relations and achievement of justice and equality.[29] A White woman born into the genteel class of the Delta area when Mississippi was still a closed society and named for one of Margaret Mitchell's characters in *Gone With the Wind*, Neilson grew up in a hurry in the turbulent metamorphic period of the 1960's and 1970's in the state. She had her baptismal experience in the transformative process as she went to work for Robert Clark, first Black Representative to Mississippi State House since Reconstruction, in his campaign for United States Congress in 1982. Her experiences of change and those of her father, depicted in her autobiographical work, *Even Mississippi*, are a reflection of the crossroads experience of all of Mississippi, including Meridian and Lauderdale County and all of east central Mississippi.[30]

Describing her first venture into the formerly forbidden territory, Neilson states,

> When I went to work for Robert Clark in his 1982 campaign for the United
> States Congress, fifteen years after his historic victory as Mississippi's first
> Black state representative in this century, I remembered the old tension. My

first immersion into a Black crowd was shocking and total, like a plunge into icy waters.[31]

Over the ensuing years of both of Clark's unsuccessful bids for Congress, Neilson played a major role in the campaign. As she did, she found herself on the cutting edge of the painful struggle of the two societies in Mississippi, Black and White, to come to terms with their threshold experience of encountering a new era. In the political and social arena, change was taking place slowly but surely, and the masses simply were not handling it very well. But the experience of Melany Neilson and her family, especially her father, and the amazing transformation they underwent in accepting the change and promoting it in the face of great odds (harassment, threats, personal rejection, etc.) bodes well for the crossroads experience in Mississippi. There are definitely other "Neilsons" as well as Whites of lesser social stature who have made the transformation. And although there are still strong evidences of the two separate societies in the state, the crossroads experience is also very much in evidence and unavoidable by all. The Meridian area, as well as all others in the state, can easily identify with the reality expressed in the words of Robert Clark regarding the change in the state, "We may be coming slow as mules, and working twice as hard, but we're coming, and I'm going to see what I can do about it."[32]

Neilson's father, called Ed Tye, summed up the crossroads experience from the standpoint of himself and his neighbors:

Yeah, your old father is a radical. Folks around here just haven't gotten round to realizing they're in the twentieth century. Some folks are just too stubborn. They'll keep their blinders on and think, well, that's the way it's always been, so I can't support a nigra. And anyone who does, like old Ed Tye, is just a crazy radical.[33]

The stubbornness her father refers to is what seems to be the case among the Whites of east central Mississippi as well, even though they know that change is inevitable, a given that they will eventually have to accept. At the crossroads such as this, one will either cross over willingly or be swept over by the oncoming tide. From the other side, Robert Clark describes the crossroads experience from the old way to the new in a somewhat different light.

> Folks got away with a lot in those [old] days. And I wouldn't trade those days for now for nothing. Some Black folk want to grumble that things ain't that much better these days, but I know better. Oh, plenty of folk still get mighty riled up about Blacks and Whites getting too friendly and that kind of thing, but hell, this is 1984 not 1884. Despite what old Barnett [the racist candidate who opposed him in the primary] says. He can wish and get down on his knees and pray to his great White Lord and still it won't be so.[34]

It is my considered judgement that the African American strength and endurance in Mississippi, especially east central Mississippi, buttressed by a firmly grounded religious faith, a vigilant hope and love of their state, and determined group of leaders, religious and political, such as Robert Clark and Charles Young of Meridian, will bring the state over the crossroads into the new era of cooperation, justice, and equality between the races. And the African American component there will continue to reflect, as seen in previous sections of this work, neo-African religious and social character and foundations along with new world traditions encountered on this side of the Atlantic Ocean.

Endnotes

1. Sarah Graham, Interview, May 23, 1988, Meridian, Mississippi.

2. *Ibid.*

3. *Ibid.*

4. *Ibid.*

5. *Ibid.*

6. *Ibid.*

7. Horbert Kornegay, Interview, July 13, 1988.

8. *Ibid.*

9. Howard Thurman, quoted by Kornegay, Interview, July 13, 1988.

10. Horbert Kornegay, Interview, July 13, 1988, Meridian.

11. Iris Cloyd, ed. *Who's Who Among Black Americans*, (Detroit: Gale Research, Inc.), 1990–91, p. 748.

12. Iris Cloyd, ed. *Who's Who Among Black Americans*, (Detroit: Gale Research, Inc.), 1990–91, p. 1419.

13. Interview, Charles L. Young, Meridian, MS, July 14, 1988.

14. *Ibid.*

15. *Ibid.*

16. *Ibid.*

17. *Ibid.*

18. Sarah Graham, Meridian, May 23, 1988.

19. Kornegay, Meridian, July 13, 1988.

20. *Ibid.*

21. *Ibid.*

22. *Ibid.*

23. Sarah Graham, May 25, 1988.

24. *Ibid.*

25. *Ibid.*

26. Rev. Timothy Graham, Interview, Meridian, May 23, 1988.

27. Charles L. Young, Interview, July 14, 1988, Meridian.

28. Kornegay, July 13, 1988.

29. Melany Neilson, *Even Mississippi*, Tuscaloosa and London: the University of Alabama Press, 1989.

30. Neilson.

31. *Ibid.*

32. *Ibid.*, p. 163.

33. *Ibid.*, pp. 167–68.

34. *Ibid.*, p. 154.

CHAPTER 6

CONCLUSION:
New Africa in America in Perspective

"Therefore, since we are surrounded by so great a cloud of witnesses, let us also lay aside every weight and the sin that clings so closely, and let us run with perseverance the race that is set before us." (Hebrews 12:1).

One of the subtleties of Robert Clark's unsuccessful campaigns for U.S. Congress from Mississippi in 1982 and 1984 that probably escaped both him and his White press secretary, Melany Neilson, is that her being on his committee contributed greatly to the doom of their efforts. There was nothing intentional about it, but in spite of Neilson's demonstrated loyalty and devotion to the success of the campaigns, her presence on the committee, at that particular time and in that particular setting, assured the defeat. By including this genteel White woman on his staff, Clark confirmed racist Mississippi Whites' worst fears about Black men's wanting to gain power in order to achieve access to the White woman. And worst yet, he insulted them when he did not sexually corrupt this White woman as they were so sure he could not resist doing. Racist Mississippi just was not ready for any of this.

It was Clark's naivete about contemporary Mississippi society which prevented him from anticipating the impact that including Neilson on his staff would have. With good intentions apparently, Clark was trying to push the two societies together in a manner before either of them, Black or White, was ready for such. He clearly wanted to be accepted as a political candidate that would unite both societies. Yet he wound up keeping them apart. This happened because of something about contemporary Mississippi Clark, Neilson, and others on his staff did not grasp, and I'm not sure it's fully explainable. But it concerns a kind of holding pattern that exists between the two societies that are from outside appearances cooperating with legal requirements of school desegregation, voting rights, etc. Socially, culturally, and politically, however, they have made little effort to understand and accept one another. The Whites maintain their old prejudices about African Americans and have made little effort to face up to them and overcome them. Black people are eager to make progress toward getting along with the Whites and working together with them, but they know for the most part that Whites cannot be trusted where Black people are concerned. These kinds of fears and distrust faced Clark's campaigns and doomed them to failure, along with Black people's internal strife among themselves politically.

There is still a wide gulf between Black people and White people in Mississippi, as elsewhere in the country, which must be bridged before there can be real racial harmony. And politics is not the arena for the working out of the problems and ways of bridging that gulf. Religion, culture, and education will have to play a major role. I dare say that Black religion in Mississippi can be a tremendous enhancement to the total process of sensitizing, orienting, and encouraging the races in Mississippi toward mutual understanding and a sense of peoplehood. Black people in the state retain the hallmark of their African heritage—a harmonious blending of religion, and the social and political and economic facets of life—what I have referred to as the New Africa in America.

Black people in Mississippi need to understand this heritage as a great potential among themselves to enable them to come to grips with their present situation and to offer assistance to the other race in overcoming their prejudices. Black people need to understand the significance of what religion has done for them. For example, no other people have had to live under conditions such as African American slaves and ex-slaves have had to endure in American apartheid—which varied from state to state. Mississippi apartheid was a thing unto itself. It was enough to send all Black people fleeing from the state. Some did, but most did not. Those Black people who stayed, loved their home state in spite of the hardships, and most cherished the family heritage they had managed to forge there. They understood the apartheid system there and bore with it in utmost faith and rugged determination to outwit it. And to observe the state today and all the political and religious fervor and activity among Black people, one senses that they are winning.

We have seen in this book that, from those rural Black people, such as John Henry Graham, who bought land during and after Reconstruction, built churches and schools, and other structures for their families and communities, to urban families such as E.F. Young and his descendants, such as Charles L. Young, who have launched into the political affairs of the state to forge a better life for all people of the state, we have seen that Black people have profoundly strong roots in Mississippi and have what may easily be referred to as a New Africa in America. For there is nothing like it anywhere—this rich heritage and tradition. In being patient, enduring hardships inflicted from the intransigent White society when open resistance would have been suicidal, and trusting God at the same time for deliverance, these people demonstrated that they truly believed the religious teachings from the Judeo-Christian context, in contrast to their White counterparts, who demonstrated a lack of faith and trust, especially in their relations toward them (African Americans) in that they allowed their fears and insecurities to cause them to inflict hostilities and brutalities on other human beings as a means of keeping them under their control. A believing, God-fearing, religiously trusting people would have relied more on God instead to maintain their status and position, and to bring about stable and peaceful human relations, which is something the African Americans could teach their White counterpart in the society.

There were and are many religious and spiritual lessons to be learned from these captives by their captors. These captives have, in fact, become captors religiously of their political and social captors. For they have already shared with the White Mississippi society their spiritual songs, blues, jazz, and their religious zeal and power of endurance. Without acknowledging it to any great extent, both Black and White people in Mississippi have learned much from each other even as they have maintained their separateness. It only remains that they should acknowledge what they have gained and what they may yet gain from one another in seeking greater human understanding, sincere interaction, and human relations.

ARMY AND NAVY
YOUNG MEN'S CHRISTIAN ASSOCIATION
"WITH THE COLORS"

YMCA

Sep 4, 1918

Detention Camp Co 5
Camp Shelby miss —
my dear Brother I recieved your
letter today and was glad to here
from you it found me very well and
doing very well hope these few lines
will find you well and doing well
I was a proud soul to here from
you and much oblige to you for the
one dollor Bill that you sends me I
was glad to recieve it and I hope to
see you all before long I have a very
nice time down here I am helping
to train these men and I have
nothing to do but help to train
them but I do not se how long I
will be here I might be gone before
long, I seen in the papers where the
people from 18 to 46 will have to register
and that will get you all will it
I sure do want to come home to see you
all

TO THE WRITER: SAVE BY WRITING ON BOTH SIDES OF THIS PAPER

TO THE FOLKS AT HOME: SAVE FOOD; BUY LIBERTY BONDS AND WAR SAVINGS STAMPS

Letter from Ira Graham

give my love to all Tell mama and
papa I says howdy and I sure wants
to see them all Tell sister and Bud
and Odena howdy give my love to
all Tell Charlie howdy and his family
also you all pray for me. how is my
crop getting along is my cotton open
much I shore does want some goober
to eat is they ripe have you all pulled
them up. give my Best respict
to all the boys Tell them they will
be in this before long you all be
good and pray for me and I hope
to see you all again I have been
shot thril times with a nudle
about a inch and a half long once
in the right sholder and twice in
the lift sholder with licrid
medicine and they made me mighty
sick they shoots once a week
and I have been vaccanated to
on the lift arm and it made me
sick also. so I will close from
your Bro I. W. Graham

To mr John H Graham

Bro John dear Brothe
I am siting you a few
lines can you let
me have a half
a bushel of corn
if you can I will
said the money
and a sack

L. Graham

Descendants of John Henry Sr. and
Sarah Ann Anderson Graham

John Henry Graham, 1862-1956
Sarah Ann Anderson Graham (wife), 1862-1941
  I. Charlie Graham, 1883 (m. Maggie Graham)
      Wilson Graham
      Clarence Graham
      Roger Graham
      Rev. Timothy Graham
      Cleveland Graham
      Sweetie Graham
      Ruth Graham
      Stanley Graham
      Mittie Graham Radcliff
  II. Rev. Willy J. Graham, 1885-1936
  III. John Henry Graham, Jr., 1886-1986, (m. Pearlie Graham)
      Annie Graham Kent
      Clara Graham Butler
      Gertrude Graham Darden
  IV. Daisy Graham, 1888
   V. Sarah Graham Gregory, 1889-1992
      Leola Rackingson
      Beatrice Moore
        Maxine
      John Gavin
  IV. Ira Wilson Graham, 1891-1918
      Ira Graham
  VII. Arnol Graham, 1892 (died as a child)
VIII. Louella Graham Radcliff, 1894
      Wilson Radcliff
      Freddie Radcliff
      Ezella Radcliff

Sarah Ann Radcliff
IX. Bethena Graham, 1896
Daisy Mae Jackson
X. Odena Graham Gordon, 1898-1974
Sarah M. Gordon Jenkins (m. Fred Jenkins)
Hattie M. Gordon
Paulette Gordon
Joseph Sean
Sherrie
KK
Effie A. Hearon (m. Bennett Hearon)
Etha M. Hearon Humphrey
Mary M. Hearon Bounds
Barbara J. Hearon Dorris
Bennett Hearon, Jr.
Lorine Hearon Whorton
Cell D. Hearon
Jimmy L. Hearon
Dorothy L. Hearon
Eugene Hearon
Gloria D. Hearon
John Gordon
Albert Gordon
Jerry
Terry
Garry
Mary Alice Gordon Alexander (m. Dewey Alexander)
Lee Alexander
Michael Alexander
David Alexander
Paul Gordon (m. Charlotte Gordon)
Michael Gordon
Elnora Gordon Brown (m. Mazell Brown)

Josephine Gordon White (m. Harold White)

Ira Gordon

Dianne Gordon

James Gordon

Mozella Graham Gordon (m. Edrick R. Woodson)

Cynthia L. Woodson

Marcia D. Woodson

Zahra Dena-Marie Woodson

Jamila Woodson

Palmer Gordon

XI. Lula Graham Brown, 1899

Charlie Brown

John Brown

Rev. Otis Brown

Willie Mae Brown

Annie Mae Brown

Dessie Ree Brown Wilson

XII. Oscar Graham, 1903

XIII. Mabell Graham, 1905*

* List supplied chiefly by Mrs. Effie A. Hearon

Granddaughters of Rev. Jack Graham (left to right) Ezella, daughter of Bethena, Annie Kent, Effie Hearon

(Top) Mrs. Sarah Graham Gregory (left), daughter of Rev. Jack Graham, and Mrs. Annie Kent, granddaughter of Rev. Jack Graham, on the Gertrude Darden Estate. (Bottom) (left to right) Maxine, her sister, and Charlie Wilson, great-granddaughters and grandson of Rev. Jack Graham.

(Top) Leola and brother, grandchildren of Jack Graham. (Bottom) Beatrice Moore, children, grandchildren, and brother, descendants of Jack Graham.

(Top) Brothers Charlie Wilson (left) and Rev. Otis Wilson, grandsons of Jack Graham. (Bottom) Effie and Bennett Hearon, children, and grandchildren, descendants of Jack Graham.

Backview of Clara Graham Butler's home in Meridian, Mississippi, adjoining the estate of sister Gertrude Graham Darden.

(Top) Mr. and Mrs. Cleveland Graham, grandson of Jack Graham. (Bottom) Tombstones of Jack Graham and Sarah Ann Anderson Graham, All Day Cemetery.

(Top) Annie Graham Kent (left), Gertrude Graham Darden, and husband C.H. Darden, grandchildren of Jack Graham. (Bottom) Detail of the Jack Graham home built in the 1880's, the fireplace and chimney of the structure being dismantled.

(Top) New Hope Baptist Church. (Bottom) (far right) Home that Jack Graham built with his own hands in the 1880's, presently being dismantled, Enterprise, Mississippi.

(Top) Clara Butler and husband Marvin with their grandchildren (Clara is the granddaughter of Jack Graham). (Bottom) (left to right) Dewey Alexander, grandson-in-law of Jack Graham; Ira Gordon, grandson of Jack Graham; Mrs. Pearlie Graham, wife of John Henry Graham, Jr.; Ezella, granddaughter of Jack Graham.

Signs of New Africa Elsewhere in America

Within the history of the Black church exists a very significant tradition from which we can derive much theological meaning and tremendous resources for the development and enhancement of Black life. It is the tradition of the family church at the present time when rapidly increasing divorce rates, the devaluing of traditional marriage and single-parenting among young adults, increases in family tensions and problems in general are cause for great fears concerning the disintegration of the American family, and especially the Black family; teachers, preachers, theologians, and sociologists are newly stressing the values of the family church and the necessity for family counseling and ministry to the families within the church. J. Deotis Roberts, for instance in *Roots of a Black Future: Family and Church* (Philadelphia: The Westminster Press, 1980), sees the hope of the Black race as determined by the extent to which we are able to develop and foster cooperatively these two basic institutions. Roberts explores the "deeper meaning of church as family and family as church" (p. 9) and tries to present "a constructive theological statement on the Black church as an extended family" (p. 59) based on the historical situation of the Black church. He goes beyond the implication of family based on blood ties to stress the notion of the church as the extended "family of God" with the pastor serving as mother or father (pp. 89, 117, and 113).

With a similar notion in mind, I wish to call attention to a somewhat rare or unique situation within the family church tradition and to talk about ways of utilizing it and other such situations for the development and progress of the church and the society.

St. Joseph A.M.E. Zion Church, located in the South Norfolk borough of Chesapeake, Virginia (one of the four cities of the Tidewater, Hampton Roads area including Norfolk, Portsmouth, and Virginia Beach) has, as so many of our A.M.E. Zion Churches, no doubt, a somewhat unique historical background which along with its present make-up, renders it a very valuable resource for the development and progress of the church, as well as the community and the society at large.

The church was founded in 1905 under the pastoral leadership of the Reverend Miles Gordon by a group of Methodists who had grown weary of walking long distances to church and attending churches of other denominations within their neighborhood (interview with Mr. John Parson, December 22, 1980). The members organized at Israel Hall, West Munden in Norfolk County, two miles west of the present location. The first building bearing the name "St. Joseph" was established in 1907, under Rev. Gordon's leadership, on Higgins Street, one half mile from the present location. The first edifice on Atlantic Avenue was built in 1917 under the Reverend A.L.Woods. The latest at the same location was built under the Reverend E.L. Coleman in 1967 (*Saint Joseph's Day*, souvenir booklet, April 25, 1971).

Ordinarily, the name of the church, "St. Joseph," would not be a source of concern. One naturally assumes the church was simply named for the biblical figure of Joseph, the earthly father of Jesus. But this case is not as simple as that. Furthermore, in the A.M.E. Zion Church, as well as other church traditions, churches are usually named for either biblical persons or places, as memorials to former bishops or other famous persons within the history of the church. And in most cases, the person for whom a church is named is no longer living. One remembers especially the numerous Hood Temple A.M.E. Zion Churches throughout the country named for Bishop James W. Hood; or Shaw Memorial, Shaw Temple, and other churches named for Bishop B.G. Shaw; or Tubman church named for the famous Abolitionist and many others.

St. Joseph Church, however, was named for two of its founders, the late *Joseph* Edney and *Joseph* Parson, who happened themselves to be named for biblical figures (either the son of Jacob, Joseph of Arimethea, or the earthly father of Jesus, or any number of other Josephs that may appear in Scripture). The church was named for these two men within their own lifetime because of their deep devotion, sincere dedication, and valuable participation in the church and the community. These men were actually "canonized" in the new African American tradition by the addition of "saint" to their names. I have thus far been unable to trace Mr. Joseph Edney or his descendants any further than the founding of the church in 1905. But from the line of Mr. Joseph Parson have sprung a network of descendants that comprise the present St. Joseph Church along with very few other members not connected with these families (numbering altogether between 150 and 200 members). Therefore, St. Joseph is literally an extended family and as such it functions very smoothly, efficiently and harmoniously as a church. The lines of four other family groupings intersect with the Parsons within the church: the Cuffees, the Overtons, the Griffins, and the Wilsons.

A brief historical sketch will make this clear. Joseph Parson (1859–1913) was married to Mary Alice Cuffee (1857–1936). Both were born and reared in Norfolk County, Virginia (now a part of Chesapeake), and in their early life they were members of the Gabriel Chapel A.M.E. Zion Church in Hickory, Virginia (now a part of Chesapeake, also). The Cuffees still live in that area and many are still members of Gabriel Chapel. Joseph was considered a pillar of the church; he was a choirmaster and teacher of music in the Norfolk County area. His wife, Mary A. Cuffee Parson was a devoted companion in every facet of his work. In her own right, she was a midwife in the South Norfolk/Norfolk County area. The two of them reared nine children of their own: Aruetta, Olia, Laura, Rufus, William, Dora, Mattie, Vernon, and Joseph, Jr., all of whom grew to adulthood as faithful members of the church. As is usually the case with families today, some moved away at maturity to other cities. Mainly by way of Vernon and Rufus Parson, whose descendants remain at St. Joseph, the church members are connected with the other families. Like his father Joseph, Rufus had nine children, three of whom are presently active members of the church: Marian Parson Ruffin, Leonard and John Parson (Interview the Mr. John Parson, Dec. 22, 1980).[*]

Vernon Parson married Sopora Overton (still an active member of the church in 1980), and the union produced four offspring, two of whom are still members of the church: Grace and Elouise. Elouise Parson married James Griffin, the two of them producing nine children, all of whom were reared in the church — all but one still active. Mrs. Sopora Overton Parson's first cousin, Mary Overton, married a Josiah Wilson (who has numerous descendants still at St. Joseph Church including Mary, Louise Wilson Griffin, Doris Wilson Macdonald, George Wilson,[*] Dorothy Mae Wilson Morris, and Bernice Wilson Williams and their numerous offspring). Some of the other families married into the basic line of St. Joseph families. Notable are Mrs. Delores Leary Wilson who married the grandson of Mrs. Evilener Doxey, and Mr. Phillips; and Mrs. Arnetta Parson, one of the daughters of Joseph Parson. Louise Wilson, in turn, married Richard Griffin, the brother of James Griffin (both the sons of Mrs. Eveline J. Griffin Doxey — 1895–1965, also a staunch member of St. Joseph). Mrs. Louise Wilson Griffin's family (nine children) are therefore twice-related to Mrs. Elouise Parson Griffin's family (nine children also). All but two or three of the Mary Louise Wilson Griffin/Richard Griffin offsprings are still active at St. Joseph, including their own families. Doris Wilson married Kenneth MacDonald, a union producing four children who grew up in St. Joseph. Others of the Wilson brother and sisters, such as Bernice, George, and Dorothy also reared large families in St. Joseph. Some of the grandparents/great

---

[*] Since the 1980 interviews some of these persons have passed away.

grandparents still around at the writing (1980) to serve as guiding lights from the past are Mrs. Elizabeth Overton Granby, Mrs. Justine B. Woodhouse (mother of Mrs. B. Cuffee Holloman), Mrs. Sopora Overton Parson and Mrs. Delia Parson Charleston (ex-wife of Rufus Parson), as well as others not directly related to the extended family, such as Mrs. Abrams and Mrs. Sawyer (interview with Mrs. Elouise Parson Griffin, Dec. 23, 1980).

Behind the history and present composition of this church lies much theological, religious, cultural, and social significance both for now and for the future development of the church and the community. In the first place, we observe a kind of social mechanism which reflects the African heritage, the very strong and stable family ties and the reverence for kin, both living and dead. Although the formalized myths and rituals and rites of passage are absent, the values remain much intact and informal practices incorporate some of the principles of the African system while assimilating Christian beliefs and ideas. What seems to have occurred is that, as in the African past, the family kinship system remained as a strong medium of discipline and control, while the Christian church (St. Joseph) replaced the African myth and ritual that served to reinforce family values and principles. The church and family played complementary roles in the lives of the people.

According to Mr. John Parson, the family and church brought influence and strength for the members. There existed always a sense of personal security and dignity along with public recognition and reputation for the family and church members. Mrs. Elouise Parson Griffin states that the church gave all of the families a sense of value.

All members of the families tended to be highly respectable, moderate, and mild-mannered. There was no trouble with the law among any of them. She does not remember any serious problems in school, community, or church. They always seemed to try to get along with one another and with persons outside the family. They were never rowdy, and rarely did there appear to be alcohol or drug problems among them (interview, Dec. 23, 1980). Mrs. Griffin's daughter Carolyn Griffin, who was then superintendent of Sunday School, was especially cognizant that, unlike in many situations in the larger society, the males in these families tended to excel more, even more so than the women, in many cases. She felt very positive about the fact as they were all brought up in the church with a solid and strong sense of values and morals. Miss Griffin could recall no tension, rivalry, or feuds within or between any of the families. Also the general problem of young adults between the ages of 18 and 30 drifting away from the church has not been prevalent at St. Joseph, seemingly because of the family unity, harmony and cooperation (interview, Dec. 23, 1980, confirmed by Mrs. Mary Louise Wilson Griffin and family, Dec. 28, 1980).

African and Christian elements are also seen in the origin and make-up of the church. The people's naming of the church for Joseph Parson and Joseph Edny (whose names, of course derived form Biblical figures) and the affixture of "Saint" to the name was in a sense an unofficial canonization of humans in their own lifetime. It was as well, the establishment of a Christian patriarchal tradition that has had a tremendous influence on the families involved, and still does even to this day. Also, we might call the St. Joseph experience an American version of the African clan or small tribe with the ancestor Joseph Parson as the tribal head. Though the system is not consistently maintained by myth and ritual, yet the church is proud of its family traditions and does have infrequent founders' day or homecoming programs or family reunions which commemorate the past family and church membership.

As to the enrichment of the community at large, these families people every level and all areas of the society. Housewives, mechanics, public servants, electrical engineers, doctors, dentists, teachers, architects, musicians, preachers, college professors, program administrators, and business men and women are only some of the occupational pursuits in which they participate.

A dynamic theology is also evident within this particular family church tradition. For the various families, the Spirit of Christ was incarnated or embodied in the figure of the ancestors. The spirit is also carried in the collective peoplehood. There exists among them an unwritten, unexpressed reverence for the ancestors and the Christian spirit that has 'been inculcated within the group and is passed on from generation to generation. This reverence has had a powerful character-building influence upon the family members. The descendants of this family tradition are not themselves fully aware of the spiritual myths which lurk within the tradition and binds them to their culture and way of life.

Mythically speaking, the union of *Joseph* Parson and *Mary* Alice Cuffee, both bearing the names of the earthly mother and father of Jesus, provided the link for all the families within the network and thus produces as offspring a church which is, as Scripture would have it, the "body of Christ." In this way the people here have rather subtlety appropriated the gospel by making the sacred history their own. The process has both immediate and eternal significance. They have actualized the concept that we are of the family of God — younger sisters and brothers of Christ, the Son of God.

With its highly meaningful family tradition, St. Joseph Church could become the hub or center of a progressive and unified and developmental church family. That is, it could become the nucleus from which the community around it could draw together in a family type bond and become much stronger as a Christian community. This church could be a leader in exemplifying and encouraging strength for the other families in the community. In other words, it could be instrumental in helping turn the trend around that moves toward family disintegration, crime, isolation, loneliness, drug addiction, alcoholism, and the like. The families through the church could then perform a healing service and become, on a much broader scale, the "household of God," as described by Roberts (J. Deotis, p. 18). Roberts claims: "When the Black church is viewed as a family all persons, whether married, single, or divorced, will come to sense a kinship in the church as the family of God" (pp. 132–133). Certainly such a possibility exists at St. Joseph. In fact, the church has already moved in this direction to some extent. Other reputable families that have blended in well with the basic family groupings include the Long family, the Lee family, the Spruills, Manleys, Ecklins, Barcliffs, Dearings, Whitmores, and Powells. The church is also standing as a "family of God."

Martin Luther King, Jr. Memorial Studies in Religion, Culture, and Social Development

This series is named for Martin Luther King, Jr., because of his superb scholarship and eminence in Religion and Society, and is designed to promote excellence in scholarly research and writing in areas that reflect the interrelatedness of religion and social/cultural/political development both in the American society and in the world. Examination of and elaboration on religion and socio-cultural components such as race relations, economic development, marital and sexual relations, inter-ethnic cooperation, contemporary political problems, women, Black American, Native American, and Third World issues, and the like are welcomed. Manuscripts submitted must be equal in size to a 200 to 425 page book. Two copies must be submitted.

Mozella G. Mitchell
Religious Studies Department 310 CPR
University of South Florida
Tampa, Florida 33620